MW01632876

Once in every few decades, a brilliant innovator makes a quantum leap in the way we relate to and care for our bodies. Dr. Burdenko is such a person. His genius lies in discovering the power of water and land exercises to enhance health, accelerate healing, and prevent injury.

Dr. Andrew Geller, M.D., M.P.H.

In the race between conditioning and aging, conditioning can win if it is diversified and fun, as it is with Dr. Burdenko's techniques. I am now 73 years of age and have been seeing him for 27 years!

Professor Lester Thurow
Former Dean, MIT Sloan School of Management
Author of 17 books, including several NY Times bestsellers

Dr. Burdenko's work is revolutionary. The Burdenko Method must be taught to every medical student and every athletic trainer.

Henry Shterenberg
CEO, New England Sports Academy

Igor Burdenko's methods emphasize a strict discipline of attention to detail and an understanding of body motion. He exudes enthusiasm and humor in leading the injured to maximum potential. I have experienced the value of his water-land methods with an amazing recovery of a nerve injury. Igor is a master!

Dr. Benjamin E. Bierbaum
Clinical Professor of Orthopedic Surgery, Tufts University
Chair, Department of Orthopedic Surgery, New England Baptist Hospital

The brilliance in the Burdenko Method is its intense focus on the very essentials of human movement. It has revolutionized the way I look at rehabilitation, conditioning, and training. I've used its foundations every day since I graduated physical therapy school in 1997, and have had outstanding results for my patients and for myself.

Paul J. Salvi, P.T., OCS
Medical Director, Back on Track
Master Certified Instructor, Burdenko Method

In my 20 years as an exercise physiologist, I have found the Burdenko Method to be the single most effective system for rehabilitating, conditioning and training the human body. My clients always experience an "awakening of their body" through doing Burdenko Method training, which is empowering to them and a privilege for me to be a part of.

Mike Siemens
Master of Science in Exercise Physiology
Head of Exercise Physiology, Canyon Ranch
Master Certified Instructor, Burdenko Method

Nineteen years ago, I worked with Igor Burdenko following surgery for a herniated disc. His innovative techniques, both in water and on land, helped to restore my strength, agility, and flexibility. My experience working with him gave me the confidence in my body that led to an unanticipated ten-year stint as a competitive bodybuilder.

Dr. Rick Silverman
Associate Professor of Surgery, Division of Plastic Surgery
University of Massachusetts Medical School
St. Elizabeth's Medical Center, Boston, MA
Author of "Bodybuilding: Muscle Over Myth"
WNBF Pro Bodybuilder

Dr. Igor Burdenko has such a rich depth of therapeutic experience! I am honored to have worked with, and learned from, such an esteemed colleague.

Ruth Sova
President, Aquatic Therapy & Rehab Institute

I have been involved in sports medicine for over 30 years. My area of expertise is in rehabilitation. The Burdenko Method is the most innovative and effective intervention I have been exposed to for many years!

Marjorie A. King, PhD, ATC, PT
Director of Graduate Athletic Training Education
Associate Professor, Plymouth State University

In 1990, I came to Igor Burdenko to work on my flexibility and strength at what I thought was the end of my career due to knee injuries. I was not even 25 years old. Igor gave me much more than a set of exercises -- he gave me an outlook that inspired hope and a second wind that helped me to earn spots on the 1990 World Team and a Silver Medal in the 1992 Olympic Winter Games.

To this day I use his methods and techniques as I train for athletic feats much lesser than the Olympics! I train young skaters (and my own children) the Burdenko Method for their careers and lives. I still enjoy skating and working out!

Paul Wylie
1992 Olympic Silver Medalist, Men's Figure Skating
U.S. Figure Skating Hall of Fame

I am an old runner. I mean really old. Igor Burdenko's wonderful fitness training enabled me to keep moving into my 90's, taking gold, silver, and bronze in the 2009 US National Senior Games in the 90–94 age grouping. Thank you Igor.

Bill Stern, Engineer (Retired)
Bedford MA

THE BURDENKO METHOD

Restore and Maintain Health with
the Fitness Wisdom System of
Water and Land Therapy

by IGOR N. BURDENKO, PhD

Edited by Vladimir Goltsov

BOSTON • 2012

The Burdenko Method
by Igor N. Burdenko, PhD

Edited by Vladimir Goltsov

Library of Congress Control Number: 2012946844
ISBN 978-1-934881-89-7

Published by M•Graphics Publishing in cooperation with
The Burdenko Water and Sport Therapy Institute

Editor: Vladimir Goltsov
Design and Layout: Paul Kraytman
Illustrations: Paul Kraytman and Scott Biehler

M•Graphics Publishing
Phone: 781.990.8778
mgraphics.books@gmail.com
www.mgraphics-publishing.com

Printed in the United States of America

Dedicated to all of the Burdenko
Master Certified instructors,
who help bring this knowledge
to the world

DISCLAIMER

The therapeutic procedures in this book are based on the training, personal experiences, and research of the author. Because each person and situation is unique, the author and publisher urge the reader to check with a qualified health professional before using any procedure where there is any question to its appropriateness.

The publisher does not advocate the use of any particular treatment, but believes the information presented in this book should be available to the public.

Because there is always some risk involved, the author and publisher are not responsible for any adverse effects or consequences resulting from the use of any of the suggestions or procedures described in this book. This book is as timely and accurate as its publisher and author can make it; nevertheless, they disclaim all liability and cannot be held responsible for any problems that may arise from its use. Please do not use the book if you are unwilling to assume the risk. Feel free to consult with a physician or other qualified health professional. It is a sign of wisdom, not cowardice, to seek a second or third opinion.

Contents

EXERCISES WITH TUBING

Acknowledgments

I would like to very much thank my dear wife Irina, my partner and love, for her belief in my work and deep participation in all my projects and ideas, and my wonderful, talented daughter Nelli for contributing her chapter and sharing with all of us her valuable ideas and knowledge.

I would like to thank Vladimir Goltsov for his tireless editing, revising and corrections, and for his courage to share his story.

I also want to thank Scott Biehler, for his willingness to share his experience and knowledge, and for his illustrations which are in this book.

I would like to thank Dr. Andrew Geller for his thoughts and ideas, Esther Greif for her comments and for practicing the Burdenko Method for many years, William Barrett for his reading and corrections, and George Shamis for his technical support.

I would like to say "Thank you" to the Master Certified Instructors of the Burdenko Method: Sylvia Aizpurviete, Erik Alikpala, Tom Barbeau, Joe Carroll, Elaine Drawbridge, Laurie Fucigna, Alex Heath, Lisa Illg, Taylor Kruse, Susan Lauring, Susan Manero, Rick McAvoy, Dottie Rau, Paula Ray, Janis Redlich, Paul Salvi, Beth Scalone, Mike Siemens, Steve Victorson, Tony Zemlinsky.

I am very thankful to Michael Minayev, my publisher, and Paul Kraytman, the designer, for their patience, understanding, and professionalism throughout this project, and others who continue to bring to the public awareness of this new methodology available for anyone interested in innovative techniques in health, fitness and sport.

With great appreciation and respect,
Igor N. Burdenko, Ph.D.

Foreword

I am very pleased and honored to write an introduction to the Burdenko Method. This text represents the distillation of more than 50 years of work by the first author in the area of physical exercise and water therapy rehabilitation. Dr. Igor Burdenko is known throughout the world as a great innovator and promoter of the concept of mind and body rehabilitation for both his land-based exercises and in particular, his work with water-based exercises.

I first met Igor in 1981, and I've had the pleasure of interacting with him and sending him patients who have the most difficult problems with rehabilitation. Inevitably, he has responded to these challenges—my patients experienced decreased levels of pain and improved levels of function, whether they are elite level ballet dancers, figure skaters or simply people who wish to live a life more productively and in greater comfort.

In addition to the rehabilitation aspect of his work, Igor's patients have been able to continue a systematic and thorough program of exercises which will last them for the rest of their lives and improve their health and function.

I would give my greatest recommendation to the readers of this book to study it carefully and to realize that this represents the distillation of a focused career in sports medicine and rehabilitation which is truly unique in this field.

Lyle J. Micheli, MD
Director, Division of Sports Medicine, Children's Hospital Boston
Clinical Professor of Orthopaedic Surgery, Harvard Medical School
O'Donnell Family Professor of Orthopaedic Sports Medicine
Secretary General, International Federation of Sports Medicine (FIMS)

It was the spring of 1992 when I had the fortunate pleasure of meeting Dr. Igor Burdenko. I did not know at the time that this meeting would change my life.

I grew up and studied sports in the 1970s in North America. During that time, as many of us remember and as was portrayed in our culture, we were the "good guys," fighting the good fight against the Communists. We heard all about the big bad Soviet Union. The news reported and movies portrayed how they cheated and manufactured athletes.

When I met Dr. Burdenko, who worked at the highest levels of professional and Olympic sports in Moscow, wrote hundreds of articles in sports journals and several books, including the main manual of physical fitness for the Soviet school system, I knew right away that something was amiss with what we had been sold. Listening to him describe his work and methodologies, I began to understand the reasons for so many Soviet medals.

Dr. Burdenko told me about the Soviet approach to physical fitness. He told me how much they focused on health and performance, without ulterior motives. He told me of how research and education was coordinated throughout the entire country. Dr. Burdenko told me how excited he was, as this was a time of amazing progress and discovery for human health.

I was amazed with Dr. Burdenko's education and knowledge. I joked that he has as much education as a full university faculty. I knew that I wanted to learn his methods. I studied with him and became Master Certified in the Burdenko Method, and over the years have continued learning, becoming something of an apprentice to the master. After almost 20 years, I am still learning from Dr. Burdenko. For you, this book is a way of receiving information from a man I believe to be a master of his trade.

A woman from England once said in a Burdenko Certification class, "Dr. Burdenko, he is a healer." How true. Dr. Burdenko told me that when he was ten years old, he carried his father, who had returned from war with many wounds, down to a pond. He watched as the magic of water healed his father. This was the beginning of Dr. Burdenko's interest in water therapy.

I truly believe that Dr. Burdenko is a healer. He follows and uses the research, but he also follows his intuition, his "gut instinct," and most importantly, his experience of what works. Dr. Burdenko often says, "It's results that count. Don't be afraid to try new things. Be creative. If one thing doesn't work, keep trying. Don't give up. *We don't know the limits of human potential.*" His philosophy and his ability to work with people so enthusiastically with a unique methodology creates positive results in his clients often far beyond prognoses of doctors. In this profession it's all about results—and he gets results.

Dr. Burdenko and the Burdenko Method have contributed to my life both personally and professionally. To say that he has helped me a great deal would be a gross understatement. The knowledge I have gained from the Burdenko Method and from Dr. Burdenko's teaching techniques have opened many doors. I am now Master Certified in the Burdenko Method, and have had the opportunity to teach Burdenko Method certification courses around the world and at universities. I have worked with aspiring athletes, professional and Olympic athletes. I have coached at three Olympic Games. I would never have had the opportunity to do these things without the expertise learned from Dr. Burdenko. I remember once telling him, "I used to coach my athletes with the knowledge I had, while you coached your athletes with your knowledge. My athletes did not have a chance."

Since introducing the Burdenko Method to the Waterville Valley Ski Academy, the young athletes I coach have experienced very few injuries, and achieve greater results from their training.

My family calls Dr. Burdenko "Uncle Igor." He helped my wife recover from herniated discs without the surgery her doctors recommended. Her doctors were surprised to see the discs had slid back into place. But it wasn't magic. Dr. Burdenko had designed a program for her in water and on land to give her body the ability to heal itself, with assistance from the hydrostatic pressure of water.

He has also helped my son grow into a healthy young man and an excellent athlete, successful in college basketball.

As for my own health, Dr. Burdenko has not only changed my life, but saved it. When I was diagnosed with cancer, Dr. Burdenko designed a program for me which included diet, massage, breathing exercises, and a plan to keep my mind and body in shape, on task, coordinated with each other and my goals in life. This built my vitality and confidence to a level where I knew I would return to my normal lifestyle.

Though I had surgery to remove the cancer, I never missed a beat. I taught at a ski camp in Austria a few weeks after the surgery. I subsequently underwent chemotherapy, and three days after my last treatment, taught a Burdenko certification course. Seven days later, I was coaching teenage ski racers in Colorado. I have been moving forward ever since because of "Uncle Igor" and his method.

I refer to the Burdenko Method as all encompassing. This means someone may use only this one method for rehabilitation, conditioning, training and recovery. It can produce a healthy world-class athlete, and it can keep a 54 year old fellow such as myself going strong, keeping up with teenage athletes, and doing what I love for as long as I like.

It is a common belief in western culture that we can only keep going for so long before the body falls apart. Dr. Burdenko says the human body can stay healthy until it is at least 125 years old. Dr. Burdenko calls this "Fitness Intelligence." Fitness Intelligence trains the 6 essential qualities of fitness (balance, coordination, flexibility, endurance, speed, strength); balances what is eaten; balances exercise, rest and meditation; and balances the body with proper alignment and proper breathing. This allows the young ones to stay injury free, and us old ones to last to a ripe old age with vigor and health. We do not only wish to move gracefully, efficiently and safely, we want to age that way too.

Please take the time to read and learn from this book. Hopefully you will see results that will change your life.

Tom Barbeau
3-time Olympic Coach
Hall of Fame, McGill University 2009
Athletic Director, Waterville Valley Ski Academy
Master Certified Instructor, Burdenko Method
M.Ed., McGill University

Introduction

I believe that many people agree with me that human body is the most perfect organism. How to secure good health, energy and the right spirit for many years to come is very important. There are many people in the world working on this subject in many different countries. I am one of those people and have devoted most of my life and experience to make it happen.

The Burdenko Method that I developed, practice myself and teach, brought very convincing results and changed the lives of many people to the better. This method is illustrated by stories written by my students and clients. Everybody is different, everybody is unique, but there are certain general principles. The Burdenko Method is the practical application, based on principles of fitness intelligence. Learning and practicing this method will add joy and many healthy years to your life.

Contained within this book is the knowledge I have acquired over the course of over 50 years working with people of all ages, abilities, and fitness levels. Based on this knowledge, research, and experience, I developed the Burdenko Method: a system of innovative water and land exercise programs which help prevent injury and promote recovery from injury with exceptional results, generating a healing process that is more efficient than working exclusively with land-based therapies.

My approach is to work with the whole person, not only the injured area. All aspects of a person—physical, mental, and spiritual, contain important pieces for recovery. Use the *fitness wisdom* principles in your workout to achieve results.

The Background of the Burdenko Method

As a young boy growing up in the former Soviet Union, I was very interested in sports. I played hard, and like most young athletes, had occasional injuries.

During World War II, my father was wounded on five separate occasions, the last one being a strafe from a machine gun. Many people told him, and

I truly believe, that the only reason he survived was that he exercised his whole life, was very athletic, and was in great shape. In my home town of Kiev after the war, there were no doctors, hospitals, physical therapists, or even medications. There were no wheelchairs for those who were disabled. After returning from war, my father was in constant pain and could hardly move or walk. At his request, I helped him to a pond nearby.

When in the water, my father was able to move and do various exercises. I asked him how he could function given all his injuries. He replied that being in water was the only way he could get relief from his pain. Over time, his abilities improved enormously.

My father benefited enormously from his belief in the healing power of water. As I grew up, if I had pain, bruises, or any sort of injury, my parents advised me to go in the water.

There were no pills or medications, and if I was injured, I was not told to sit on the couch in front of the TV (there were no TVs!). I was told to be active, to go in the water. If I hurt my knee, if I had a headache, I was told to be active and go in the water. To this day, in my mind, doing nothing is associated with giving up. Nothing comes from nothing. If you want to change your situation, you must be active in whatever way is possible.

I learned that I could exercise in water after an injury, and if I did so, my pain decreased and that my recovery time was significantly reduced. I also discovered that exercising in water is fun. All this sparked an interest that led to my using water as a therapeutic modality throughout my career.

My fascination in health and fitness continued, and as a young man I competed in cross-country skiing and speed-skating events. I obtained a Master's Degree in Sports Medicine, a Ph.D. in Training and Human Performance from Moscow Pegagogical University, and a Rehabilitation Specialist degree from Moscow's First Medical School.

Afterwards, I began work as a coach and a teacher. I designed and implemented conditioning programs for athletes to prepare them for competitions. In Moscow, I worked with a wide variety of athletes, including members of the cross-country skiing team, soccer team, gymnastics team, track and field team, weight lifters, speed skaters, rowers, and others. I wrote a manual for physical education which became the main book for teachers of physical education in schools in the former Soviet Union, from grade four through high school.

Not satisfied with anecdotal results, I became interested in establishing scientific study to test the techniques and methods I had developed for the use of water therapy to condition and rehabilitate athletes. I was fortunate to have had the opportunity to head a research project sponsored by the Ministry of Sports and Education. Members of the project included engineers, medical doctors, orthopedic specialists, athletes, biochemists, physicists, a dermatologist, an obstetrician, and many other professionals. The goal was to bring the 240 million Russians a program that would help with conditioning for able-bodied people to maintain good health, training for athletes, and rehabilitation from injuries.

We began studies with animals, then progressed to research with people of all ages, from young children to the elderly. The tests and experiments were conducted on both the healthy and the injured. Much of the study focused on athletes who, almost by nature, push their limits, are well organized, and are disciplined in their approach to physical fitness. Our research showed that animals and people recover from injury faster and develop muscles that are stronger and of better quality when using water as a therapeutic modality, compared to control groups who practiced traditionally on land.

We applied discoveries of this research to the development of programs for conditioning the Soviet Union's top athletes.

I then had an experience that changed the course of my career. One of my friends was a very talented athlete training for competition in gymnastics. While high in the air, practicing his elements on the balance beam, his safety belt broke. He landed on the beam, breaking his spine. This once-strong athlete was left quadriplegic. He had many plans for his life, including wanting to be a writer. Now the only way he could write was by using a pencil with his mouth.

From that point on, I took a special interest in helping people overcome injuries. At the time there were few books available and little information on the subject. I adapted my program to address the special needs of the injured and physically delayed, worked with my friend and others.

I immigrated to the United States in 1981. Before leaving Russia, my friend regained the use of his arms, including fine motor movements, which enabled him to write with his hands again.

In the United States, I continued working in the field of rehabilitation, conditioning, and training. I was fortunate to have the opportunity to begin working with members of the U.S. Special Olympic team in 1983. I based my methods on the techniques I had developed in Russia for use on athletes recovering from sports injuries. I designed a program for wheelchair users, which led to my participation as a coach and rehabilitation specialist for athletes in the 1984 World Handicapped Games in Stoke Mandville, England.

I have built upon my experience and developed a method that is extremely effective in helping people recover from injuries. It is a thrill for me to see my clients improve their physical condition, recover from injuries, and in many cases, even regain the use of their paralyzed bodies. Working with people with physical challenges always provides a source of great joy and personal satisfaction.

Over the years, I have studied many different theories and treatments, from ancient techniques to the current practices of today. I have traveled the world to observe and test many rehabilitation and training modalities and techniques for maintaining a state of good health. I have attended and presented at over 70 national and international conferences, presented the Burdenko Method to the American College of Sports Medicine, the Fourth World Geriatric Congress in Germany, the SPIN Summit in Vancouver, and to universities, hospitals, professional and amateur sports teams, and many others.

There are over 300 people certified in the Burdenko Method around the world who have worked on every continent. Over the course of the last thirty years working in Boston, I have refined my techniques and worked to condition professional athletes as well as rehabilitate people recovering from severe injury.

Burdenko Method Class at the U.S. Research Station in Antarctica taught by Lisa Illg, PT

Scott Biehler's Story

At the age of 41, I was enjoying a career as an account manager for a computer graphics company in the Boston area. My wife, my two sons, aged 9 and 16, and I had just finished an active summer. We went bluefishing on Martha's Vineyard and hiking in the Grand Tetons; we visited Yellowstone and attended a National Wildlife Federation family summit in Big Sky, Montana.

I have had a passion for riding motorcycles since I was a young boy. Over the years I have owned a variety of different models and was thrilled to have just purchased a Ninja ZX-10. I had owned the motorcycle for about two months when I took it for a ride one lovely autumn afternoon.

While trying to impress one of my friends, I lost control going around a curve. The next thing I remember, I was on my way to the hospital in a helicopter. My back was broken and I was paralyzed from the chest down.

After the accident, all my medical evaluations resulted in the same prognosis—short of a medical breakthrough, I would not be able to walk again. I was told that I needed to accept my fate and learn to live with my limitations in order to get on with my life.

Adding to this, I had chronic pain that seemed incurable as well. After visiting several neurosurgeons, I was finally told that my life was going to be different from now on. I would have to accept the fact that I could only look forward to accomplishing a small percentage of my goals. I would have to learn to settle for less, since "less" is all I would be capable of achieving. Essentially, I was told that I was a subset of my former self.

Some doctors were cruelly blunt, painting a bleak picture of the future. Others were polite, and tried to candy-coat their words, but the message was the same.

I kept hoping I would find a doctor who was smarter than the rest or knew something the others didn't. I pursued the normal channels for rehabilitation, including an endless stream of medical specialists, therapists, medications, traditional treatments, and alternative methods of healing. My family and I moved from the Boston suburbs to northern New Hampshire, in hopes that the fresh air and peaceful setting would help me rest and give my body time to heal.

The people who sold us our home asked if we had moved there to work with Dr. Burdenko. They assumed I knew of his accomplishments in working with handicapped and disabled people and thought that I had come to visit The Burdenko Water and Sports Therapy Institute in Waterville Valley. This was how I first learned of Dr. Burdenko—by chance. He and I subsequently met to discuss my situation, and I discovered that he has helped other people in my situation recover from paralysis.

Dr. Burdenko has an entirely unique philosophy about the way the human body heals from injury. He treats all his patients as though they were athletes in training, trying to build up their bodies to the best possible condition. His system includes conditioning the mind and taking care of the body, especially in water. He believes the body has the power to heal itself.

When Dr. Burdenko and I began working together, I couldn't even maintain my balance to sit up straight. My muscles were weak, and I had difficulty getting around and transferring to and from my wheelchair. I soon discovered that working in water is fun. While in water, I was able to move my body with less pain and greater flexibility. Within months, my strength and stability had dramatically improved. After six months, my wife saw my legs begin to move in the water for the first time. We laughed and we cried. It was a small movement, but it was something, and it was something every doctor told me would never happen.

The more I worked with Dr. Burdenko, the more I believed I could make progress. I didn't know how far I could go, but became a strong believer because the level of my mobility was completely different in water.

I discovered I could turn, be vertical, be horizontal, and even move independently in water. I could do these things for myself, unlike on land. That was the biggest breakthrough. I didn't expect I would be able to navigate in water independently.

On land, I couldn't turn over on my own, and was in constant pain. My body wouldn't respond to what I wanted it to do. But in water, I could turn over on my own, and pain was vastly reduced. I felt my mind and body connected. The ability didn't come right away. It was slow, but the slow progress was much further and faster than I expected.

I have been elated with my progress so far. I have regained control of some of the muscles below my injury and am looking forward to making further recovery. The best thing for me, as a result of working with Dr. Burdenko, has been the change in my motivation and attitude. Dr. Burdenko's program has paid off many times over in my personal satisfaction alone.

Why Did We Write This Book?

I write my books with my clients. Who better knows the circumstances of people who lost their ability to move? Who better than those who were injured to explain how they have overcome their difficulties? Who better than the voice of experience to show others a way?

There are so many books for people with all sorts of difficulties, but few materials to encourage people with practical techniques to overcome severe injuries.

I do not pretend that the Burdenko Method is the only way to heal, or that everyone should work this way. I created this program because my clients motivate me. Before starting to work with people with physical challenges, I searched to find programs that already existed, so as not to reinvent the wheel. I did not find anything. Handicapped people would ask me, "Where can I find information for people in my situation? Where can I read about the method you teach?"

My clients told me that when they tried to speak with their doctors, they usually did not have time to listen and directed them to find their own sources of information. Many doctors are not familiar with alternative medicine. Surgery and prescription medication are but two of many options. I want to educate people about possibilities.

Many people are confused about paths to health because much of the health industry is more focused on business than health. One example—there are so many programs that focus on core muscles. This is like telling a centipede, "Forget about all those legs, only use the first few of sets of legs." What about all the other legs?

You have 650 muscles in your body. Why would you ignore all of those? Your body is not your core! Core is the buzzword now. It used to be strength. All the late night commercials were about strength. Before that it was stretching. That was the buzzword. It is not about your body. It is about business.

The latest fad I see are programs focused on sweating and working yourself to exhaustion. ***Pushing yourself to extremes does not have anything in common with health.*** Where is the focus on posture? Where is the focus on alignment? Where is the focus introducing a foundation for health and educating people on what they are doing and why? It's go go go go go. I never recommend my clients exercise in this way. The future of working yourself in this way is that your body will fall apart with aches and pains. Fitness is an act of intelligence, not foolish mimickery of one-size-fits-all exhaustive workouts. Fitness is an act of intelligence—how to move your body, feel your body, and use your body, and engage your mind as a part of the process.

We do not do exercise for exercise. We do exercise for everyday life and sport. I think 90% of people have never heard this. They hear a completely different message from those who are meant to teach them. ***All exercises should complement everyday life.***

When most people exercise, they are occupied only with how to lose weight, or tire themselves, not with enhancing daily functioning. Or they are concerned with building muscle without focusing on the quality of muscle they are building. They believe hitting their limits is the goal of exercise, and they exclude their brain from the exercise process. This is a recipe for injury. The exercise process must include the whole body, including engaging the mind.

We wrote this book because I want to share what I have taught people my entire career of over half a century—the awareness and educate to move your body gracefully, efficiently, and safely. I have spent my life bringing people to the best shape they can be in, for recovery, for sport, ***for life.***

PART ONE

THE FOUNDATION OF THE BURDENKO METHOD

The Burdenko Method: A system of movement in rehabilitation, conditioning, and training programs in water and on land based on principles of Fitness Intelligence and the six essential qualities of everyday life and sport—balance, coordination, flexibility, endurance, speed/quickness, and strength.

Fitness Intelligence: Exercise is an act of intelligence. Fitness Intelligence is the ability to process information and use it for fitness performance: how to move the body gracefully, efficiently, and safely, in different environments and activities, based on education, knowledge, and experience.

Fitness Intelligence activates and interacts with emotional and analytical intelligence during health and fitness activities. The individual becomes capable of absorbing and incorporating increasingly complex activities, and harmonizing the six essential qualities of everyday life and sport: balance, coordination, flexibility, endurance, speed/quickness, and strength.

To achieve Fitness Intelligence, one follows a program of exercises reflecting a logical progression from simple to complex. Change and variation is emphasized, so exercises are done in different starting positions (horizontal, vertical, side, etc.), and in different environments (in water, on land), as well as with different speeds (slow, medium, fast).

A variety of movement patterns and attention to full range of motion provide a constant challenge. Activities are never boring or repetitive, and they continue to challenge the body and the mind, while providing an energizing, life-enhancing exercise experience.

Exercise Choreography: The ability to create programs from simple to complex according to the physical, emotional, and spiritual condition of an individual. The principles using exercise choreography in the Burdenko Method progressively challenge the individual to adopt new and more interesting patterns of fluid movement.

Choose logistics to develop one of the qualities you want to focus on, and move from one exercise to the next without stopping, in one fluid motion, so that the end of one exercise is the beginning of the next exercise.

Also, add challenges and new twists. For example, if we moved only one arm, perform the movement with both arms, or in another direction, or another speed. Change or add to the movement in a way that creates a challenge and learning experience. Show this fluidity from one movement to another movement with full control and without losing alignment, balance, or range of motion.

Choreography is not only for the ballet. Choreography is for everyday life and sport.

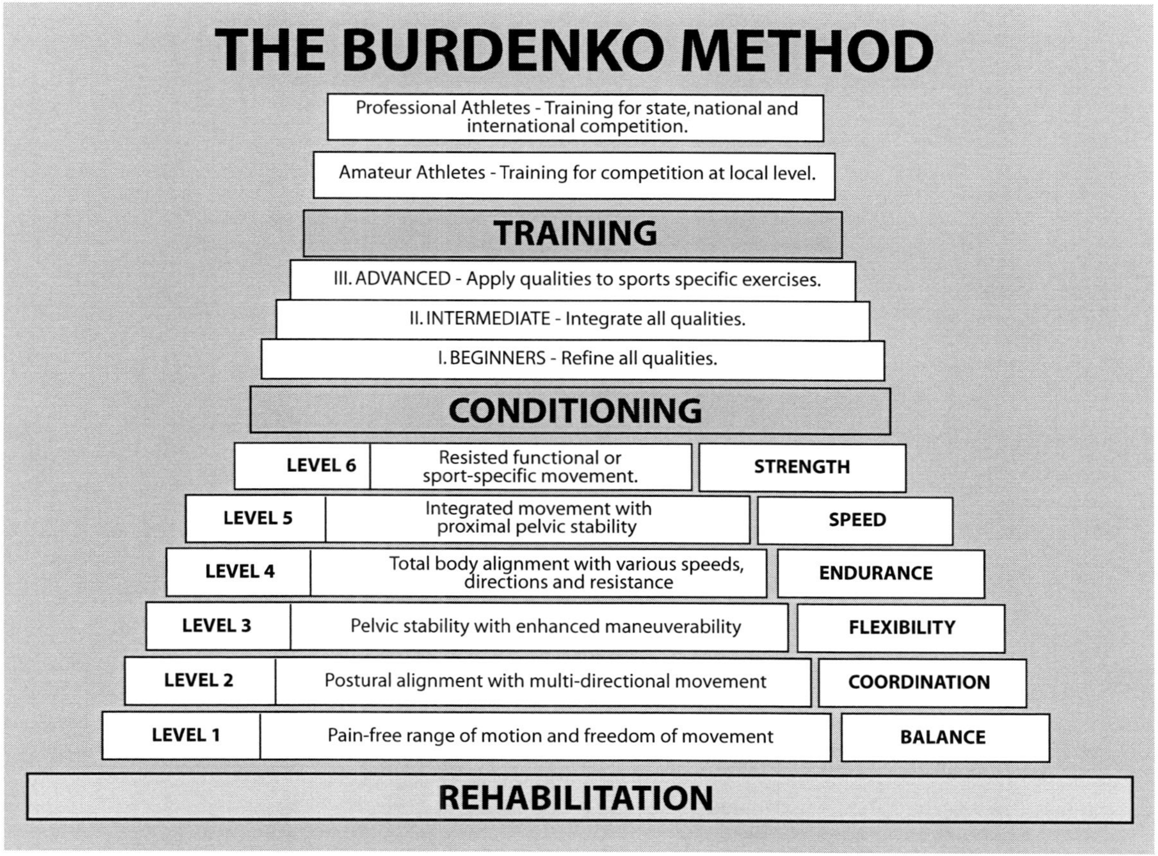

THE BURDENKO METHOD

Professional Athletes - Training for state, national and international competition.

Amateur Athletes - Training for competition at local level.

TRAINING

III. ADVANCED - Apply qualities to sports specific exercises.

II. INTERMEDIATE - Integrate all qualities.

I. BEGINNERS - Refine all qualities.

CONDITIONING

LEVEL 6	Resisted functional or sport-specific movement.	STRENGTH
LEVEL 5	Integrated movement with proximal pelvic stability	SPEED
LEVEL 4	Total body alignment with various speeds, directions and resistance	ENDURANCE
LEVEL 3	Pelvic stability with enhanced maneuverability	FLEXIBILITY
LEVEL 2	Postural alignment with multi-directional movement	COORDINATION
LEVEL 1	Pain-free range of motion and freedom of movement	BALANCE

REHABILITATION

Chapter ONE

Destination: Recovery

My whole life I have walked the edge of the knife, often breaking through my own limiting beliefs about what the human body can and cannot do. Over the course of my career, I discovered that the human body has an enormous capacity to heal and an enormous capacity for physical achievement. I have incorporated my studies and experience into a program called the Burdenko Method.

Dr. Burdenko's Philosophy

As of this writing, I am 77 years old. I have spent five decades working in the fields of rehabilitation, conditioning, and training. I have learned a wide variety of techniques in different countries and at many institutions. I have searched for the best and most efficient techniques to help my students and clients. After years of experience comparing many modalities, I have concluded that in order to consistently produce the best results in a safe and enjoyable way, it makes sense to work with the whole body, not just the injury, and use a combination of water and land exercises *without pain*. Pain is the biggest obstacle of recovery and progression.

It is possible to stimulate and enhance the natural healing capabilities of the body. *I have found the healing power of a combination of water and land exercises to be more effective than pills, surgery, or traditional modalities.* Exercising, especially in water, literally changes the body's physiology.

Many people do not realize that when they are in water, the performance of all their organs is enhanced and stimulated. Water produces an environment which allows the organs to perform their functions more efficiently. Of particular importance are the stimulation of the heart and liver, which promote efficient blood circulation (a key to healing all injuries) and the cleansing of toxins from the body (another key to healing all injuries). Being immersed in water stimulates the release of Dopamine and other chemicals in the brain which promote happiness, a positive outlook on life, help resist depression, and reduce pain. These are among the reasons that I believe water helps create the best environment for promoting the body's healing process.

The use of water therapy has always been an important part of my life's work in rehabilitation, conditioning, and training. When people ask me if they can achieve the same results without using water, I reply that in my experience, progress is much, much slower, and it is more difficult to achieve the same level of recovery.

Key points of the Burdenko Method philosophy include:

- Moving gracefully, efficiently, and safely.
- Pain is a language—listen to your body.
- Perform actions when you have prepared yourself physically, mentally, and spiritually, and you feel you are ready for them.
- Plan your work in logical order.
- Progress from simple to complex actions.

An essential part of recovering and staying well is maintaining the right attitude. For this, I have a simple philosophy—The Five Fs:

1. **Future**—Life without a future is senseless.
2. **Fitness**—If we are not fit and able to function, we cannot enjoy living and have a positive future.
3. **Family and Friends**—We need to share the excitement of our lives with the people important to us.
4. **Fun**—We need to enjoy ourselves! Life without fun is like being in the shower without soap.
5. **Fantastic!**—When you have the first four Fs, then you are automatically fantastic!

I don't like complicated things. Life is complicated enough. I make simple explanations of my philosophy, the way I live, and what I believe.

Educate Yourself

Educate yourself and learn what works for your body and your mind, because no specialist or anyone can know you better than you know yourself. You know what you like, what you do not like, what you can do, what you cannot do, and how you feel when you do or do not perform certain actions. You have your own experience of how to tolerate pain and stress. You know the best ways that you learn and enhance your knowledge. Elderly people have tremendous experience of what it took to make it through their lives. Life experience is like radar that guides you through your life.

I do not have patients. I have clients, and I consider them all to be students. It is important to be a student. Learn and practice, learn and practice. That is what being a student is all about. You use your education for the rest of your life. This is what I need you to understand. You have come to what I call human university. Life is human university.

The word patient has a lot of connotations. When people think of themselves as a patient, it creates a certain image in their minds which is not easy to overcome. This image and thought pattern changes the level of participation people are willing to take in their recovery. Those who think of themselves as patients may not engage in activities because they lack confidence in their abilities and are afraid to believe they can be active. Generally, someone who feels he is a patient is not ready and eager to consider and process options and creative solutions regarding the information given about his condition. He believes someone else will do the thinking for him.

Not everyone is a doctor, but people need to understand information about their health, ask questions, and actively engage themselves in their own healing process. People should not be passive about their fate.

When I share these thoughts with my clients, they often tell me they do not know anything about medicine. That is fine. But it is your body. Ask yourself how you can be involved. Learn and be a part of your healing process. Be active. Participate in your healing.

Trust your doctor. But his word is not gospel. Obtain opinions from many experts in different fields. And educate yourself. Do your own research. These days with the internet it is very easy to find many sources, and also to connect with others who experience similar issues.

I have come across many cases of people who do not consider themselves to be patients. I know people with heart problems who are active, strong, participate in everyday life and competitive activities. I do not recommend not following doctor's orders or performing actions that endanger one's health. I do want to make a clear statement that a prognosis is not set in stone and that health professionals cannot know your body as well as you do. You know yourself better than anyone. Bring your character and your strengths to the forefront of your healing.

I would like to illustrate my recommendation with one of my students, Vladimir Goltsov. He refused to be a patient. He did not accept answers he was given, and he did not accept his prognosis—that he would likely spend his life in a wheelchair. He stimulated his mind, kept his body active in water and on land, and held on to an unquenchable thirst to improve and try every alternative non-invasive treatment available.

Every morning and evening, he spent an hour meditating, practicing breathing techniques, and practicing yoga movements he could make. He often did far more physical activity than he was told he should do, because he felt energetic and could do so without pain. He came to physical therapy early and stayed late, working on his own. Other times he refused to do as his physical therapists instructed, because his body did not feel ready for those activities or because it was painful—a clear sign from his body to slow or stop.

A physical therapist makes educated guesses, but cannot know what his body is ready for. He knows how his body feels and uses those feelings as a yardstick to judge when he needs to push, and when he needs to stop. He also engaged help far and beyond what was recommended to him. He sought out acupuncture, herbal medicine, energy healing, and other traditional methods of medicine.

You must be an active person finding a way to overcome injury and succeed. While guided by your health professionals, you must involve your own feelings. This creates an incredible synergy between you and your health practitioner for achieving your goals to better health. When you take life by the reins and actively participate in your healing process rather than passively allowing it to be dictated to you, you are no longer a patient. You are an active person finding a way to succeed.

I do not have patients. I have students. I tell people that I will train them, for three reasons. One, I do not want anyone to become dependent on me. I want others to learn what I know and apply it for themselves. Two, I want people to have an active role in their rehabilitation, conditioning, and training. Three, I want people to have the knowledge, experience, and skills to use for the rest of their lives. I think this approach leads people to focus, learn, and apply what works for them today and in their future.

I have many long-term students and clients, not because they are in poor health, but because they desire to learn more and improve their level of health and athletic performance.

My students and clients schedule appointments with me looking for a checkup and to advance to the next level of their development. This type of approach creates very strong ties between health practitioners and their clients, allowing the clients to use this knowledge for the rest of their lives, and share it with their family and friends.

When you plan your program, start simply and progress to something more complicated. There may be an overwhelming amount of information from different sources. Do not overload yourself. Move one step at a time.

Educating yourself helps you to plan, because you know what is available and what works for you. You are not creating a general plan. You are creating a plan for you. Your education and knowledge helps you focus and create a plan that is just right for you.

A Healthy Lifestyle

A healthy lifestyle includes knowing how to de-stress, how to stay emotionally stable, being outdoors, sleeping enough, eating right, not overworking or hitting your limit with physical activities, and knowing when and how to implement your plan.

Plan how many hours you will spend on aspects of your healing program. Planning is a part of achieving a healthy lifestyle and a discipline in your everyday life.

One or two poor habits can have significant impact on a healthy lifestyle and the body's healing ability. For example, many people smoke but think it does not have consequences because their lifestyle is otherwise healthy.

I am not judging anyone, yet I want to note that people who smoke regularly or drink heavily or overeat, or have improper alignment, do not have a healthy lifestyle. These choices have consequences on their bodies. Every aspect of a person's lifestyle that is under their control should be healthy. One or two poor habits do matter. A few poor habits can destroy a healthy lifestyle.

People who are not satisfied with their health status need to reevaluate what they are doing to keep themselves in shape. If the answer is clear, it is important to focus on scheduling the activities that will move them toward the condition they desire. Many people do not see a way out from their condition. These people should find health practitioners who can help guide them to their goals.

Everything can be changed. Obstacles can be overcome. It is a matter of how much effort is put into this goal. People understand that if they work more, they can change their financial situation. A health condition is the same. It requires work. It is not for sale. It is never too late. Just like love, you can find health at any age.

The important message is that you make a commitment to take care of yourself. Once you have made this commitment, you can start changing your habits. The time to begin is now.

Give your body the supplies it needs to heal and stay healthy. This means an abundant supply of oxygen, nutritious foods, and plenty to drink. Consider the use of herbal and natural remedies, which allow you to be deeply engaged in and have control of your healing process.

We Don't Know the Limits of the Human Body's Healing Capacity Let's Start Work and Try

I have worked with a wide range of injured people, from everyday Joe's to Olympic athletes, from quadriplegics told they would never walk again, to those with double hip replacements told they would never ride a horse again, to those with multiple bulging disks told there was no solution outside of surgery.

By applying the Burdenko Method, some have been able to walk again and no longer require the use of their wheelchairs. Injured athletes told they could not possibly compete brought home medals. People told they had no alternative but surgery delayed it for years or avoided surgery altogether.

It takes time, determination and hard work, and often a radical shift in thinking. One way I believe thinking needs to change is that after surgery, people are told to go home and take it easy. I do not believe in this concept. I believe it is important to move safely and without pain. This is possible in a no-impact environment such as the deep end of a pool. Covering wounds with waterproof tape and CastGuard keeps wounds dry, and people are able to go in the water days after surgery—stimulating rather than delaying the healing process, and keeping their spirits up rather than fighting lethargy and depression later.

Sarah Lamb, prima ballerina of the Royal Ballet in London, was told that her ballet career was over. Refusing to accept this prognosis, she arrived at the Burdenko Institute in Boston with her foot severely injured and in a cast. She worked hard for two years, then returned to her position as prima ballerina in London, where she continues to this day. She says she now dances as well or even better than she did before her injury.

I worked with Alexandre Despatie, severely injured and limping just a few months before the Olympics. He competed in the Olympics and won a silver medal.

Nancy Kerrigan arrived at the Burdenko Institute with a severe knee injury just 5 weeks before the Olympics. Doctors believed the Olympics were a long shot. She worked very hard, went to the Olympics, and won a silver medal.

I give these examples and provide so many stories within this book because my clients exemplify that people can heal and even compete at world-class levels after severe injuries. I believe in the power of the human body to heal if given the right tools and techniques. My message is to show that these results are attainable. Not everyone is an Olympic athlete, and this book is filled with stories of everyday people who achieve extraordinary results.

The human body needs to move in order to heal most efficiently, and I believe using water as a modality for healing is one of the best methods available to promote the healing process of the human body. Everyone is different, and everyone will experience a different level of healing. When people ask me if I can help them, I answer, "I don't know. Let's start work and try. We don't know the limits of the human body's healing capacity." When you try, and believe that trying in and of itself can bring a breakthrough, amazing things may happen. Recovery from one's injuries and the motivation to heal are directly related. The desire to be independent is a powerful driving mechanism for anyone who has been injured.

Although an essential part of this program involves rehabilitation in water, this book is not aimed at swimmers. It is not necessary to know how to swim to practice the Burdenko Method. We use various buoyancy devices for all activities in water. Staying afloat is not an issue, so you can simply relax and let the water help support you.

My goal is not to merely teach a program, but to educate people to move the body gracefully, efficiently, and safely. It is well accepted that a program of physical conditioning is beneficial to most anyone. Studies have shown that people who exercise live longer and are in better health, regardless of age or physical capability. Taking care of one's body is just as important for injured people as it is for anyone else.

The approach of the Burdenko Method for recovery after injury and for physical conditioning is threefold.

- Take care of your health with proper breathing, eating, and liquid intake.
- Work on the abilities we need for everyday life. We rebuild balance, coordination, flexibility, endurance, speed/quickness, and strength.
- We must help the body heal itself by stimulating and attempting to wake up damaged muscles and nerves. We focus on engaging the whole body, not only the injured area.

Life is Movement

Many programs of exercise refer to the old adage, "Use it or lose it." This takes on special meaning for physically delayed individuals, as well as for the disabled, who may have already "lost it" as a result of injury.

Yet nothing comes from nothing. People should be very active. I cannot imagine progress without action.

Many people are told by their doctors, "Take it easy." They are often prescribed prescription medications. I disagree with this notion. I do not want you to take one medication for pain, another medication for depression, and another to sleep. Prescription medication should be the last resort, not the first option.

My message is to move, and as soon as possible after injury or surgery. The sooner you start moving, the greater your chances of recovery.

Find a way to move without pain. ***Pain indicates the absence of healing.*** Pain is a language. Pain is a message. If you ignore pain, you will create damage within yourself. And you disconnect yourself from reality. The reality is that you have pain. If you disconnect, you cheat yourself.

Movement should not be arbitrary. Move with a plan, and with a clear understanding of what you are doing. Move because you believe in the power to heal. If you choose to practice the Burdenko Method, move because you want to execute a plan which has helped many people achieve tremendous results, and believe it may help you.

Several years ago, I was invited to participate in a study where eight doctors asked me to discuss my methods with them. Each doctor was a prominent specialist who had pioneered advanced techniques in their respective field. They said to me, "We all tell our patients to take it easy after surgery. You tell people they need to move, and your clients consistently achieve excellent results. Why does moving result in more positive outcomes?"

The answer is very simple—*being active safely and without pain as soon as possible after injury or surgery is vitally important for recovery*. The results show that being active is more beneficial to the healing process than taking it easy. When a person is active, blood circulation increases, and they do not experience a loss of motor skills or range of motion. They are also less likely to lose motivation and become depressed.

Additionally, what does "take it easy" mean? It will mean entirely different things to a child, a young adult, and an elderly person. It will have different meaning for a person with a joint replacement or a bulging disc. "Take it easy" is not a direct message to follow and does not help people to feel empowered in their own recovery.

Life is movement. Never stop moving. Do not lie in bed saying, "I tried it, it didn't work." Keep an open mind and try many different methods. Try the methods in different ways, in different directions, in different settings. Keep trying over and over. Never give up! Work as hard as you can, and do not forget to smile. When you smile, you reduce stress and relax 250 muscles.

The Burdenko Method uses two environments—water and land. The water environment can be used to move safely and pain free. People can move their bodies and perform exercises in water in ways that are difficult to perform on land. If and when people are ready, they progress to exercises on land. We have practiced in this way for over half a century.

The water environment decreases the effect of gravity on one's body. Exercising in water helps reduce pain and swelling, and increases range of motion. The water environment helps promote a positive mood and outlook, increases energy levels, and stimulates a relaxation response in the body. Floating in deep water while wearing a floatation device provides natural traction. Most exercises in the Burdenko Method are performed in the vertical position. The vertical position is the natural functional position of the human body.

On land, we must spend energy to fight gravity. In water, gravity does not affect the body in the same way. This allows the body to save energy as it does not need to fight gravity to move. We know from physics that energy does not disappear. Energy the body saves is directed toward other body functions, including the healing process.

All these factors combined create a healing environment in which people are able to move safely and with less pain. By blending water and land therapy with additional modalities explained within this book, such as massage, acupuncture, meditation, and deep breathing, we nourish the healing process exponentially compared to lying down all day.

Using the Burdenko Method to Overcome Injury

I never make any claim that the Burdenko Method outlined in this book will solve all your problems. What I offer is that for many people, the Burdenko Method has worked where other options have failed. I hope it will work for you. The degree to which you succeed will vary. My goal in designing the Burdenko Method is to provide an environment in which the body can do its work at the highest level possible. The important thing is that you never give up!

When following the recommendations within this book, do so safely. Consult with a health care professional you trust, who understands your condition and knows your fitness level. Communication with your health care practitioners is very important.

The reality is that many practitioners do not have a great deal of awareness about the health benefits of working in water, and have not had a chance to study water therapy. It is not their fault. Few universities teach it. There is less research about water therapy than other aspects of healing. How can a health practitioner recommend something they have not learned about or experienced?

Find people who know the value of water therapy or have experienced the Burdenko Method. Find people who understand that waterproof tape and CastGuard can keep a wound safe and dry in water, while giving you a chance to start the healing process and active movement much earlier than might otherwise be possible.

You can go in the water with a cast that is covered and sealed from water. You can go in the water wearing a brace, splint, or Aircast that is covered. You can go in the water after having your appendix removed by putting waterproof tape over your incision and stitches. Be careful, be safe, and be smart. Yet understand that lying in bed inactive for a week will delay the healing process and build depression and frustration.

Some people can go in the water two or three days after surgery. Others need a more time. But as soon as you can, go in the water.

I have cases of people who, contrary to their prognosis, regain speech after a stroke and even return to conditioning and sports. I have worked with a number of prima ballerinas who return to the stage for many years after sustaining what their doctors called a career-ending injury. ***My strong belief is that there is no limit to the capability of the human body to overcome injuries.***

For those who experience nerve loss, remember: ***By constantly stimulating the nerves and attempting to move muscles, you excite nerves and recondition the body***. At first, there may be no movement, but with persistence, nerves start to tingle, and muscles begin to respond. Then you will begin to experience micro-movements.

By applying a comprehensive approach that includes water and land exercises, a constant diet of good food, fresh, oxygen-rich air, visualization, meditation, cold laser therapy, massage, and alternative treatments such as acupuncture and herbal therapy, the body has the opportunity to heal in ways that medicine alone may not achieve.

There are different degrees of recovery. Any improvement in attitude, pain, balance, coordination, flexibility, endurance, speed, or strength is a step toward recovery. We always seem to want what we do not have. The trick is to set realistic goals and participate in a program of activity to achieve them. You can revise your goals from time to time based on the full understanding of what you have been able to achieve along the way.

A common mistake people make is they cannot make priorities, or they choose the wrong priorities. If they have not set the right priorities, it is hard to achieve all that can be done. Make a priority to exercise every day, if you really want to recover quickly. Other important priorities: build up a lifestyle which will give you enough hours for sleep. Attain knowledge to take in the proper foods and nutrition. Do not push yourself to the point of injury in your exercises or everyday life.

Scott Biehler:
When speaking with doctors about rehabilitation, they usually offered me traditional therapy, modalities, and treatment. The Burdenko Method offers enhancements to traditional rehabilitation. The focus is on waking up and revitalizing the body and using water as a modality for healing. The Burdenko Method provides the exercises and conditioning one needs to gradually return to a state of good health. The degree of health one can achieve is limited only by ambition and abilities.

The results achieved with the Burdenko Method have shown that *physical limitations can be overcome*. My experience and the experiences of many others have proved this. Our bodies respond to conditioning. I have met people who used this method and regained the use of their legs after over a decade in a wheelchair.

The Burdenko Method for Lifelong Health

Everything you learn and practice now is an investment for the rest of your life. When you are first born, your body is like a high-performance vehicle. With proper care and maintenance, it can last and last. Without a proper maintenance program, the vehicle will fall apart. In the same way, our bodies require care and maintenance.

Injured and physically delayed individuals can live fulfilling lives whether or not they regain full use of their bodies. However, after an injury, it is easy to fall into a pattern of neglect that causes physical damage and mental distress. A positive attitude is essential to avoid adversity and get on with life.

The biggest injury to the human body is stress. Stress creates most of the injuries and illnesses in the human body, and ***stress inhibits the healing process***. Stress affects everything—your mind, your organ function, your mood, your spirit. Many people under a great deal of stress feel and act as if they have lost touch with themselves. Do not hit your limit. It will lead them to a better life.

The significance of stress on the human body is being recognized. Recent studies have shown that 75% - 90% of visits to primary care physicians are stress related. The World Health Organization called stress "the *health epidemic of the 21st century*." Using water as a modality for healing is a strong method for stress reduction. Water's healing power is demonstrated by the therapeutic reactions of the human body and brain when one is immersed in water.

Moving helps you stay positive and helps your body heal itself. ***Life is movement.*** Movement helps you to reach a level of achievement you could not reach without moving your body and mind.

The Burdenko Method covers a wide range of activities, mental, physical, and spiritual, based on the philosophy that the body has *the power to generate the healing process*. After an injury, it is our job to get our bodies into the best possible condition to allow this natural healing process to take place.

It is much easier to prevent injuries than to cure them. Learning to prevent injuries as well as cure them is extraordinarily important.

THE MAIN CHARACTERISTICS OF THE BURDENKO METHOD

It takes hard work and dedication to get your body into a state of good health and fitness. The focus is on the following key points:

- Exercising in water and on land
- Working with the whole body
- Developing the six essential qualities for everyday life and sport: balance, coordination, flexibility, endurance, speed/quickness, strength
- Performing exercises in a vertical position in deep water
- Performing each exercise in multiple directions
- Performing each exercise at multiple speeds—slow, medium, fast
- Practice what you learn regularly with a solid schedule

Exercising in Water and on Land

Water has special qualities that make it ideal for rehabilitation. Exercising in water is an essential part of the Burdenko Method. We always use a flotation device (vest or belt) when in water, so the body can float freely without effort required. A flotation device also helps ensure safety while working in water.

Water exercises are a gentle means of stimulating and reconditioning the body. In deep water, movement is more relaxing and easier, and there is less stress on the body. When creating a program for rehabilitation, we usually start work in deep water, a non-weight bearing environment. Nearly all exercises in water are performed in a vertical position.

After mastering exercises in the deep end, we progress to shallower water. As soon as you touch bottom, you begin to experience the effect of gravity on the body and a partial weight bearing environment is created as. Progress by working in water up to your neck, then waist-deep water, then knee-deep water.

When in water up to the neck, a person experiences 10% of the body weight. When standing in water up to the waist, he/she experiences 50%

of the body weight. When standing in water up to the knees, he/she experiences 70% of the body weight. When floating in deep water with a floatation device, a person experiences being virtually weightless.

After mastering water exercises, we progress to exercises on land. Exercising on land is more demanding than in water, as a person experiences the full effect of gravity on his body.

On land, we start exercises in a horizontal position, which is partial weight bearing. We slowly progress to exercises while sitting. Then we move to exercises in a standing position, which is full weight bearing. Then we progress to dynamic movements—progressive weight bearing.

As you regain the use of your body, we once again move into water with challenging exercises which build up further mobility.

Depending on your level of recovery, you may spend more or less time in water, but always use a combination of both water and land-based exercises for each exercise session.

For those who are not injured and wish to use the Burdenko Method for conditioning and training, we use this progression in reverse—start on land and finish in water in the deep end at the end of each session. Start in a horizontal position on land. Progress to exercises in a sitting position, then a standing position, then dynamic exercises. Then move into shallow water and progress toward the deep end.

Water cools the body and reduces stress after a workout. I have used this technique with lay people searching for conditioning and training, as well as professional sports teams, with results that startle the athletes and their coaches—fewer injuries, and improved performance.

Research and experience has shown that working in this way is less stressful for the body, and produces greater results than traditional methods. The progression of working in different ways and at different weight bearing levels helps to achieve better results for recovery compared to land-based therapies alone. The combination of working in water and on land has consistently resulted in the greatest levels of healing in a wide range of injuries, from strokes, to hip replacements, to paralysis, to limitations of range of motion.

Exercises are usually more effective when performed outdoors. The environment is more pleasant, the air contains more oxygen, sunlight promotes vital vitamin D generation, and you feel less tired during and after the session. Whenever possible, exercise outdoors in fresh air, both in water and on land.

Working with the Whole Body

Some health practitioners focus their attention primarily on the location of an injury. I have found that working the whole body is of extreme importance. Considering the function of a client's heart, lungs, liver, and the whole body as one unit, is of equal importance to working directly with an injury. When you improve the function of the whole body, the healing process speeds and attains levels difficult to achieve by focusing on an injured area alone.

The mind is an important part of the whole body. Just as the body needs nutrition and exercise, the mind needs to be educated to meditate, control pain, and deal with stress and demanding situations. Essential elements of the Burdenko Method include using the body's ability to visualize and generate the healing process taking place.

Good nutrition plays an equally important part of working with the whole body. The quality of food you consume and air you breathe determine the nutrients and compounds your body will have to fuel its self-healing process. Not only is what you eat important, how you eat is also important.

Many people with artificial joints walk differently after their operation. They have different walking patterns, and might limp or lean, or stand or walk wrong. They develop habits that do not look good or feel good. These patterns are created because certain muscles are weak. We need to balance the muscles. People do exercises on one part of their body, but other parts are weak.

Much attention must be paid to moving, massaging, and exercising injured or paralyzed muscles and stimulating nerves following an injury. Yet that is only part of the rehabilitation process. Stimulating the entire body to promote the healing process is very important.

Working on one muscle at a time creates isolation instead of integration. The human body is an integrated mechanism. Muscles do not perform alone. Exercising by performing movements in an integrated way helps in the ability to transfer these skills to everyday life.

Compensating for Injured Areas

Working with the whole body and raising levels of function in the whole body helps compensate for injured areas.

For example, when working with people who have lost cartilage and have bones rubbing directly against each other, I have found that *muscles can compensate and substitute for weakness and injury in joints.* This can happen when the muscle is of good quality, developed with the right programs, and when there is enough muscle mass.

In addition, the traction of water helps create space within the joint and loosen muscles and soft tissue. It also creates an environment for better blood and lymph circulation, which speeds the healing process. In time, the muscle builds up and compensates for the joint to recover pain-free function. I have seen this occur many times, from housewives to business people to professional athletes.

I worked recently with a star basketball player in the NBA. I told him that if he developed the muscles surrounding his injured knee and moved in proper alignment without pain, he would find his way back to the court. He said to me, "Didn't you see my X-rays? The bones in my knee are rubbing together. I'm in constant pain!" He was very surprised at how quickly he found his way back to the basketball court without surgery. It helped that the rest of his body was in good shape, that he was open to learning new patterns of movement including relearning how to walk and jump. He was also a very disciplined hard worker and followed the program.

When our clients are at this stage, we usually recommend the following:

- Precisely follow your health practitioner's recommendations to increase mobility as much as possible, without increasing your pain level.
- Pay special attention to reduce impact to injured areas while walking. Be especially aware on stairs -- walk slowly, and step softly on the balls of your feet, rather than landing your foot flat on the step. Hold the railing.
- Temporarily use crutches or a cane as needed.
- Don't lock your knees and ankles - keep them loose, when walking and standing.
- Learn the right way to sit down, stand up, walk, make turns, and bend the body. See Chapter 3 for instructions.
- When picking up objects, bend your knees (not spine). Don't lean forward.

You can achieve pain reduction and increased mobility in the deep end of a pool, a virtually weightless environment. This environment reduces compression on nerves and reduces muscle tension, which increases blood circulation and reduces swelling. This enhances and speeds the healing process.

We highly recommend massage therapy, Epsom salt baths, mud application, and cold laser therapy.

Try to take a nap during a day. Think positive, keep your mind occupied reading books, watching DVDs, talking to a friend, etc. Try not to be alone. Have the company of friends, animals, everyone and everything that you enjoy. Pay special attention to your selection of food and liquid. Food is your fuel for recovery.

And smile!

Completing the Healing Process

During rehabilitation, we have the opportunity to work with the whole body, which helps complete the healing process so that the body is in as good or better condition as it was before the injury.

It is often the case that after an injury, strong parts are weakened, and weak parts become weaker, as the injury limits one's ability to move and perform daily activities.

Let me give you an analogy. You are camping on a damp, cold day, and want to start a fire. The fire is difficult to start, but you are able to do so by using the right sized wood placed in the right way. You grow the fire by adding the right kind of wood at the right time. As the fire grows stronger, it becomes warmer and continues to need fuel. You can't stop adding wood, or the fire will go out.

It is the same with the healing process. You should not stop your healing before it is complete. Some of my clients, especially the young ones, stop their recovery before it is complete. They desperately want to finish, do not feel pain for a short period of time, and believe they are done. It is very common for people to discontinue rehabilitation when they experience less pain or no pain. Often difficulties such as pain and limited function return, and become chronic difficulties. Restarting the healing process takes longer and requires more energy than it would have if completed fully to begin with.

People on the road to recovery should be focused until the very end on complete healing. What is complete healing? Complete healing includes being consistently pain-free for a long period of time, and not having restrictions on function or range of motion. Complete healing means being able to return to the activities they previously participated in without pain. If a client cannot jump and turn, for example, or if he feels pain while doing so, he is not done. When the pain disappears, consistently and in the long term, he's completed.

With debilitating problems such as paralysis, completing rehabilitation may mean getting into a routine that makes you feel better. If you have a good day today and a difficult day tomorrow, you are probably not finished. You may be finished with your rehabilitation if you continue with your routine for a period of time, your condition and pain levels do not fluctuate, and you feel better compared to when you started. You should have experienced physical indication of progression—perhaps you no longer need crutches, perhaps you no longer need medication, perhaps you can sit down or stand up easier, perhaps you have experienced movement and sensation where there was none, perhaps you have returned to skiing or other activities.

If you did not experience an improvement, you have not finished. Someone who runs 24 miles has attained a great feat, but she did not finish the marathon. Do not stop your rehabilitation until you have finished.

Be patient and understand that these things take time. Several stroke victims I worked with climbed stairs for the first time after a year living on the first floor.

People must also understand that it is important to continue to work on their conditioning even after rehabilitation is completed. The rehabilitation should be the foundation of a future routine. It is like brushing your teeth. You do not have pain, but you brush your teeth to preserve them. It is the same with a conditioning program. Conditioning should be a consistent part of your everyday life. It does not matter how old you are, where you live, or which profession you hold.

After experiencing what was believed to be a career-ending injury, Sarah Lamb of the Royal Ballet spent two years without dancing on land. But she danced in water—the jumps, the turns, the plie, all of it. Two years after her injury, she danced on land again, and returned to her position as prima ballerina of the Royal Ballet in London.

Many people believe a pill will solve their problems. That is not the message I preach. The pill may help symptoms, but actively taking part in your recovery with your whole body and mind is how your system heals best and most efficiently.

Developing the Six Essential Qualities for Everyday Life and Sport

The program for returning to a state of excellent health and developing fitness occurs with a logical progression of exercises. It is most efficient to build one quality before proceeding to the next, although every exercise works multiple qualities. The art of my profession is to recruit as many qualities as possible with each exercise, while maintaining focus on one quality.

The first step is to perform exercises that build balance, then coordination, then flexibility. Then move on to exercises that build endurance and stamina. As your physical condition improves, the next step is to work on improving your speed and quickness.

After building the first five qualities, you will be ready to build up strength to condition and tone your muscles. One cannot utilize strength without balance or coordination. Many body builders cannot run—they do not build up enough endurance or flexibility.

A car designed to function on four wheels does not run well with only three. In the same way, the human body has many qualities. Ignoring some of the qualities will cause the body to function inefficiently. It is very important to build up harmony between the qualities for everyday life and sport.

When I immigrated to the United States, I was amazed to see that most people use this pyramid upside-down. Most people pay attention to strength as the main quality. Yet how can you utilize strength without balance? How can you utilize speed without balance? How can you utilize endurance without coordination? It became absolutely clear in my mind that I need to explain to my students and clients why the pyramid I use requires a strong foundation. I believe it is very important to educate people on methods to build all six qualities. Many people have knowledge to build strength, but not balance, coordination or others.

If we work with this strong foundation, building one quality after another, the human body will develop much safer and more efficiently, with fewer injuries and better results than working in the opposite direction.

The Six Essential Qualities for Everyday Life and Sport

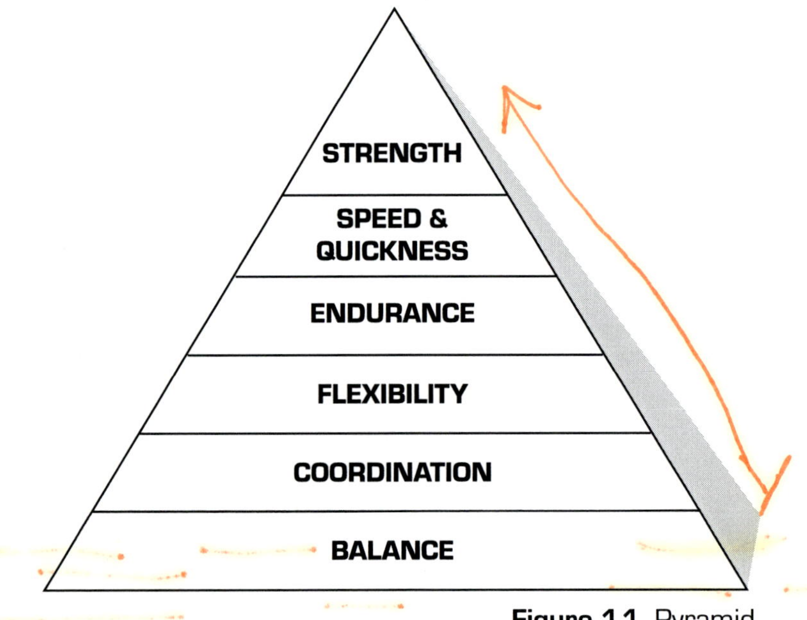

Figure 1.1 Pyramid

BALANCE

One of the first abilities we develop as infants is the ability to maintain our balance. Balance plays an essential role in our daily functioning, yet we tend to take it for granted. As people grow older, they often lose this quality very quickly. For many people, especially following an injury, maintaining stability can be difficult. Even if your muscles are strong, you cannot function properly without good balance.

You need to be able to hold your body erect and make controlled movements without wobbling or falling. Without balance, you cannot properly develop strength and endurance. Focusing on and concentrating on improving balance is always a priority.

Key points of working with balance include alignment, pelvic awareness, and pelvic stability. Alignment awareness is not only about the spine. The entire body, from the lower extremities to the head, must be in alignment. The pelvis is the foundation for the spine and is among the heaviest bones in the body. The pelvis should always be in alignment with the shoulders.

Dynamic movements are very important to coordinate arms and legs when walking or running, and head position should be straight.

Introduction to Methods for Building Balance

In Water

Practice maintaining a vertical position in deep water both sitting and standing on a barbell or Burdenko Board. Progress to jumping and turning while standing on a barbell or Burdenko Board. Exercises and equipment are detailed in Chapter 8.

On Land

Practice maintaining balance while lying down in a horizontal position on a half-roll. This position is safe, easy to practice, and low weight bearing. The next step is to maintain balance while in a sitting position on a half-roll, then a standing position. Then perform exercises and movements while on the half-roll. Practice movements forward, backward, and sideways. Practice various exercises while standing on one leg. After that, practice balancing while performing dynamic movements with turns and jumps. Exercises and equipment are detailed in Chapter 9.

COORDINATION

Coordination is the ability to use parts of the body together harmoniously. To move your body uniformly and perform the activities you desire, your muscles need to work together, properly flexing and extending in a coordinated manor.

Additionally, your muscles and tendons need to be able to move your bones through the full range of motion that your joints allow. As the human body grows from infancy, it acquires coordination through normal development. Your movement becomes an unconscious activity. When you have lost the ability to move due to an injury, illness, or lack of exercise, you must learn how to control your movement again.

A person's movements may become stiff and uncoordinated due to lack of motion, or because muscles do not receive the right signals following an injury. Reconditioning becomes a conscious activity of focusing on each muscle and joint.

People who have limited use of their legs or other parts of their body must especially work on their coordination as nerves and muscles repair themselves and wake up. It is important to focus on and coordinate the signals sent and received by the brain together with actual movements of the muscles. There are over 650 muscles in the human body. The goal of the Burdenko Method is to reach and develop all of them, working together in harmony.

The latest research shows that improving and maintaining coordination may slow or even prevent the onset of neurodegenerative disease, including dementia and Alzheimer's disease.

Many people regularly wear clothing that restricts their movements. To many people, the clothing on the body is more important than the body that wears the clothing. Yet physical beauty does not come only from the clothing one wears. Physical beauty comes from the harmony of the body and its movements.

Introduction to Methods for Building Coordination

In Water

Perform various exercises with long and short barbells. Practice "walking" forward, backward, and sideways while floating in a vertical position in deep water. Practice tossing and catching balls of various sizes, from tennis balls to soccer balls to beach balls. Further exercises are detailed in Chapter 8.

On Land

Start in a horizontal position, just like with balance. Progress to sitting, standing, standing on one leg, then dynamic movements. When working on coordination, we utilize long tubing attached to the arms and legs in prone, supine, and horizontal positions. We use exercises with the Burdenko Stick while sitting, standing, and in dynamic movements. These are detailed in Chapter 9.

FLEXIBILITY

Flexibility is the ability to bend, twist, and turn without breaking. Muscles should have a lot of elasticity. When working on flexibility, one should never experience pain. Pain is a sign that you have reached your limit of elasticity and continuing will cause the opposite of what you are trying to accomplish.

Once muscles begin moving, you need to concentrate on stretching and loosening the joints. Wheelchair users especially need to have very flexible movement of their arms and upper bodies in order to overcome the limitations of living in a world designed to accommodate walking people.

It is important to understand that flexibility refers to a quality of muscle, while range of motion is the performance of a joint. A muscle can be flexible. A joint cannot be. A muscle can be elastic. A joint cannot be. A joint may however, be stiff or locked. You cannot have flexibility without range of motion. You cannot have range of motion without elasticity.

Before working on flexibility, it is very important that your body and muscles be warmed up. I usually recommend starting stretching with the upper body, then progressing to the trunk and spine, then lower extremities.

It is very efficient to work on flexibility using a combination of stretching and shaking, while visualizing the layers of muscles that you are stretching. (Shaking and visualization are detailed in Chapter 2.)

Large muscle groups should be stretched for longer periods of time and more often. The hamstrings, quads, and gluts, for example, are relatively large compared to the rest of the muscles in the human body. They require more focus and varied ways of stretching.

I have found the most efficient way to stretch is in water. Warm water helps the body keep a warm temperature. Exercising in water provides a gentle way to build flexibility, as does using exercise tubing, in water and on land. I also highly recommend massage as an effective way to stretch muscles.

The best way to build flexibility is with dynamic movements, not static exercises (i.e., stretch and hold). It is important to stretch gradually, in multiple directions, from different positions, and at different speeds, so that you can feel the limits of a particular muscle.

Flexibility should be achieved using proper alignment. The pelvis should be under the shoulders. The head position should be straight. Try to stretch with your foot and toes pointed up (dorsiflexion).

Be aware not to overstretch. Pushing past limits creates damage that is difficult to fix. It is very common for a coach or personal trainer to push against someone's limbs. Yet this is a very easy way to go past your limit. It may feel good, but is harmful in the long term. Overstretching muscles may decrease flexibility or create capillary bleeding. This is not the best way to stretch. It is important to have a connection with your body. How much can your body do today? A month from today? A year from today? Be very patient and keep trying. Never experience pain when you work out.

Additionally, active range of motion can only be developed by moving actively, not when someone moves your joints for you. When someone moves your joints for you, or stretches your joints for you, this excludes your brain, and demolishes rather than builds mind-body communication that we work so hard to create. We use water, exercise tubing, and other equipment to help people be actively involved in their own movement. In this way I have seen the best results. Assisting someone in their movement may be helpful, yet doing it for them is another story. Always remember the importance of patience, and never give up.

Introduction to Methods for Building Flexibility

In Water

Practice performing a breast stroke with your arms while sitting on a barbell or Burdenko Board. Perform various exercises with exercise tubing, and long and short barbells. Practice "walking" forward, backward, and sideways while floating in deep water. Practice tossing and catching the Burdenko Stick and balls of various sizes, from tennis balls to soccer balls to beach balls. Further exercises are detailed in Chapter 8.

On Land

Practice exercises with long tubing while standing and lying down. Practice exercises with the Burdenko Belt and Stick. Practice bending to the side (as shown in Land Exercise 14). Further exercises are detailed in Chapter 9.

ENDURANCE

Endurance is the ability to sustain muscle movements over a period of time. Most textbooks on physical training emphasize strength before endurance. I believe this should be in reverse order. To develop strength, one must first have the endurance to build muscles. Endurance is a quality that requires a lot of movement. A lot of movement builds quality muscle mass. It also develops heart strength and cardiovascular performance. The Burdenko Method slowly builds endurance by having you perform simple exercises, then increasing the number of repetitions in water and on land. Performing exercises at different speeds—slow, medium, fast—is a foundation for building endurance.

I highly recommend building endurance outdoors. Exercising outdoors brings many benefits to the body, including more oxygen-rich air and a stimulating, changing environment which engages all the senses and lessens adaptation.

Endurance should be practiced in a variety of ways. For example, walking or running up and down hills, on flat surfaces, and stairs. Do not practice only in one way.

While working on endurance, be aware to emphasize breathing. Air is the fuel for muscle performance. Otherwise, muscles will fatigue quickly and the heart will quickly tire and be in pain. Ensure your body receives enough air.

Be aware of your coordination and alignment while working on endurance.

Some of the best methods for building endurance include cross country skiing, long distance swimming, long distance running in water and on land, and jumping at different heights and intensities. After an endurance routine, shake and go in the water to promote a relaxation response.

Introduction to Methods for Building Endurance

In Water

Start with simple exercises. In deep water, walk and jog forward, backward, and sideways at different speeds with turns, in multiple directions. While walking and jogging, jump and turn 90 degrees, 180 degrees, 270 degrees, and 360 degrees in different directions. Try walking and jogging in water and on land with a Burdenko Belt or while tethered with long exercise tubing attached your arms, waist, or feet. Try practicing dolphin kicks. In the shallow end, continue the same routine (except for dolphin kicks). Also practice high knee kicks and butt kicks. Further exercises are detailed in Chapter 8.

On Land

Perform the same exercises as in water (except for dolphin kicks). Also walk and run with a Burdenko Belt, at different distances, including hills with varying inclinations, and stairs. Further exercises are detailed in Chapter 9.

SPEED AND QUICKNESS

Improving speed includes conditioning reflexes and reaction time. For normal daily living, we must perform certain functions quickly to avoid injury. For example, we must stop ourselves from falling if we slip, or catch a glass from falling off the table. Wheelchair users must be able to turn or move their chairs quickly if the situation calls for it. In high levels of training, as in most sports, speed is a measure of performance.

Changing the speed of activities in everyday life is the best way to practice speed and quickness. Walk and move at different speeds. Then combine walking with turning—walk and quickly turn to the right; walk and quickly turn to the left; walk and quickly stop. Learning to move at different speeds will improve the quality of everyday life as well as help avoid injuries.

While speed and quickness are similar, they are distinct concepts. Quickness is agility, the ability to change direction and move from spot to spot. Speed is a sustained velocity, for example when running, swimming, or biking.

For some people, practicing speed and quickness is difficult due to limitations in their joints or muscles. That does not mean they should not try. They should practice and develop their skills. For example, to develop quickness in hands, practice playing the piano, typing, or manipulating a tennis ball in your hands. Practice throwing and catching to develop speed and quickness in your arms.

Introduction to Methods for Building Speed and Quickness

In Water

Move your legs as if running while horizontal on your chest in deep water. Then allow your legs to drop down move through the vertical position to a horizontal position on your back. Practice other exercises in which you move from the horizontal to vertical position. Practice running on your side. Run on your side while your body turns in a circular motion. Practice all of these exercises both forward and backward. Run while tethered with long exercise tubing attached to your arms, waist, or feet, while the attachment is to your front, back, or side. In the shallow end, practice jumps and turns. Further exercises are detailed in Chapter 8.

On Land

Run with high knee kicks and butt kicks. Quickly jump while running. Quickly turn while running. Quickly jump and turn while running. Practice running downhill. Jump and split your legs sideways or forward and back, then bring them together and land softly. Further exercises are detailed in Chapter 9.

STRENGTH

Strength is the physical power of the muscles. Strength is developed by conditioning the muscles with exercise. Muscles that have withered due to underuse as a result of illness, injury, or neglect need to be built to a healthy working level. You cannot resume your normal functions if muscles are not properly developed. Beyond rehabilitation lies conditioning and athletic training, where strength is a key factor.

One of the best ways to know how strong you are is to see how you can move your body. Can you do push-ups, chin-ups, and squats? Some people lift weights, but cannot do a squat.

Rather than focusing on weights, focus on your own weight—how many pushups, chin-ups, and squats can you do, from different starting positions?

At what speed are you able to perform these movements? Practice 3 slow, 3 medium, and 3 fast. Build up to 10 slow, 10 medium, and 10 fast.

The use of weights may be dangerous for people recovering from injury. Exercise tubing provides a practical, inexpensive, and safe alternative for strength training, that can be used both in water and on land.

If you cannot do pushups, chin-ups, squats, or lift objects without pain, it is important to build strength to a level where you can do these things. Then progress to weights. Gradually build up the weight used. Do not succumb to the belief that more is better. Gradually build up the repetitions you can do both with and without weights.

Remember, the quality of muscle you develop is exceedingly important. What good is strength if you cannot use it? You need to have balance. You need to coordinate the muscles with each other and with your intention. You need to be flexible. Your muscles need the ability to move at different speeds in different situations. And they need to have lasting power so you can do what you want and need without getting tired. You need to do all these things before using weights or getting on a machine and developing muscle mass that is not coordinated, balanced, or flexible. Think about the quality of the muscle you are developing.

Introduction to Methods for Building Strength

In Water

In deep water, practice vertical jumps and squats with barbells, Water Walkers, or Burdenko Board. Practice chin-ups with hand-bars next to the pool or gymnastic rings above the pool. Practice squats in the shallow end. Further exercises are detailed in Chapter 8.

On Land

Practice jumps, pushups, chin-ups, and squats. Vary your starting position, sometimes starting standing, sitting, or lying down. Vary the exercises. For example, sometimes do chin-ups with bent knees, and other times with legs straight in front of you, bent at the hip. Practice squats on both legs and on one leg. When you begin working with weights, I highly recommend dynamic movements with kettlebells of different weights. Further exercises are detailed in Chapter 9.

Performing Exercises in a Vertical Position in Water

The vertical position is the natural functional position for humans. When you are upright, your spine, all your joints and internal organs are in their natural alignment. During rehabilitation, conditioning, and training, the body works best and most efficiently in the vertical position for achieving its full potential. Wearing a flotation vest or belt in water allows you to maintain an upright vertical position with little or no effort.

The vertical position promotes traction and better alignment. Traction in water is the one of the best stretching methods available. Active movement in water enhances traction, rather than stretching passively.

Most traditional exercise routines are conducted sitting or lying down. This is not the natural position for exercise and physical conditioning. Exercising in water in a vertical position allows the healing process to occur most efficiently. This is especially important for the many people who spend most of their days in a sitting position, particularly those confined to a wheelchair, who rarely have the opportunity to be in a fully vertical position.

One of my instructors calls the machines in a gym "fancy chairs." You are sitting the whole time! You are isolating every muscle to work individually. Any movement is better than nothing, but the human body is one piece—everything is integrated, and functions at maximum capacity while vertical, moving dynamically, and engaging as many muscles as possible simultaneously with each exercise.

When doing any kind of exercise, you must be aware of your alignment. It is the signature of your performance.

Performing Each Exercise in Multiple Directions

The muscles in our bodies work in pairs commonly referred to as flexors and extensors. Our muscles work in pairs because muscles push only in one direction. For example, your bicep bends your elbow while your tricep rests, and your tricep straightens your elbow while your bicep rests. We need to balance exercises to equally develop all the muscles. Muscles that are not equally developed result in poor coordination and balance, and create flabbiness in that part of the body.

Developing muscles in both directions builds incredible strength and body harmony. Traditional rehabilitation techniques often overlook the importance of balancing muscle development. How often do you see people walking backwards? How often do you see someone turning bicycle pedals backwards? How often do you see people turning and jumping or jumping and turning in different directions?

Any exercise or movement that occurs in one direction should also be performed in the opposite direction. If you move forward, you should move backward. If you move left, you should move right.

If you want to walk forward well, you must know how to walk backward. If you want to run forward well, you must know how to run backward. This is one of the best ways of balancing muscles, improving mind-body awareness, and maintaining equilibrium. This helps prevent falls, something especially important for those who are injured, and for all of us as we age.

How can you build strength and ability by performing repetetive actions in one direction, without building the foundation for the muscles that support the opposite movement?

People who never walk backwards lose control and ability, and become afraid to move backwards. This creates limitations in the human body. Yet most methods focus only on walking forward, pedaling forward, stretching forward, or pushing against resistance in one direction only.

Exercising in multiple directions helps the body perform efficiently, stay in harmony, and increases the six essential qualities.

Additionally, when possible, **perform exercises facing different directions and in different environments**. This stimulates the senses and helps prevent adaptation. When the same motions are performed in the same environment, we lose awareness, mental focus, and do not pay attention. We become adapted and lose communication between the mind and body, which increases possibility for mistakes and injuries. Engaging the mind and body with varying movements of varying speeds helps prevent this.

We strive to create stimulating movements in a stimulating environment to increase the mind-body connection, promote body awareness, mental focus and sensory stimulation, all of which are vitally important in enhancing the body's healing response.

Performing Each Exercise at Multiple Speeds—Slow, Medium, Fast

Life does not move at one speed. The exercises and routines in the Burdenko Method are meant to prepare you for everyday life. Many people cannot recall the last time they ran, or the last time they jumped. It is important to move at different speeds, not only for your health, but for your life. When a life situation requires fast movement, a person not in practice may injure himself, overstrain his heart, or fall down if unable to catch himself.

Changing the speed of exercises builds healthy patterns of motor skills and cardiovascular conditioning. It also encourages healthy chemistry in the body—it helps regulate body temperature, enhances organ performance, and improves the mindset.

Performing exercises at multiple speeds increases the alertness of mind and body function, and helps prevent adaptation and loss of concentration. Moving at varying speeds requires more attention and helps us stay focused. It also creates a different flavor to the workout, trains motor skills, every organ, and the entire system.

Practicing in this way helps you receive the most benefit from exercise. The efficiency of workouts will be much higher for the same time spent and ***you will achieve greater results on many levels for the same amount of time and effort.***

The way we put this concept into practice is as follows: When first learning an exercise, use a speed you are comfortable with in order to learn the exercise and practice it with proper form. When you are able to perform 10 repetitions at a speed you are comfortable with, progress to practicing the exercises at three speeds—slow, medium, and fast. Perform 3 repetitions at slow speed, 3 at medium speed, 3 at fast speed, and 1 at slow speed.

Performing repetitions at slow speed gives you time to understand and learn, build body awareness, enhance the mind-body connection, and be aware of feelings you have when practicing the exercise.

Continuing repetitions at medium speed helps you practice and implement what you have learned, and builds the structure and pattern of the exercise within the mind and body. Practicing at medium speed with proper form requires increased levels of awareness and focus compared to practicing at slow speed. This stimulates and engages the mind in addition to the physical benefits received.

Practicing repetitions at fast speed without losing the momentum or structure of the exercise, and while maintaining proper alignment, help you feel lively and energetic, and enhances the mind-body connection. We are not mindless emotionless robots, and we should not lose the mind-body connection during the performance of exercises, even when performed very quickly.

Too often, people do not understand the necessity of this connection, nor do they practice building it. People watch TV while exercising, or read, or listen to loud music. They are completely disconnected from their body and what they are doing, they do not have feelings or communication between their mind and body, and they are not aware of their alignment.

People who exercise without proper feelings and alignment learn the wrong patterns. These wrong patterns ultimately do more harm than good.

Performing each exercise at multiple speeds during each session is something that is commonly absent in rehabilitation, conditioning, and training. Those who try it will discover greater results from their efforts.

Practice What You Learn Regularly with a Solid Schedule

It is important to work out every day. Do not use excuses. Just like you brush your teeth, make an exercise routine a part of your daily schedule. It does not matter what your age or how busy you are. Practicing an exercise program daily brings a totally different flavor to your everyday life. And it increases your ability to overcome injuries and achieve the results you desire. People who are in good shape have a greater chance to survive, no matter what happens to them. If you want to be in good shape and avoid complications in your life, I highly recommend practicing an exercise routine every day.

SUMMARY

- Life is movement
- Develop the six essential qualities for everyday life and sport
- Engage your entire body
- Perform exercises in a vertical position in water.
- Practice what you learn
- Complete your rehabilitation fully

Paul Carney's Story

An unseasonably late snowstorm in May of 1977 had iced over the roads. The day before had been sunny and warm, and I had been playing softball. I had just finished my first semester at college and was looking forward to the summer. As I was driving that day, my car skidded on the ice, and I crashed into a wall. I felt a tingling creep up my toes and legs just before I blacked out.

Later that evening, I overheard the doctors tell my mother that if I survived the night I would be quadriplegic—essentially a vegetable for the rest of my life. I spent the next twenty-two months in the hospital undergoing all kinds of experimental medications and treatments. A side effect of the steroids I had taken caused severe bone damage, and I endured several hip replacements.

This was devastating for me. I had always been athletic and loved to compete. I felt deep down inside that somehow I would beat this thing and find a way to walk again.

After I was out of the hospital for seven years, a friend of mine—Charles Laquidera, a famous Boston disc jockey—recommended that I see Dr. Igor Burdenko. Igor had helped Charles recover from a painful back injury, and Charles said Igor worked wonders. I met with Igor and discussed my situation. At the time, both of my hips were broken. Even though I had just replaced them, the bones were weak, and I was in so much pain that I didn't realize the extent of the damage. Igor evaluated my situation and explained how he could help me, using a combination of land and water exercises. We agreed to work together to get me into shape.

At first, we worked in water and on land with no equipment—just performing basic exercises. Igor would not allow any negative thinking. He was always positive, encouraging me to strive to do better and pushing me to achieve more and more. He shared with me his philosophy of the mind—he told me to believe in myself, that I am who I want to be, and that I can achieve my goals with positive thinking, a competitive drive to win, and hard work. Prior to my accident, I had been a hockey player. As an athlete, I agreed with his intensive conditioning and training methods. Igor was like a start-up button to get me going.

It came time for me to have my hips replaced once again. I decided to get into the best physical condition possible before the operation. I believed Igor could help me like no other person I had ever met. I made a commitment to work intensively with Igor for one month. We went to the island of St. Thomas and started working out in earnest.

We began each day at 6 a.m. by swimming in the ocean, followed by vigorous exercises with rubber exercise tubing in the water and on the beach. It was amazing how my body responded to the water exercises. For some moments, I could forget my limitations. Water gave me freedom of movement and relief.

After a healthy breakfast, it was more exercises and a walk with crutches in the sand. In the afternoons, we went to the health club to work out with weights and exercise equipment. Then, back home for more exercises in the pool and supper. After a day of hard work in water and on land, Igor would have me undergo relaxation therapy. This included several types of massage Igor developed to stimulate nerves and muscles, and a different massage to relax. We spent time daily conditioning my mind with positive thinking and visualization of my body healing. I learned how to establish communication between my mind and body. After a good night's sleep, we'd start the whole process over again in the morning.

While we were at St. Thomas, for the first time since my accident, I took a step on the beach by myself without the aid of any crutches. I was so excited! It was a wonderful feeling to be walking. Igor's encouragement to never give up, and to try, try, try, had really paid off. When we returned to Boston, my mother saw me walking unaided for the first time in seven years at the airport terminal and started screaming with joy. Everyone was in tears—happy tears.

My life changed since working with Igor. I am pursuing my dreams. Professionally, I am a writer. Personally, I am happily married and just recently had a baby girl (another achievement the doctors said would not be possible).

Scott asked me if I had any words of advice I'd like to share in this book. I say, "Believe in yourself. Don't let even a tiny speck of negative thinking sink in to keep you from achieving your goals."

Chapter TWO

The Importance of Using Water as a Modality

According to our experience, research, and observation, recovery from injury occurs faster, more easily, and with less pain in water than when the same therapy techniques are used on land. I have seen over the years that using water not only affects a person's healing process, but impacts their vision, spirit, and life overall.

People who cannot swim typically do not ask for water therapy and believe they are not candidates for water therapy. This is common, and should not be the case. Our experience shows that people who have not swam for their entire lives can get in the water with a floatation device, achieve incredible results, and feel wonderful.

The public tends to believe that water is for recreation rather than rehabilitation. Yet using water for therapeutic purposes should be a big part of our lives. Maybe today you have back problems, or liver problems, and one day you may have arthritis. Water can help prevent these things before they occur, or help overcome them if they do, so that you can continue to live an active, healthy, pain-free, happy life.

Picture yourself taking a shower after a long work day. Right away you feel better. That is how the body responds to water. In a pool the response is much stronger, because you are immersed in water and virtually weightless when floating with a floatation device. Your muscles and whole body remain relaxed for a period of time after leaving the water. Studies confirm these common feelings—they show that immersion in water stimulates the release of chemicals in the brain which promote a positive mood, and that this continues even after leaving the water.

Water therapy is like doing homework. Water therapy requires active participation in one's rehabilitation. Taking pills is not like doing homework, as pills are not an active part of your life. When you are active, you will have better results than when you are passive. Taking three pills a day is not active. Going to the pool several times per week is active, and in my experience, achieves greater long-term health.

I want the public to be aware that pills and surgery are not the only answers to physical ailments. In my practice I have worked with people to prevent joint replacements doctors said were required, or delayed surgery for a decade or more, while clients maintained active, healthy lives.

If you are motivated, and have the right setting, using water as a therapeutic modality is a prescription to prevent injuries, heal injuries, and sustain good health for the rest of your life.

I want to help open the eyes of the general public to using water to help prevent and overcome injuries. Be aware that there is always a way to help yourself.

Scott Biehler:
Prior to my accident, I enjoyed going in water for fun and recreation. I loved going to the beach and swimming in the ocean, relaxing in a pool, and playing around with my kids in a lake. After my accident, I believed I simply could not do those types of activities anymore. I had heard of physical therapy in a pool, but my mental image of that was being strapped in a bulky life jacket, with a physical therapist, doing the same rehab exercises as on land.

Boy, was I wrong! The first time I got into water after my injury, it was exhilarating. I was able to float and swim with a specialized thin flotation vest called a Wet Vest without worrying about tipping over or going under. The flotation vest was thin and lightweight, allowing me to move without feeling restricted. Being in water became fun again. Dr. Burdenko encouraged me to relax, move around, splash, and enjoy myself. He would often say, "I want to see you smile." In water, this was no problem.

The first benefit I experienced from water was psychological. I was able to do something I had done before, and it was fun. In water, I found I was able to move much more easily. My mobility was better and less restricted. My body felt light weight, and I was free to lean, roll over, or even do a somersault! I could move and stretch in ways that were impossible on land.

There was no need to worry about losing my balance or falling the way I did during land-based activities.

To my surprise, all this activity caused much less pain than less activity caused on land. I could easily make movements in water that I could not do on land, as they hurt too much. In water, the slightest movement of my body could be seen, unlike land-based exercises, where attempts to move my legs seemed fruitless. The ability to see such immediate results helped my motivation a great deal.

Water provides a gentle medium in which to work the body. Dr. Burdenko's program includes the use of flotation devices, such as long and short adjustable buoyancy water barbells, a floatation board he designed that has straps which allow you to secure the board to your legs or hands, and Water Walkers which provide more resistance when moving legs and achieve more muscle mass and strength.

These simple devices make it easy to perform a wide variety of exercises and motions that are difficult to achieve on land.

PHYSICAL PROPERTIES OF WATER THAT MAKE IT IDEAL FOR REHABILITATION, CONDITIONING, AND TRAINING

Water has been used as a therapeutic modality since ancient times. Ancient Romans understood and used the healing properties of water. Their spas were for healing as well as pleasure.

Since that time, there has been a great deal of research and experience using water for healing purposes. Today, there are locations worldwide with extensive facilities that specialize in water treatment, including Carlsbad in Czech Republic, Tskaltubo in Georgia, Balaton in Hungary, and many others.

Water has a number of properties that make it an ideal therapeutic environment. These properties make exercise in water safer, less difficult, and less painful than on land. Using water as a modality is also less dramatic, less invasive, and in my experience, more effective in creating long-term health than many traditional recommendations.

Many people spend much of their time with part or most of their body sedentary. Pressure sores are a constant concern. Water provides a medium in which the body is virtually weightless when floating with a buoyancy device. This environment allows one to escape the effects of gravity, helping to reduce pain after a medical procedure or injury. When in a vertical position with a buoyancy device, traction is created, which creates more space between joints and stretches muscles.

Water provides assistance, support, and resistance, and decompresses the body, helping to loosen muscles and creating a relaxation response. This further reduces pain levels, allowing for increased mobility, thereby generating a stronger healing response.

Healing is not occurring efficiently when you feel pain and are immobile. Reducing pain, compression, and stress, while increasing movement and blood circulation, is vitally important in promoting a healing response.

A common problem for people with a spinal-cord injury is spasticity (muscle spasms). These can take the form of muscle contractions where the muscles are rigid and hard, or muscles may contract and relax sporadically, causing arms or legs to twitch. A water workout provides relief from spasticity for many people. The muscles are exercised, circulation increases, and movement is produced in areas that are usually restricted, providing those areas with vitally needed increased circulation, oxygen and nutrient supply. You feel less pain, more comfort, increased mobility, decrease overall tension in your body, and reduce spasticity.

Many people believe working in water does not address bone density issues. This is far from the case. Exercising in shallow water with one's feet touching the bottom allows us to work with bone density in a way that would be difficult on land—the partial weight-bearing environment of shallow water allows us to perform exercises and movements that would be difficult or impossible on land.

The water environment enhances recovery and allows those recovering from injury to be active and safe.

Hydrostatic Pressure

If a submarine submerges too deep, the pressure will cause it to implode. This force is called hydrostatic pressure. This property of water is described in Pascal's Law: Fluid pressure is exerted equally on all surface areas of an immersed body at rest at a given depth.

When you are immersed in water, pressure pushes against your entire body evenly from all directions. This even pressure helps create proper alignment in joints and vertebrae, generates increased circulation within the body, and helps blood return from extremities to the heart. The heart works work more efficiently, and your pulse and heart rate will decrease in water as a result, allowing a more vigorous workout with less stress on the system. Hydrostatic pressure also helps the body remove lactic acid from muscles, so you will not feel as sore as when performing similar exercises on land.

Hydrostatic pressure, along with the increased circulation that it promotes, helps prevent and reduce swelling. On land, people often wear compression stockings to reduce swelling. People are often surprised that swelling and edema decrease after working out in water.

Hydrostatic pressure makes breathing slightly more difficult when immersed in water. Although you may not be consciously aware of it, the muscles in your lungs work harder to inhale the same volume of air as on land. The simple act of breathing while immersed in water is a form of exercise in and of itself. This stimulates and improves respiratory ability, increasing your breathing capability on land.

The increased circulation, reduced swelling, promotion of proper alignment, improved respiratory ability, and more efficient removal of waste materials all combine to greatly enhance the healing process.

Density

Relative density determines whether or not an object sinks in water. If an object is denser than water, it will sink. The human body is slightly less dense than water, and therefore floats. This allows water to support us and provide a cushion for our work.

Muscle tissue is denser than fat, so people that are lean and muscular have a higher relative density than those who are not. When floating in deep water with a floatation device, the right buoyancy is such that the neck and head should be above the surface of the water. Apply enough buoyancy devices to ensure that this is the case. If more buoyancy is needed, one option is to use a floatation vest and belt together.

Parts of the body that are swollen after an injury or due to edema (chronic swelling) retain fluid. This fluid is lighter than muscle tissue, so they tend to float more easily, as those parts of the body have a low relative density. Therefore it takes significantly less effort to raise weak or swollen extremities in water than it does to lower them.

Fluid Resistance

Fluid resistance is the force that tends to oppose or retard the motion of an object through fluid. The fluid resistance of water is caused by density, friction and by the clinging action of water molecules to the object. When moving through water, you have to push your way through it, slowing you down. The physical properties that explain this are viscosity, adhesion, and cohesion.

Viscosity is the degree to which a fluid resists flow under an applied force. This resistance is caused by the friction your body makes as you move through water molecules. Cohesion is the attraction of similar molecules. Water molecules tend to stick together, which is one of the reasons it is difficult to push through water. Adhesion is the attraction between dissimilar molecules—water molecules stick to your body.

Fluid resistance is beneficial for water therapy in two ways—it supports and resists movement. Fluid resistance supports movement by creating a supportive cushion which helps hold you in position and slows movements. You will not fall over or lose balance as readily as on land. Slower movements allow you more time to process information, correct movements as necessary, and provide the opportunity for additional awareness and control. This increases mobility and reduces the risk of injury.

Fluid resistance resists movement by causing movements through water to be much slower than through air. The same action in water is more difficult than on land, and engages more muscles. This challenges the body and increases the effectiveness of water workouts, developing strength and building muscles. Fluid resistance is dynamically adjustable from moment to moment—move faster for more resistance, or move slower for less resistance.

The first quality we develop in the Burdenko Method is balance. The fluid resistance of water makes it an ideal place to perform balance exercises. Water is very forgiving and allows time to react and relearn how to maintain proper balance in a gentle environment.

Turbulence

Part of the fun of being in water is splashing, making waves, and hearing the water make a whooshing noise. These are the result of turbulence. Turbulent flow is the motion of the water as it moves at changing speeds and pressures, caused by a disturbance.

Moving through water causes pressure to build up in front of you and creates waves. At the same time, pressure drops behind you, creating drag that swirls the water in a circular motion. The combination of these differences in pressure causes turbulence.

Turbulence provides therapeutic effects in the form of massage and resistance. The movement and pressure of water on your body act as a gentle massage. This helps increase circulation and ease pain.

Turbulence eases pain because nerve receptors are filled with sensations of water from all over the body. This wave of sensations causes the brain to ignore or reset some of the other signals your body is sending, including pain.

The continual sensations from all over the body also serve as a walk-up call for nerve receptors, as nerves attempt to communicate these non-stop sensations to the brain. Any stimulation, whether pressure, touch, heat or cold, creates the potential to stimulate and heal damaged nerves over time. Being immersed in water creates so many continual sensations all over the body that the potential is greatly increased for stimulating damaged nerves to restore communication pathways and create new ones. Over time, this may restore feelings and movement to parts of the body where nerve damage has occurred.

Feeling the turbulence of water helps us feel more alert and more alive. It provides an additional source of resistance, helping to further exercise muscles during a water workout. This resistance can be varied by changing the speed and direction of your motions.

The jets of a Jacuzzi or hot tub also create turbulence in a pleasant way, creating a massage, increasing circulation, easing pain, and stimulating nerve function.

The combination of these properties helps restore function and greatly enhances the body's healing capability. Water provides a medium in which a person recovering from injury or surgery can be active, upright, and participating in his or her own healing. This helps create a positive outlook, which in turn allows for greater enthusiasm and further healing. Compare this to the physical condition and mood of a person lying in bed for days or weeks.

Knowing the characteristics and physics of water allow us to develop exercise programs which help people achieve results that are difficult to attain with land-based therapy alone.

Traction

Traction is one of the strongest benefits of water. When floating in deep water with a floatation device, water creates natural traction in your body. Traction can also be created by hanging from a pool side pull-up bar or rings suspended from above a pool.

The buoyancy of water (and a floatation device) pulls you up. Gravity pulls you down. The pull in both directions creates more space between joints and stretches muscles, creating traction. Natural traction in water is the best and most efficient method I have seen for stretching—gentle, efficient, pain-free, and safe.

More space between joints and stretched muscles increases circulation and allows for more freedom of movement, enhancing range of motion and flexibility. It also helps reduce or prevent nerve compression. Traction is especially important for those with joint injuries and arthritis, as it can relieve pain and allow for an efficient workout that might otherwise not be possible. Traction helps stretch back muscles and creates more space between vertebrae, helping to align the body, reduce stress, and increase circulation, vitally important for those with back injuries.

Decompression

Warm water provides a relaxation response for the whole body, relieving pressure and tension throughout the body and loosening muscles. Compression on nerves is reduced, helping to reduce pain and enhance receptivity between nerves. Decompression creates better conditions for healthy blood flow, helps alleviate muscle spasms, improves range of motion, and creates an environment in which the body can heal efficiently.

Traction and decompression are different forms of therapy which intend to achieve the same goal through different means. Warm water provides a medium in which both methods are provided.

Buoyancy

Buoyancy is the upward thrust that a fluid exerts on an object less dense than itself. Archimedes, the ancient Greek mathematician, described this force in what has become known as Archimedes' Principle: When a body is fully or partially immersed in a fluid at rest, it experiences an upward thrust equal to the weight of the fluid displaced.

Buoyancy has a wonderful therapeutic effect—it decreases the effect of gravity on the body. The body weighs less—90% less when neck-deep water. A 150 pound man weighs just 15 pounds when neck-deep in water. This allows more freedom and ease of movement, which is especially important for those with physical limitations, injuries, arthritis, and those who are overweight or pregnant. A person weighs 50% less when in waist-deep water; 30% less in knee-deep water.

Floating in deep water with a floatation device creates a virtually weightless, non-weight bearing environment where movement does not cause impact to bones, joints, or muscles, greatly easing the ability to move and perform exercises.

Shallower water (up to the chest, hips, or knees, for example) creates a partial weight bearing environment where the level of impact, the effect of gravity, and one's weight can be easily adjusted by moving into deeper or shallower water.

Traditional exercises are performed on land in a clinic, gym, or physical therapy room. Land-based exercises rely upon muscles to resist gravity and carry the weight of the body. The body must continually exert energy to counteract the force of gravity. When using water as a modality for rehabilitation, less energy is required to counteract gravity. The energy your body saves by not fighting gravity can be redirected toward rehabilitation and healing.

The reduction of the effect of gravity reduces pain and creates a feeling of comfort. It also reduces tension in muscles and joints, making movements significantly easier. This is particularly beneficial when attempting to move parts of your body that are stiff, weak, or paralyzed.

The buoyancy of water assists, resists, and supports movement. It assists movement by counteracting the force of gravity, letting your body experience weightlessness while floating. Movements toward the surface of the water are assisted by water's buoyancy, making the movement easier.

Movements away from the surface of the water are resisted by water's buoyancy, making the movement more difficult.

The buoyancy of water is supportive as it counteracts gravity, so you do not have to spend energy fighting gravity, allowing you to have more power available for exercise.

Vertical Position

The properties of water allow us to float in a vertical position while virtually weightless. The simple act of relaxing and floating in water in a vertical position while wearing a floatation vest or belt has an enormously healthy effect on the body.

Most people associate water with swimming in a horizontal position. We use water for rehabilitation, and the main position for this purpose is the vertical position. The vertical position is the human body's functional position. Those who are injured spend much of their time lying down or sitting, including during therapy. *Yet being in a vertical position generates a chain reaction of healing processes throughout the mind and body.*

Floating in a vertical position in deep water (a non-weight bearing environment), promotes more efficient heart and liver function, aids in digestion, bladder function, increases circulation, and promotes a positive mood, positive thinking, and better focus. The vertical position is the most efficient position for organ function and body processes in the human body.

The vertical position also provides for reduced stress compared to a horizontal position, as it allows people to maneuver more easily, be more alert and aware of their surroundings, better able to see and communicate with others, and generally feel comfortable and safe.

Those who are injured are often not able to be in a vertical position on land for long, if at all. Floating in water with a floatation device allows for the ability to easily sustain a vertical position, enhancing and promoting the healing process, and restoring balance, while warding off lethargy and depression, which are all too common in those who are largely sedentary.

Dr. J.B. Smith—author, educator, and researcher discovered that "the submersion in water increases the circulation of blood and creates more efficient breathing as well as mood improvement. Water immersion increases the blood flow by 22% in older people and 59% for younger people—just from immersing the body in water."

In my opinion this is the best investment in your health.

SUMMARY

Physical Properties of Water that Make it Ideal for Rehabilitation, Conditioning, and Training

Vertical Position

- The properties of water allow us to float in a vertical position while virtually weightless.
- The vertical position is the human body's natural functional position.

Buoyancy

- Buoyancy has a wonderful therapeutic effect—it decreases the effect of gravity on the body.
- The reduction of the effect of gravity reduces pain and tension in muscles and joints, making movements significantly easier.

Hydrostatic Pressure

- When you are immersed in water, pressure pushes against your entire body evenly from all directions.

Traction

- Traction is one of the strongest benefits of water.
- Natural traction in water is the best and most efficient method I have seen for stretching—gentle, efficient, pain-free, and safe.
- More space between joints and stretched muscles increases circulation and allows for more freedom of movement, enhancing range of motion and flexibility.

Decompression

- Decompression creates better conditions for healthy blood flow, helps alleviate muscle spasms, improves range of motion, and creates an environment in which the body can heal efficiently.

Density

- The density of water allows it to support us and provide a cushion for our work.
- When floating in deep water with a floatation device, the right buoyancy is such that the neck and head should be above the surface of the water.

Fluid Resistance

- Fluid resistance supports movement by creating a supportive cushion which helps hold you in position and slows movements. This increases mobility and reduces the risk of injury.
- Fluid resistance resists movement by causing movements through water to be much slower than through air. This challenges the body and increases the effectiveness of water workouts, developing strength and building muscles.

Turbulence

- The movement and pressure of water on your body act as a gentle massage. This helps increase circulation and ease pain.
- Being immersed in water creates so many continual sensations all over the body that ***the potential is greatly increased for stimulating damaged nerves*** to restore communication pathways and create new ones.
- Using water as a modality for recovery, condition and training brings remarkable results.

Recovery from injury occurs faster, more easily, and with less pain in water.

Merrill Ashley's Story

The life of a ballerina is filled with injuries, but the hip pain that afflicted me in 1990 seemed to defy the expertise of the many orthopedists I consulted. At the time, I was a Principal Dancer in the New York City Ballet where I had begun my professional career in 1967. Although I was nearing the age when many ballerinas retire, I still felt strong and was convinced that without my hip pain I could continue to dance the many difficult roles in my repertoire. However, the pain in my left hip made it very difficult to raise my leg in high extensions, a crucial movement in ballet. At first I tried rest, but that only made the pain worse. None of the doctors could tell me what to do to stimulate healing—their only advice was a frustrating "keep resting". However, the more I rested, the more restricted I became. In addition to my increasingly limited movements, walking and sitting started to become very uncomfortable, and standing up became an exercise in slow motion. Sleeping on my side was impossible. Any and all forms of exercise proved equally detrimental—even swimming was painful. The hope of ever being able to dance again began to fade, and soon the prospect of living a life with constant hip pain became a looming reality.

During the many months of rest, I made many visits to different doctors in many different fields of the healing arts in New York. I tried chiropractic, acupuncture, Feldenkrais therapy, cranial-sacral therapy, energy therapy, massage therapy and even faith healers! I was desperate to find a solution to my problem. I decided to see doctors in other parts of the country, and even the world if necessary. I didn't want to give up the hope of finding the cause of my pain and curing the problem. I wanted so badly to go back to what I loved the most, dancing in the New York City Ballet. But if I couldn't dance, I at least wanted to be able to do some type of physical exercise or movement. I was tormented by my inability to be physically active.

I went to Boston to see Dr. Lyle Micheli, the orthopedist for the Boston Ballet, He was mystified by my pain, but recommended I go to see Dr. Igor Burdenko, who specialized in rehabilitation in the water. He said Igor had a high success rate with difficult cases, and had worked with ballet dancers many times before. Igor worked in the suburbs of Boston, so I contacted him and set up a consultation. I was immediately impressed by his knowledge, enthusiasm and positive attitude. His plan for me was doubly appealing: his program consisted of a broad variety of exercises on land and in the water and it bore no resemblance to anything I had ever tried before.

I approached his program with excitement tinged with trepidation because past attempts at exercise had only aggravated my problem. However, in my first session he had me moving around the gym floor doing numerous exercises, many related to ballet movements I would need to be able to do. It felt wonderful to move again! Importantly, he wouldn't allow me to do anything that was painful. If an exercise caused pain he could usually find a way to modify it so it would work the same area without discomfort. Failing that, he quickly gave me a different type of exercise to work on something else. There was infinite variety. He focused not only on improving my range of motion, but also emphasized balance, coordination, strength and stamina, and all the other aspects of movement that he knew so well. My excitement grew with each minute that passed. The exercises he gave me when we proceeded to the pool were a revelation. I had never imagined doing exercises in the pool like the ones he gave me. I felt so free and light, compared to the way I felt on land. And my restrictions seemed less severe in the water. Finally, I could see that at the very least, there would be a way to exercise and get my body back into condition. And that fact brought back hope that one day I might dance again. I was ecstatic. My spirits rose even higher after my first session was over because although I was tired from the exercise, my hip pain was no worse. It fact, it was a tiny bit diminished. It seemed like a miracle.

Igor's approach provided me with an added benefit: I could work by myself on the exercises while I was in New York. With all the other therapies I had tried, I had to be with the practitioner in order to be treated. Igor's goal was to make me independent, and able to work by myself. Of course I spent many hours working directly with Igor, since he knew the best progression of exercises for me. Each time I went to work with him for four or five days in a row. I would then go back to New York with more advanced exercises and more variations of basic exercises. I would work alone for several weeks and then go back for more help from Igor. Little by little my restrictions diminished and my conditioning improved, making a return to the stage a distinct possibility.

In time, Igor's program brought my body to peak physical conditioning. In many ways, I was stronger than I had ever been before. I still had some restrictions in lifting my legs, but I had improved enough to return to performing! What a joy to be back on stage doing what I loved so deeply.

The happy ending to this story is that thanks to Igor, I was able to dance another four years. Today, a decade after my retirement and well into my teaching and coaching career, Igor's exercises keep me in good physical condition. I also am able to teach young dancers the benefits of his exercise programs, which will help reduce the number of injuries they may incur and accelerate the rate of recovery from injuries they do sustain. Meeting Dr. Burdenko, working and learning from him has been one of the most valuable, satisfying and enjoyable events in my life. I am forever in his debt.

Chapter THREE

Principles and Techniques

A significant portion of this book is dedicated to exercises and movements of the Burdenko Method. It is important to note that preparing for an exercise session is just as important as the session itself. You might be thinking I am referring to the warm-up and cool-down period. Those are vitally important, but they are a part of your exercise session.

I'm referring to a number of techniques that need to be used outside your exercise sessions, which will allow you to gain maximum improvement, both physically and mentally.

Part of my philosophy is the necessity of conditioning the whole body, not only the injured area or the small set of muscles receiving focus at a particular moment.

Proper techniques such as breathing, relaxing, and acquiring the proper mindset are vitally important. Learning to walk properly and knowing how to climb and descend stairs properly, whether you are injured or not, is vitally important. *Practice taking care of your body both in and out of exercise sessions, or we are wasting our time during the sessions.* Everything outlined in the Burdenko Method is geared toward improving the quality of our everyday lives, not doing something for its own sake. *We don't do exercise for exercise. We exercise for everyday life and sport.*

To return to full health, the Burdenko Method incorporates a comprehensive method to create a lifestyle that will change one's body and help build a rewarding life.

Often people tell me they barely have enough time for a few hours of exercise per week. I ask them, "Do you have time to take a shower?" Of course they do, they make time. Find the time, make the time, squeeze the time in. This is the time for life transformation. If you do not find time, especially after an injury, you may spend more time in the hospital in the long run, being forced to make time.

I recommend incorporating the following principles and techniques into your daily routine.

PHYSICAL CONDITIONING

So many people do exercises, but do not see the reflection of the exercises in their everyday lives. Yet it is vitally important to bring everything you learn in exercise sessions to your everyday life. For example, in everyday life, many people sit at a computer for long periods of time. It is important to know how to sit, how to write and type, and how to hold the body in a healthy way.

Everyday life must include exercises. From time to time, participate in something you do not usually do. Seek out and try something new. Keep your mind fresh and excited. Learn about what interests you. And ask questions about your new experiences and knowledge. If you do not have any questions, either you are very educated and advanced, or you do not fully understand the message.

Once again, it bears repeating, we do not do exercise for exercise, we do exercise for everyday life and sport. That is what physical conditioning is. If you are in good physical condition, your life will be more enjoyable, you will be able to do the things you love, and God forbid you have an injury, you have a greater chance of recovering.

Visualization

Physical conditioning starts with visualization. Visualizing your healing process will help your recovery tremendously. Visualization is a powerful tool to use while exercising to wake up your mind and body. Visualization involves picturing your goal actually happening. For example, if you have difficulty moving your legs, picture your legs moving in your mind as you attempt to move your legs, even if you feel like nothing is happening. If you wobble while you work out, imagine staying erect. Remember how you felt before your injury. Think about what muscles are used in sitting erect. By visualizing, your mind will stimulate the nerves and muscles that have been damaged or neglected.

Picture yourself in the activities you plan on performing. Visualize your body performing actions in a lying down position, a sitting position, and in dynamic movements that include jumps and turns.

Remember how you used to run. Remember how you used to swim. Remember how you used to play sports. When you recollect these movements, your nerves will fire. There will be micro-movements. The visualization, the firing of your nerves, and the micro-movements are a wake-up call to the entire process of healing.

Imagine that you can see inside your body. As you breathe, visualize oxygen entering your lungs, passing into the bloodstream, traveling out through arteries, branching out through the body, leaving the bloodstream, and going into the neurons (nerve cells). Picture your neurons healing. See them branching out and regenerating. As you work your muscles, picture them taking in the oxygen and nutrients from your blood to revitalize and strengthen. See them developing and growing.

In your mind's eye, picture yourself in good health—walking, running, playing, and back to normal. Keep generating positive signals to help stimulate your body's natural healing response.

During an exercise session, visualizing what you want to do is very important. For example, I find many times when people start to work on balance, they lose their balance. One of the ways I help is to tell them, "Hold a vision of how you want to be moving, and do the action." That's visualization.

If you hold something with your vision, that vision supports your actions. Another way is to create a vision of a model in your mind, visualizing moving the model the way you want to move.

Passive visualization is visualizing an end goal already completed, or visualizing an action and performing it afterwards. ***Active visualization*** is visualizing your actions and the actions of your muscles as you are performing the movement. Best of all, visualize your movement followed by contracting your muscles and doing what you visualized, while still visualizing.

This creates very strong patterns and habits for performing your actions. You create patterns for performance with awareness and feedback from your muscles, organs, and brain. Increased awareness of your body gives you a strong ability for visualization, which in turn allows for greater body awareness. Altogether this promotes stimulating the action you want to achieve.

Later on, visualization and the subsequent movement will become automatic, and you will avoid mistakes and injuries. Try to go from passive to active visualization.

An excellent way to visualize is to work with your breathing:

- Visualize your lungs full. Practice your visualization.
- Visualize your lungs empty. Practice your visualization.
- Visualize your lungs half full. Practice your visualization.
- Visualize your lungs a quarter full. Practice your visualization.

This is also an excellent training tool for respiratory function and for people who have injuries which affect the breathing system. Further breathing techniques are described later in this chapter.

Alignment

Maintaining proper alignment must be at the very beginning of everything related to health and fitness. The rehabilitation process starts by addressing alignment. Without addressing alignment, the efficiency of exercise is diminished and you will not have the results you expect. Stretching and exercising with improper alignment creates an environment which produces injuries, and is not a healthy environment to prevent injuries or heal from injuries. This is a common mistake, but is not commonly addressed.

People with bad posture are not in good health. It is like having a Mercedes with bad shocks. No matter how good everything else is, the car is not functioning properly. You must maintain proper alignment when you sit, stand, walk, or exercise. **Your body is in alignment when your pelvis is under your shoulders.** Throughout your day, whatever you are doing, your pelvis should always be under your shoulders, unless there is a specific circumstance which deems otherwise.

People who feel fine today do not understand that things like holding their neck out of alignment with their spine, or sitting with a rounded back, will likely cause them back problems or breathing difficulties one day. As goes the famous line from Casablanca, "You'll regret it. Maybe not today. Maybe not tomorrow, but soon and for the rest of your life."

Posture alignment is not only about the spine. It is about maintaining a vertical position in alignment with all of your joints. Everything in your body is interconnected, and everything should be aligned. If you walk with one leg out of alignment, you will lose cartilage and destroy your joint. If you walk with one of your feet facing outward, it will give you problems. If you favor one leg out of habit or injury, and have improper weight distribution, that leg will be overloaded and exhausted. Your hips, joints, and muscles become at risk for injury.

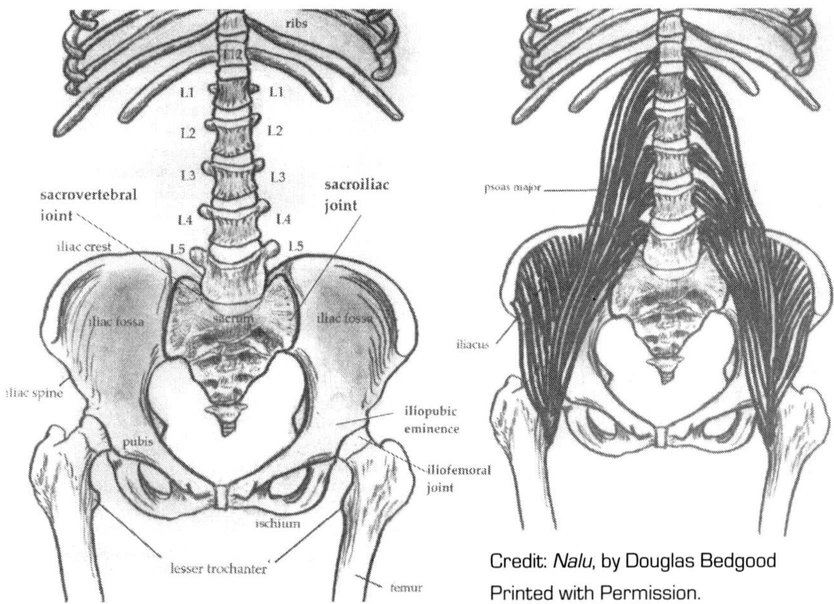

Credit: *Nalu*, by Douglas Bedgood
Printed with Permission.

Figure 3.1 Everything in the body is interconnected.

Your feet should be parallel. The distance between your feet should be the distance between your hips. When you walk, swing your arms. A lot of people walk without swinging their arms. If you do not swing your arms, you lose coordination and balance. Balance is the foundation to everything. Without balance we do not have any way to move our bodies.

A lot of people put their head down when they walk. Walk with your chin up and shoulders open. Walk at different speeds. Most elderly people never change their speed, and often shuffle forward rather than lifting their legs and bending their joints.

All of these factors reflect on your body performance and the safety of your movements in exercise and everyday life. A car with improper alignment is not functioning properly, no matter how powerful the engine. The tires will wear out faster and it will not perform well. What are tires on a human body? They are your joints.

I always tell people, **"Posture is your signature."** The unique way you carry your body changes the way you experience life.

Sitting, standing, and walking properly are guided by principles of biomechanics. ***Biomechanics*** uses engineering principles to study biological systems. It is not common for people to be taught the proper way to sit, stand, walk, or climb stairs. Yet doing so helps the body function more efficiently and prevents injuries. Moving properly also enhances the ability of the body to maintain internal and external alignment.

Sitting:

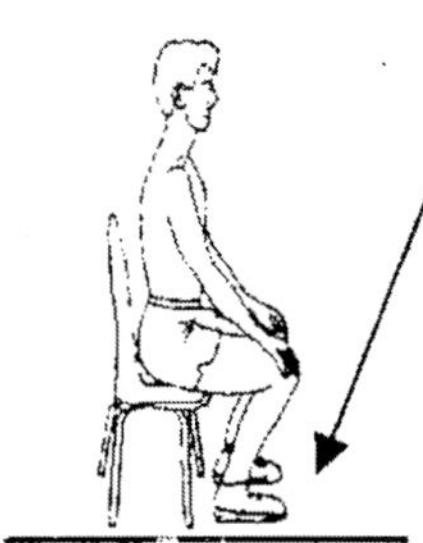

Sit straight. Keep your feet parallel to each other and on the floor. The distance between your feet should be the width between your hips. Push your glutes back into the chair and keep your pelvis under your shoulders. Keep your shoulders open and your chest out.

Try not to cross your legs. This creates misalignment and compresses the groin area, which reduces blood flow and lymph flow.

Sitting properly will contribute to remaining energetic even when sitting and working. It will also be easier and produce less stress to stand up from this position.

Standing up:

Put your palms down flat on the seat of the chair, while moving your upper body forward to the position where your knees are over your toes. Then swing your upper body back, forward and up, while simultaneously pushing your hands down against the chair as you stand up. This creates momentum and redirects the effort required to stand from the legs to the arms, legs, and body momentum, making it much easier to stand up.

Many people sit for long periods of time. When they begin to stand up, the muscles are not ready to lift the body's entire weight. People strain to stand up, creating tension, stress and contraction in the body. They then carry these feelings with them throughout the day.

Standing up properly saves energy and keeps the body relaxed and loose. People who stand up and sit down wrong many times daily may become tired and tense much more easily. Standing up properly is especially important for people with injuries for whom standing up is difficult, as well as elderly people who may have muscle weakness.

Sitting down:

Stand close to the chair so that the back of your knee or calf is touching the edge of the chair. Slowly lean forward and lower your hands straight down so they hold the edge of the chair. Use your arms like shocks to lower your weight to the sitting position, allowing yourself to be supported on your legs and arms as you lower yourself to the chair.

It is good to have a habit to get dressed in a sitting position, rather than standing and trying to balance yourself while on one leg or putting a shirt over your head.

It is good to sit when you put on and take off your shoes. This will help prevent injuries. Additionally, if you put your shoes on while standing and trying to balance, you add stress, tension, and compression to your body, which you may carry with you throughout your day.

Standing:

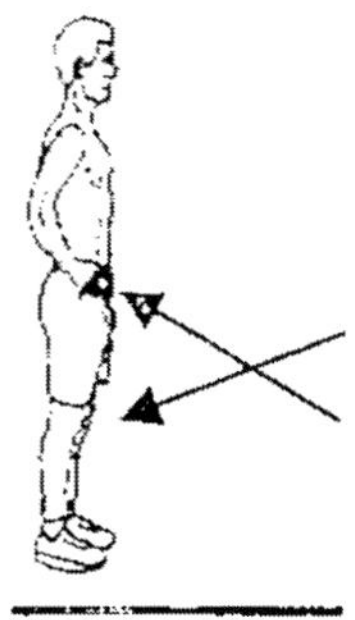

Stand with your back straight, chin parallel to the ground, looking forward. Ensure your shoulders are open, with your chest out. Keep your weight evenly distributed between both legs and do not lock your knees. Keep your pelvis under your shoulders. From this position, you are better able to have good balance, be more alert, and move more efficiently.

If you are slouching with your head down and your knees locked, your balance is affected, your body is not prepared for movement, and it is very easy to lose balance and sustain injury.

If your knees are locked, your pelvis is out of alignment and vertebrae issues may result. Locking your knees also wears cartilage and may create orthopedic issues.

Habitually looking down may weaken your neck muscles and create alignment difficulties and discomfort. The neck muscles support the head, provide stability for the vertebrae and support for the shoulders. Everything is connected.

Standing properly makes your body ready for movement. You will feel energetic and balanced, and others may notice that you look more vibrant.

Walking:

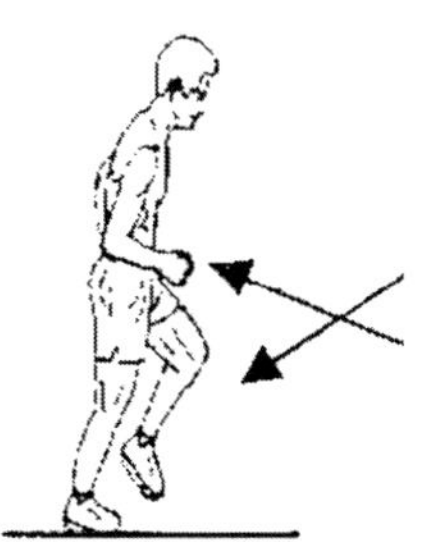

Keep your shoulders open, chin parallel to the ground, pelvis under your shoulders, with feet shoulder-width apart. Swing your arms while walking.

Keeping your feet shoulder-width apart is simple biomechanics. It creates even weight distribution and body stability.

The pelvis is the foundation of the body's alignment. Pelvic stability and awareness are necessary to develop proper alignment. It is also the foundation for good motor skills.

Swinging your arms while walking contributes to balance and gives added mobility. Open shoulders help create respiratory comfort and contributes to proper breathing.

Lifting legs is crucial. Sometimes people do not lift their legs when walking, particularly as they age or after injury. The sense of balance is removed without lifting legs while walking. If you cannot lift your legs high, lift them the way you can. They should be lifted as the knees bend, rather than keeping knees locked. People who do not lift their legs while walking train themselves to lose balance. They lose muscle mass as well.

Feet should always be parallel to each other when walking, rather than twisted inward or outward. This provides even weight distribution and stability, as well as alignment for the whole body. Twisting your foot creates misalignment in the ankle, knee, hips, and spine.

Walking barefoot helps expose the body to varying environments and temperatures, providing stimulation for the senses and strengthening the system. However, I recommend walking barefoot only on soft ground, like a sandy beach or soft grass. I do not recommend walking barefoot on hard surfaces. This creates greater impact and pressure on cartilage and joints, and weakens the arches in the feet. The body will also lose heat and be vulnerable to cuts.

Climbing Stairs

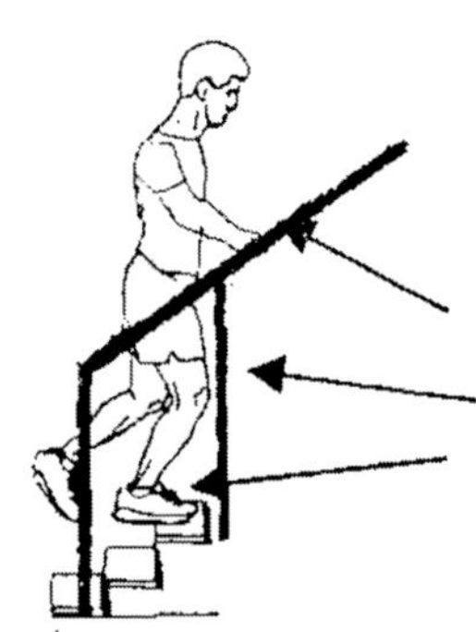

Keep your body straight, shoulders open, and look forward. Use the railing to assist your movement. Do not lock your knees while going up or down stairs. Allow the movements of your ankles, knees, and hips to be soft and fluid.

When climbing, place half of your foot on each step. When the ball of your foot is on the step, and your heel is hanging off the step, you create a spring in your foot. In this position, you use your feet the way they were designed—as shock absorbers. This position provides for efficient use of your legs, and making each step easier. It may be more difficult at first, but will become natural as you become accustomed to moving in this way.

One of the biggest obstacles for many people of every age is carrying their entire weight on one leg, as is required when climbing stairs. It is important to use the railing to reallocate a portion of your weight from your legs to ease pressure from your joints. Keep one hand ahead of you on the railing when climbing and descending stairs.

When descending stairs, it is very important not to lean forward. Do not look down all the time, or you will lose your balance. Watch your step, but maintain body alignment, and always use the railing for support.

If it is difficult for you to climb stairs, start with the stronger leg and put the other leg next to it on the same step, rather than climbing to the next step. This pattern helps you climb and descend stairs without discomfort or pain.

Proper Breathing

In the Burdenko Method, breathing takes on new meaning. Breathing is no longer an absent-minded function. Pay attention to your breathing and be conscious of it when you exercise and throughout your day.

Growing muscles and repairing nerves requires an abundant supply of oxygen. Your entire metabolism ultimately relies on oxygen consumption. Those who spend time in a hospital after a serious injury usually receive oxygen to aid in recovery.

Breathing cleanses your system. When you exhale, your body removes toxins and waste, and stimulates the lymph system—your body's waste removal system. By consciously deep breathing, you are activating your body's natural purging mechanisms. Make deep breathing a daily priority.

The most important thing I suggest is to breathe fresh air as much as you can, including fresh air of varying temperatures. Some people think they can only breathe outside when it is warm. Breathing cold air helps build your immune system. Use common sense—do not stay outside so long that you get a chill, because you may get sick and that is defeating the purpose. But most anyone, even on a cold day, can poke their head out and get a few minutes of fresh air.

Indoors, temperature is always about the same. Outdoors, it varies greatly. That difference stimulates body mechanisms and helps promote very efficient breathing.

The more you go outside, the more opportunity you have to breathe air that is fresh and oxygen enriched. When possible, I highly recommend breathing air from mountains, the ocean, or desert.

When people have physical or emotional problems, breathing must be addressed. Most doctors do not address this, and most people do not know how to breathe properly. It is vitally important to learn, yet few experts ever teach people about breathing. If you want to be in good shape, incorporate a system of breathing into your daily routine.

Any body movement or muscular activity that lasts more than a minute and a half requires a new supply of energy to keep the muscles functioning. This energy is obtained from a process called cellular respiration, whereby oxygen is used to break down food, which provides energy to the muscles and fuels your body movements.

As you build strength and endurance, your muscles will require more and more oxygen. Indeed, one measure of physical fitness is the maximum rate at which an individual can consume oxygen.

When we exercise, muscles demand oxygen and send a signal to the brain to stimulate an increase in the breathing rate. Running is the best example. "I'm out of breath," people often say. Why? The body demands oxygen, but the system cannot keep up, because you did not breathe properly while running, or you are running with underdeveloped lungs.

The brain also activates additional muscles in the chest which expand the lungs and increase their capacity. As the lungs are filled, the air pressure within them increases. This is similar to blowing up a balloon and feeling the air push out against the sides. The difference in pressure forces oxygen from within the lungs into the bloodstream. The way most people breathe, including during exercise, does not usually use their lungs to full capacity or move the large volumes of air the body is capable of moving.

Proper breathing will also help ensure alignment in the body. You cannot breathe deeply if your body is bent, or if your head is down. You cannot fill a balloon if the balloon is so stiff it cannot be filled up. In the same way, your diaphragm and lung muscles need the same thing all your other muscles need—they need to be balanced, coordinated, flexible, have endurance, speed/quickness, and strength. You cannot see these muscles working, so it is more difficult to imagine than your biceps, for example. Yet it is easy to feel your lung muscles, especially during aerobic exercise like running. Be conscious of breathing throughout exercise. Always be sure to avoid holding your breath.

There are many techniques for deep breathing. I find the following technique to be very effective and easy to learn. Outdoors is the best place to perform these exercises, unless the air quality is poor.

- Stand or sit up straight. Slouching compresses the space for your lungs.
- *Begin by inhaling through your nose.* Breathing through your nose filters and warms the air before it enters into your lungs.
- *Lift your chest* as you inhale. Let your chest expand and fill all the chambers in your lungs.
- *Purse your lips together and blow air out* through the small hole between your lips (like blowing out a candle). Push hard. Feel the contraction in your abdominal area. Contract your stomach.
- (Optional) *Stretch and exercise your neck as you breathe.* Each time you exhale, turn your head in a different direction: left, right, forward, up, and down. The different positions stimulate deep breathing.

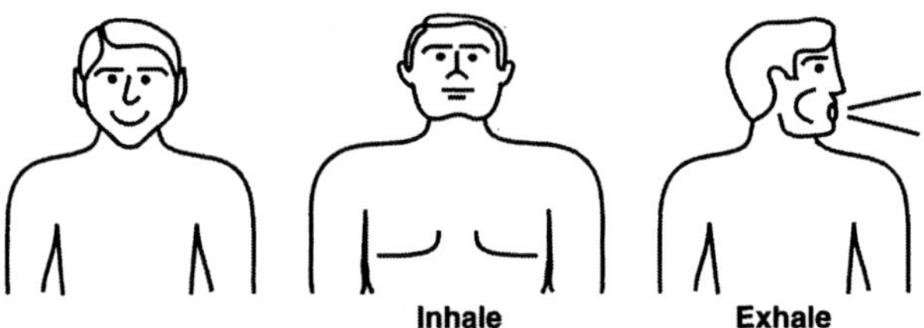

Figure 3.2 Proper breathing action.

I also highly recommend the Strelnikova Breathing system, developed by Alexandra Strelnikova, a Russian opera singer and theatrical teacher. It is a powerful technique for enhancing respiratory health, and has proven to be a great success for professional singers, athletes, and those with respiratory conditions.

The basis of the system is as follows:

- Perform a series of short, powerful, audible inhales through the nostrils. Do not exhale until you have completed all the inhalations.
- When you start, you might be able to do only 8 or 10 inhales. Try working your way up to 32.
- Exhale naturally. Repeat 1-2 times.

I use Strelnikova Breathing myself, teach it to my clients, students, as well as my own family. I have seen this breathing system make a significant impact on all those who practice it. Vladimir Popov, the famous Russian opera singer, tells me he practices the technique and can do a thousand inhales in a row.

For additional instructions, diagrams, and videos about this method, search the internet for "Strelnikova Breathing."

> "All chronic pain, suffering and diseases are caused from a lack of oxygen at the cell level."
>
> **Professor Arthur C. Guyton, MD**
> The Textbook of Medical Physiology

Shaking

Shaking is a very simple and extremely efficient way to restore body function, de-stress the body, and remove tension. It also promotes a relaxation response, decreases compression on the nerves and contraction of the muscles, increases circulation, and helps the body feel lighter. Shaking is a powerful technique that is not commonly known.

Shaking is a wake-up call to the body, a preparation to action, and a relaxation tool during the day. We shake when we feel tired or stiff or have muscles spasms. Shaking is simple and can be performed in any position. To increase the effect, it is very good to close your eyes.

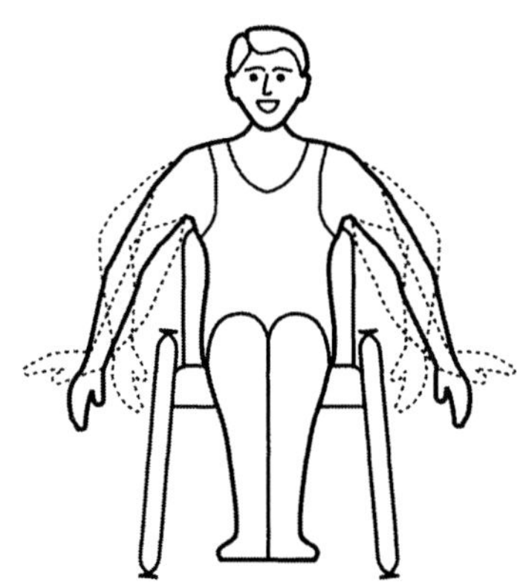

Figure 3.3 Shaking.

Shaking during the warm-up phase of exercise prepares your body to receive the benefits of exercise. When you are stiff, you are limited, physically and mentally; your muscles, nerves, and joints are compressed, and the elasticity of your muscles is poor.

Shaking relaxes muscles, increases the temperature of the muscles and whole body, loosens tight muscles and joints, and prepares you mentally and physically to perform. Physiologically, shaking stimulates better circulation and creates an environment in your system for receiving the maximum benefit from exercise. Loose, relaxed muscles with excellent circulation function very efficiently, which maximizes the benefits of exercise.

While exercising, muscles demand oxygen. Blood flows vigorously through the circulatory system, delivering the oxygen. When exercise stops, muscles are warm but sometimes more contracted than prior to exercising.

Shaking during exercise keeps you invigorated and energized. It increases circulation, helps eliminate stiffness, releases muscle tension and nerve compression. It helps restore energy levels. I highly recommend shaking after every 1 or 2 sets of exercises.

Shaking after exercising helps muscles relax so they are not tight. A massage, sauna or Jacuzzi after exercise can also be helpful to loosen muscles.

Shaking should be done with the whole body. You can start shaking from upper body down, or lower extremities up, including the head and neck. Start with **very gentle** shaking. The feeling of shaking should be pleasant. If you feel light after shaking, you have good technique. One minute after shaking, you should feel results. If you do not, try again and learn how to shake differently.

Everyone is different. The speed of everyone's shaking should be different. Some people prefer shaking fast, some slow. The body will find what it prefers. I recommend going from very gently shaking to aggressive shaking. Be sure to shake at different speeds—slow, medium, and fast—but do not shake fast right away. Performing actions at varying speeds requires more concentration and results in less adaptation. You will feel in your body the right speed for you to start.

To begin shaking:

- Start from a standing position. (If this is not possible, sit erect or lay down flat.)
- Shake for fifteen to twenty seconds.
- Feel like there is electricity moving through you, so that all your muscles are activated. Shake your upper extremities, lower extremities, and include your trunk, spine, and rear.
- Keep your feet, ankles, and hips loose. Allow your feet to tap on the floor as you shake.
- Shake on land and in water.

If your level of functioning is such that you are limited to shaking only your arms, follow these directions:

- Sit erect with your arms down at your sides. (If this is not possible, lay down flat.)
- Gently begin by shaking your arms.
- Let your wrists and hands stay loose and relaxed.
- Now shake for fifteen to twenty seconds.
- Repeat the process. Get loose!
- Next, move your arms to your sides, overhead, out in front of you, or behind you, and begin shaking again.
- Then, if you have use of your legs, stretch them, and rest your heels on the floor. Bend each knee alternately. You can also lift each leg and shake it. Make sure your entire body is relaxed while you do this.

Body Awareness

Body awareness, or *proprioception*, is the awareness of movement and location of parts of your body in relation to each other.

Body awareness includes the use of your senses to control the position of your body's performance. Knowing the precise position and movements of your body and limbs, even when you do not see them, is very important. You must feel and be aware.

Body awareness includes maintaining balance, knowing where your center of gravity and center of buoyancy is located, and paying attention to the proper positioning of each part of your body. Body awareness includes control of your breathing in your everyday life, proper alignment, and dynamic movements in your routine.

Body awareness begins with mental focus. Whenever you exercise, practice maintaining body awareness. Concentrate on performing exercises correctly. Ensure your body is in proper position.

Before you move, think about what you are going to do, especially when you learn a new movement. Think before the action. A lot of people make a movement and think later. That creates frustration, negative feelings, and injuries which can be prevented.

Many athletes, ballerinas, and martial artists exercise in front of mirrors to observe their movements in order to help them maintain body awareness. This reflection helps stimulate great communication between the mind and body.

While exercising, it is useful to have a trainer or fitness professional watch you from time to time to let you know if your balance is not right, if you are not erect, or if your elbows drop when they are supposed to be at shoulder level. This feedback helps develop awareness and correct mistakes.

Many people have difficultly maintaining body awareness when in the water. Regaining body awareness is especially important when recovering from injury, a time when sensations may be limited. There may also be limited awareness or sensations when learning a new movement.

To build body awareness, remember:

- Think before you move
- Visualize your action

The more feedback you receive, the better you will be at maintaining body awareness. Make it a conscious effort.

Remember to stay positive. If you cannot do it from the beginning, you will do it later. The best way to learn is to practice what you know.

Massage

Massage can be used by itself and in conjunction with other modalities of therapy to relieve pain, muscle soreness, and stress, and to help stimulate the healing process. The physical sensations of massage increase body awareness and helps make you more conscious of the progress you are making.

Massage is an excellent source of physical stimulation. The continual physical stimulation causes nerves to transmit or try to transmit the sensations to your brain, helping to heal and wake up damaged nerves.

Massage stimulates the healing process and contributes to recovery by offering direct benefits such as muscle relaxation, helping to improve range of motion, increased blood circulation to deliver oxygen and nutrients to the body, increased circulation of extracellular body fluids which remove waste products, and improved body temperature, which opens capillaries and helps the skin breathe. Massage helps the body regenerate and heal damaged tissues. Massage increases the elasticity of muscles, detoxifies the body, and relieves tension and stress. All these benefits contribute to physical and emotional well-being.

Massage has been used for thousands of years as a powerful healing modality by many cultures. It is well accepted as a form of treatment and relaxation therapy throughout Europe and the Far East. In Russia, massage is one of the most common modalities used in physical therapy, conditioning, and training.

There are many forms of massage, such as Shiatsu massage, Vietnamese massage, foot massage, hydro massage, stone massage, facial massage, and self-massage. Each modality has different goals and different techniques. In the United States and Europe, Swedish massage has become very popular. I recommend that you experience several different techniques. Your body may respond better to one style than another. Do not just go to a massage therapist. Select a massage professional with the same diligence you would use to choose your any of your health professionals. Be aware of qualifications and skills.

I believe massage will become more accepted in the United States as a healing modality as people grow to understand its benefits and see the results. I developed a massage technique which I taught in Moscow. When I came to the United States in 1981, I did not see massage used for medical purposes. At the present time, doctors will sometimes recommend massage for therapeutic purposes. The media has more and more useful information about the importance of massage. Doctors and health professionals are becoming educated and help their patients select the type of massage they need.

One element massages have in common is that the therapist touches the patient's body. The power of human touch provides a psychological benefit that cannot be matched by taking medications. The patient feels cared for in a personal way that creates a feeling of satisfaction and well-being. This is an aspect of the power of positive thinking, which is a key aspect of the Burdenko Method of helping the body heal itself.

There are four basic types of massage I recommend:

General relaxation massage is very helpful for relaxing muscles, reducing tension, and relieving stress.

Sports massage reinvigorates the body before and after muscles have been exercised, helping muscles that are sore or exhausted.

Selective massage focuses on a specific part of the body, such as a pulled hamstring or sore shoulders, or ankle. However, both sides of the body must be massaged—if the right leg receives massage, so must the left.

Therapeutic massage is a specific type of whole-body massage that reduces pain and increases circulation. It is used as treatment for an injury or particular condition.

I also recommend **hydro-massage**. It combines the benefits of regular massage, and decreases the effect of gravity on the body due to being immersed in water.

In most massage techniques, the patient lies still and simply receives the treatment. I use a form of therapeutic massage that is "participatory"—the patient plays an important role in increasing the efficiency of the massage using meditation, deep breathing, and visualization.

Following an injury, nerves and muscles shrink from inactivity. During a massage, I ask the client to:

- Meditate
- Visualize blood flow to injured areas or stiff muscles
- Feel muscles relaxing. With your brain, stimulate relaxation in the body
- Visualize yourself healthy—the positive thinking stimulates healing power

It is not often that a massage specialist uses visualization in their practice. I remember what Rudolf Nureyev, the great Russian ballet dancer, told me when I worked with him. During the massage session, he visualized himself dancing on stage. He said to me, "Igor, I feel like I'm dancing the whole ballet!" All his muscles "danced" while he was on a table receiving a massage.

I hope to see more doctors recommend massage as a modality for healing. It is a very powerful tool for recovery.

There are a few general guidelines I follow in administering massage that are worth mentioning:

- A massage should not be given immediately following a meal. If you generate more circulation in one area, you take it away from the stomach, where it is needed to digest the food.
- **Massage of facial muscles** is effective in stress relief. Your face is the center of all emotions. Facial expressions help your body communicate your level of stress and tension. After a facial massage, relax the facial muscles with a hot compress. Use light strokes on the head and face.

  I have been working at marathons with marathon runners for over 30 years. When they finish running, they are very sensitive to any touch. Most massage therapists start working on a runner's legs. I always start with their face. When their face relaxes, there is a wave of relaxation to their whole body. They all tell me they have never experienced anything like that before. They tell me, "I run a marathon and you work on my face!? I don't understand, I'm so relaxed now!"

When the facial muscles relax, it reflects on the whole body. They feel better right away. The results are like day and night compared to working with a marathoner's legs right away. I have tried working immediately with their legs—it takes longer for them to relax and restore circulation.

- **Self-massage** is a valuable way to help yourself. It is not complicated to learn.

If you really want to experience massage, try to educate yourself. There are many books on the subject. I recommend getting a book on massage and learning the basics.

Massage therapy should be used when needed, the same way people go to a doctor. I use massage therapy when I need it. People should know what exists, how it works, and who can perform it.

MENTAL CONDITIONING

How can I encourage a person who has given up? I tell them stories of people I have come across in my life. I encourage them to find and read stories of others who have overcome similar injuries, and to contact those people. I believe if others have accomplished something, my client can also accomplish it. I find these stories stimulate and build a belief that it can be done, not in general, but specifically with this person.

If that seed will grow, it will be the beginning of one of the major ways of generating the power of the body's natural healing process.

The most important thing is to generate the will to try. But not simply to try and that's it. I want people to try based on a belief they have heard or read—a true story of someone who succeeded in a similar circumstance.

I also introduce people to each other. Many of my clients now know each other. That is a very powerful piece of my work. In the end, they discover that they have a lot in common, and communicate with each other a great deal. They have their injury in common, pain, similar difficulties, lost mobility, conflict with their families. They share their experiences and their thoughts about how to cross or avoid obstacles and succeed. This is a big contribution to their healing. And it includes them taking action on their own towards their healing. I always encourage people to be self-sufficient.

Scott Biehler:
I am amazed at the stories Dr. Burdenko tells me about his quadriplegic patients, like Bob McKenna and Paul Carney—whose stories are in this book—who have learned to walk again, as well as stories of other physically delayed individuals and handicapped athletes who can now run marathons and compete in sporting events like swimming, sprinting, and shot put. People who had virtually given up on life now have fulfilling careers, have gotten married, and have had children. They healed their paralyzed bodies using Igor's techniques. They refused to listen to those who told them they would never walk again, and they recovered. If you believe you can accomplish something, you will find that you are capable of achieving goals that were otherwise unobtainable. The human body has no limits. Look at the world records in sporting events now compared with those of just ten or twenty years ago.

The human body has incredible powers to heal itself. We have all heard stories of cancer patients who refused to die and willed themselves to heal, and people who recover from serious illness and even wind up competing and winning in the Olympics, such as Wilma Rudolph. She was very ill as a child and had a deformed left leg and foot due to polio. Her doctor told her she would not walk. She went on to win three Olympic gold medals in track and field, and was called "The fastest woman on Earth" in 1960. Her example created a wave of people who wanted to follow.

The same thing happened when the first person ran a mile in under 4 minutes. After that, a wave of people accomplished the same feat. One person broke the mental barrier, and others followed, tapping the incredible capability of their bodies to accomplish enormous feats.

Attitude

When I speak of attitude, I think about the saying about a glass of water. It is my strong belief to see the glass as half full. If I view situations that way, it creates a special mindset for the rest of my life. It affects the way I act, the way I communicate, and the way I help people.

This attitude reflects on my clients. They do not see me down. They know I believe in what I am doing, that I believe in their healing, and that my words are heartfelt. This is more valuable than any specific words.

My example is my father. I watched him come home from war, body riddled with wounds, unable to walk, barely able to move, yet he always stayed positive and believed he could heal. In post-war Ukraine, without any medicine or medical facilities, he found his way to health. It is my strong belief that he never would have done so without believing in himself.

I believe the glass is half-full. That is who I am, how I feel, and how I act. Teaching others to achieve this view is not only about finding the right words. It is about expressing myself and acting in ways that reflect this.

It is also important to be able to focus and select the important things from those that are not important. People make a lot of mistakes because they do not concentrate on what is truly important.

As much as we can, in everything we do, bring in positive expressions, positive feelings, positive words, and a positive attitude.

Before an orchestra plays, when they are warming up, everyone is playing their own tune. It is a harsh cacophony and it sounds terrible. But when the orchestra plays together, beautiful music begins. Your life is like a cacophony. There is so much noise.

When you focus your attitude and your life on what is important, it becomes an orchestra and a beautiful tune. ***Life is an opportunity to catch positive emotions.***

Scott Biehler:
When I first began working with Dr. Burdenko, I did not understand how important attitude was. Dr. Burdenko told me I could do things that everyone else said was impossible. When I started believing in the importance of attitude, it completely changed my beliefs and directly affected the effort I put into the program. I now realize attitude is an essential part of the healing process.

Participate in activities that reinforce a positive attitude. Look in the mirror and smile at yourself. It really works! Smile when you exercise. Do not allow yourself to engage in negative thinking.

Sometimes everyone gets down. But be aware to get back to a positive attitude. Listen to CDs of motivational speakers, like Tony Robbins, Wayne Dyer, Bob Proctor or Eckhart Tolle. They have a lot of free material on their websites and on Youtube. Find in each day an opportunity to work on your recovery both physically and emotionally.

Meditation

Meditation involves setting aside a time to relax your body and focus your thoughts. It is a beneficial tool for controlling pain and achieving peace and tranquility. Meditation allows the mind to overcome limitations of the body. It is a restful time when you tap into the energy from within.

Many hospitals, schools, and other institutions offer courses in meditation. If you have not had an opportunity to meditate, I strongly recommend that you look into learning more about it. There are many books, websites, and videos about various forms of meditation.

Meditation simply means turning off all distractions and closing your eyes or focusing your eyes on something such as a candle flame. Allow yourself to be aware of and focus on your breathing, and allow whatever thoughts come to flow through you.

Meditation is not about never thinking a thought. After much practice many people reach that level, but for our purposes, meditation is about allowing yourself to calm and focus your mind. During meditation you might want to visualize yourself healthy, with the attitude you desire, with the kind of interactions you want to have with others, or as the person you desire to be. You might want to visualize your cells healing, your immune system fighting an illness, or damaged parts of you healthy, strong, and moving.

Remember, you cannot force your way into a calm state of mind. Allow whatever comes to flow through you and leave in its own time, calmly and without judgment.

It is as simple as this: close your eyes, focus on your breathing, and allow yourself to find peace. It can be done anywhere and anytime. A meditation can be 20 seconds or 20 minutes. You can be standing, sitting, or lying down.

With time, the calmness experienced during meditation becomes part of your everyday life outside of meditation sessions.

I recommend meditating daily. Perhaps for a few minutes morning and night. Perhaps you can close your eyes and find peace for a few moments while waiting for dinner to be ready, for an appointment, or in the supermarket line. Meditation does not have to be a big production. It is an available and effective tool, including (even especially) to those of us who live modern, busy lives.

Practice as often as you can. Meditating once per week or once per month is infinitely more beneficial than not meditating at all.

COMBINING PHYSICAL CONDITIONING WITH MENTAL CONDITIONING TO OPTIMIZE OVERCOMING INJURIES

Just as your mind can stimulate your body into action, so too can your body stimulate your mind into action. Physical stimulation of the body is perceived by nerve receptors and sent to the brain.

Moving stimulates your brain, stimulates your body for healing, and stimulates your progress in many directions. Physical movement not only stimulates, but occupies your mind. If the mind is not occupied, people often become depressed. In the Burdenko Method, we stimulate the mind with movement and positive thinking, rather than drugs being the first choice.

People who have suffered brain damage or nerve damage are especially encouraged to use this technique of physical stimulation. *Physical stimulation bombards the brain with nerve impulses, which helps those with nerve damage regain their senses.*

As part of your exercise routine, move the paralyzed or weak parts of your body, even if you cannot feel anything. This can be done with the aid of exercise tubing. For example, if you cannot move your arm, loop one end of exercise tubing around your hand, and other end around a pool ladder, pole, doorknob, or chair. Move your body, and your arm will move.

If you do not have feelings in your legs, loop one end of exercise tubing around your leg, and the other end around your hand. As you lift and move your hands and arms, your legs will lift and move.

Another option is to have an assistant help you move.

Be creative. Find ways to move your body in water and on land. The water environment helps produce motions that are difficult to achieve on land.

Watch closely as parts of your body move, whether you or an assistant moves them. Take that visual image and coordinate in your mind how the movements should feel. The nerves in your extremities will try to transmit those physical sensations to your body and to your brain.

When you stimulate and move your body, you are helping your nerves and your senses remember the patterns of motion. You are reactivating muscle memory, reminding your body of what it already knows, and showing your body how to do what you ask of it.

As previously stated, massage is also an excellent source of physical and mental stimulation.

This combination of physical and mental stimulation for your nerves is a powerful technique to help the body heal itself. These techniques are the heart of the Burdenko Method.

Sebastian DeFrancesco's Story

I am a C-5,6 quadriplegic, meaning that my quadriplegia is the result of injury to the fifth and sixth cervical bones in my neck. This injury resulted from a military jeep accident. I have been in a wheelchair for nineteen years. Following my accident, I have tried to keep myself in good physical condition.

I first met Dr. Burdenko in 1983 when I was in training for the Paralympic Games. Through his expertise in rehabilitation and conditioning, he was able to analyze my situation and provide me with a routine of exercises to improve my balance, flexibility, and endurance. I found Igor to be a person I could trust, who desired to help make me into a better athlete, and who has a lot of passion for what he does. We began doing many different exercises in my wheelchair using rubber exercise tubing. I never liked working with weights, and the tubing provided an easy way to get a thorough workout.

In 1984, Igor accompanied the United States Paralympic team to the Paralympic Games in Stoke Mandville, England. This was the first time that a strength and conditioning trainer had ever assisted members of the United States Paralympic team. His enthusiasm and willingness to help kept him very busy. Many of the wheelchair athletes were eager to work with him and take advantage of his experience and expertise.

Those who compete as an athlete in the Paralympic Games are placed into a class based on their abilities. After working with Igor, my training had improved so much that I competed at a higher level. The level of conditioning that Igor helped me attain in balance and mobility added to my performance and helped me win the silver and bronze medals in table tennis. I had never won medals at the Paralympic Games before.

I still use the rubber exercise tubing exercises that I learned from Igor. They help keep me in shape today.

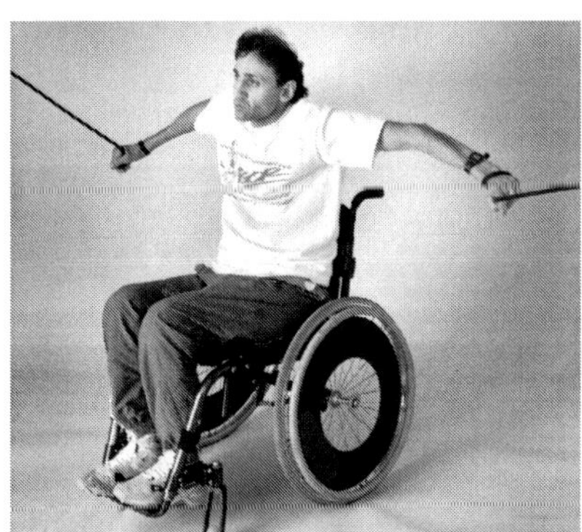

Chapter FOUR

Understanding Paralysis

Simply speaking, paralysis is the loss of ability to use muscles or feel sensations. The primary cause of paralysis is spinal-cord injury, commonly referred to as SCI. Spinal-cord injuries are often caused by vehicular accidents, severe falls, strokes, heart attacks, or gunshot injuries. Less commonly, paralysis may be caused by such conditions as infection, compression of the spinal cord, spina bifida, or cysts or tumors growing on the spine. In order to understand paralysis and its causes, let us first take a look at the spine and the nervous system.

The Spine

The spine is one of the most complex parts of the body, comprised of the backbone and spinal cord. The spinal cord is the vehicle through which the brain broadcasts messages to the body and vice versa. It consists of a group of nerves extending downward from the brain, with nerves branching out along the entire cord. The spinal cord is protected by the bones of the spinal column, or backbone. The individual bones of the spinal column are called vertebrae.

There are thirty-three vertebrae in the spinal column. The vertebrae in each area of the spine are numbered from top to bottom. The seven vertebrae in the neck compose the cervical region. The first cervical vertebra at the base of the skull is numbered C-l; beneath it is C-2 and the last cervical vertebra is numbered C-7. The twelve vertebrae just below the neck compose the thoracic area, numbered T-l through T-12. The 5 vertebrae below the thoracic area in the lower back compose the lumbar area, numbered L-l through L-5.

Below this is the sacrum, comprised of five bones which usually are not fused in children but are fused together in adults by approximately age 26. They are numbered S-l through S-5. Underneath the sacrum is the coccyx, or tailbone, usually composed of four rudimentary vertebrae fused together. Between each vertebrae is a disk which contains a soft jelly-like substance which prevents friction between the vertebrae, and allows the spine to be fluid and flexible.

The Nervous System

We control movement in our bodies via signals sent and received by the brain through the nervous system. There are two main parts of the nervous system: the central nervous system and the peripheral nervous system. The central nervous system is primarily composed of the brain and spinal cord. The peripheral nervous system is composed of a complex, interconnected network of nerves and neural pathways extending from the spinal cord to the rest of the body (see Figure 4.1).

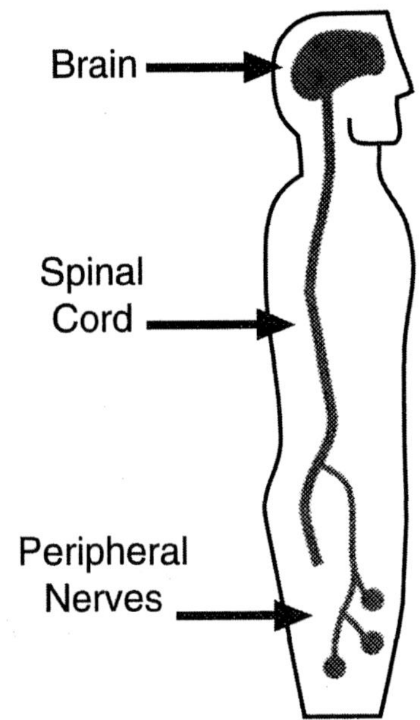

Figure 4.1 The nervous system.

Thoughts originate in our brains, are coded into signals that proceed down the spinal cord and out through peripheral nerves, resulting in, for example, our arms moving, or our legs coordinating together for walking, or moving in whichever particular manner we desire.

Nerve signals travel in both directions. Just as the brain sends signals to the body, the body sends signals to the brain. If we touch something hot, or feel pressure on our skin, or taste something sweet, the body sends a signal along the nervous system to the brain, which interprets that signal as heat, pressure, or taste. All of this happens in a fraction of a second.

The cells of the nervous system are called neurons. Each of these nerve cells has a large body with a long extension called an axon, and several other extensions called dendrites. The space between the axon of one neuron and the dendrite of another is called a synapse. It is across the space of a synapse that neurons transmit messages (see Figure 4.2).

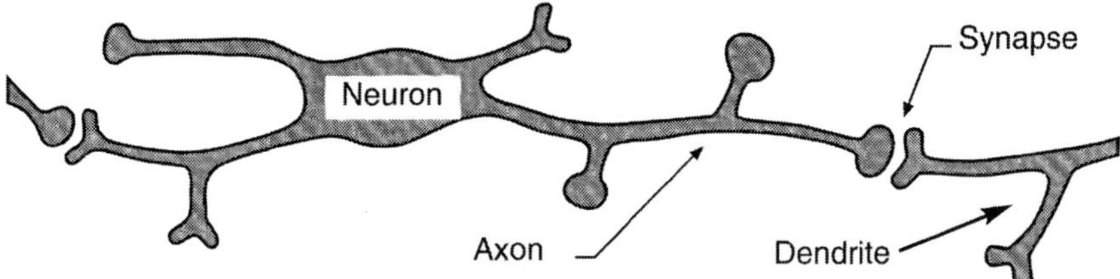

Figure 4.2 A neuron.

Neurons send messages by means of electrical currents with the help of certain chemicals called neurotransmitters. At a synapse, an axon secretes neurotransmitters, which convey the electrical current containing its message. This current is then passed on to the dendrite of the next neuron, so that this cell can receive and pass on the message (see Figure 4.3). Different nerves use different types of neurotransmitters to transmit different messages.

Contrary to common belief that the nervous system, once injured, cannot heal, research has shown that ***dendrite branches will become larger and more active in response to repeated external stimuli***, and that ***axon branches will grow if given the right environment***, such as being in the presence of nerve growth factor (explained below).

Until recently, it has been believed that axons only send messages, while dendrites only receive messages. However, the latest research has shown that dendrites have the ability to send messages (release neurotransmitters) that axons will receive. This means that neurons have an even greater potential to heal than previously thought, because every neural message or attempted message stimulates activity and the opportunity for healing. There is much greater opportunity for healing of the nervous system than is commonly believed.

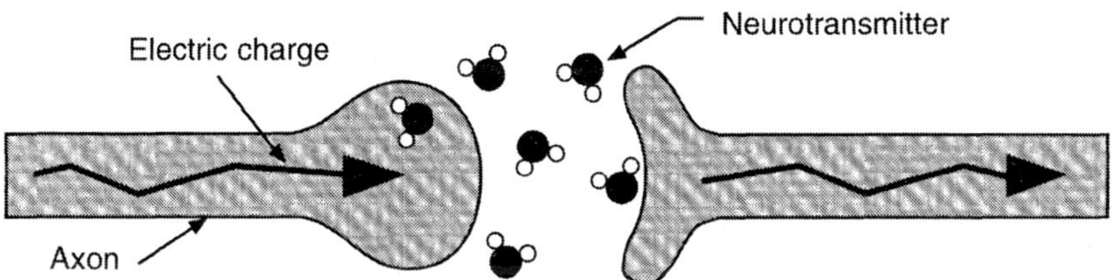

Figure 4.3 Communication between neurons.

Paralysis

When nerves of the spinal cord are damaged or severed, the flow of messages between the brain and the rest of the body becomes limited or interrupted. Paralysis, the inability to move parts of our body or feel sensations from them, is often the result.

Spinal-cord injuries are usually classified as complete or incomplete. These classifications refer to the severity of the injury. With complete spinal-cord injury, the nerves passing through the affected area are completely damaged. Doctors usually tell a patient with this diagnosis that there is little or no hope for meaningful recovery.

Injury to different parts of the spinal cord cause different types of paralysis. Injury to the area between C-l and C-5 is the most devastating. It causes paralysis of the arm and leg muscles, as well as the muscles needed for breathing. It is usually fatal. Injury to the C-5 to C-7 vertebrae causes paralysis of the legs and some paralysis of the arms. Injury to any of the thoracic vertebrae causes paralysis of the legs and varying degrees of paralysis of the trunk. Injury of the lumbar and the S-l to S-2 vertebrae causes some type of leg weakness and numbness. Injury to the S-3 to S-5 vertebrae causes loss of bladder and bowel control, and loss of feeling in the anal region.

Paralysis is generally categorized as one of three types—paraplegia, quadriplegia, and hemiplegia.

Paraplegia

Paraplegia is paralysis of the lower portion of the body, particularly the legs. The back and abdominal muscles may be affected as well. Symptoms include loss of motion, sensation, and reflexes. With complete spinal-cord injury, a patient may lose bladder and bowel control and sexual function.

Quadriplegia

Quadriplegia is paralysis of the body below the level of injury, and of the arms and legs. Quadriplegia is usually the result of an injury to the spinal cord in the area between the fifth and the seventh cervical vertebrae.

Hemiplegia

Hemiplegia is paralysis affecting one side of the body. This may be the result of a stroke or brain tumor. Infantile hemiplegia affects infants as a result of insufficient oxygen received in the womb, a brain hemorrhage at birth, or a fever during infancy.

How the Nervous System Heals

Healing occurs when a healthy oxygenated blood supply flows through injured areas. Nerve cells require a constant blood supply, which provides the oxygen and nutrients required by cells to function properly. ***Blood supply is the most important aspect of healing.*** Without a healthy, oxygenated blood supply, healing will not take place. The body can only heal itself with the necessary resources a healthy blood supply provides. This is one of the reasons the Burdenko Method stresses movement, breathing exercises, massage, and other techniques which increase blood circulation and oxygenation.

Blood contains and transfers everything your body needs to heal—oxygen, vitamins, minerals, fluids, plasma. Without oxygen, neurons will degrade. Neurons deprived of oxygen for too long will die. In the case of spinal-cord injuries, nerves are usually not severed, but rather suffer damage due to bruising and swelling, which restricts adequate blood supply.

When blood supply is replenished, neurons will attempt to repair themselves, especially when stimulated. In living neurons, axons and dendrites will work to return to their healthy state and allow communication to be restored. If neurons have been permanently damaged, the nervous system will try to bypass the old network and establish new communication links.

What does this mean for you? People need to move if they want to have increased circulation and a healthy blood supply. Additionally, exercise stimulates nerves by causing the brain and body to strive to send and receive signals. The signal to move originates in the brain and is sent through the nervous system to the muscles. The sensation of the movement of your body is picked up by peripheral nerves, which send signals back to the brain.

When healthy nerves are stimulated, axons and dendrites branch out to send and receive neurotransmitters. Previously separated neurons will link and create new neural pathways (see Figure 4.4). The ability of neurons to branch out is influenced by their environment and the amount of stimulation they receive. A constant supply of electrical impulses causes neurons to strive to reconnect. When there is little or no stimulation, nerve activity decreases or ceases.

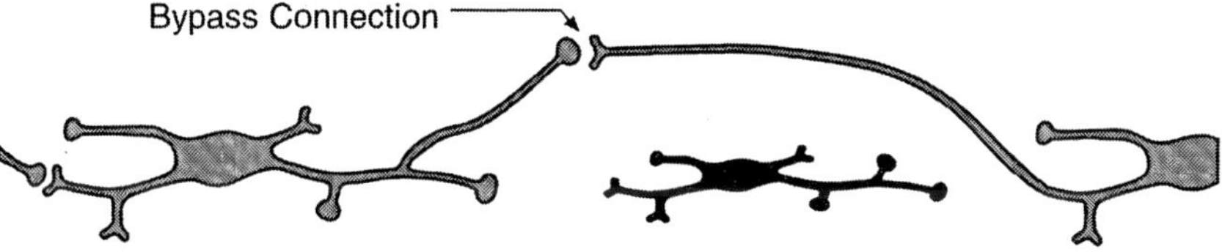

Figure 4.4
The nervous system's establishment of alternate comminication links.

The continual sensation of water moving around the body stimulates nerves to create or restore pathways. Nerves are also stimulated during massage as the sensations of touch, heat, pressure, and movement are sent to the brain.

Mental stimulation also causes the body to secrete chemicals which transmit nerve signals. Feelings of joy, sadness, and fear, for example, cause the body to secrete certain chemicals. Laughter and happiness cause the brain to secrete endorphins and dopamine, providing feelings of joy, as well as functioning as the body's natural painkillers.

When there is less pain, there is less muscle contraction, less tightness, and less swelling, enabling your body's healing system to function more efficiently and without interference.

By providing large amounts of physical and mental stimulation, and creating an environment for optimal healing, we enhance and speed the healing process and provide a means for attaining levels of healing beyond those traditionally thought possible.

The use of steroids for preventing paralysis has been effective in many cases if administered within twenty-four hours of a spinal cord injury. Steroids help reduce swelling and promote the healing of neurons, but the effectiveness varies from patient to patient and depends upon the extent of the injury.

Some people who suffer a spinal cord injury are able to recover shortly after their accident. If the swelling is controlled and the neurons in the spinal cord do not die, function will most likely return as the neurons heal. As previously stated, healthy neurons may branch out and bypass damaged cells to connect with other healthy neurons.

Nerve growth factor (NGF) is also produced in response to physical and mental stimulation. NGF was discovered in the 1950s but not recognized as important until the 1980s. Its discoverers were awarded the Nobel Prize in Physiology or Medicine in 1986.

Research has shown that NGF promotes increased nerve activity, neuron regeneration, and causes neurons to grow, heal, and lengthen branches. NGF also reduces or prevents neural degeneration, has been shown to accelerate wound healing, and is effective against a number of psychiatric issues including depression. NGF also promotes homeostasis of the body's functions, helping to create the best environment for healing.

Exercise, meditation, and yoga have been shown to promote the production of NGF, as does experiencing awe, bliss and love. A study published in Psychoneuroendocrinology in 2005 found that couples who had recently fallen in love demonstrated nearly double the NGF levels of a control group.

Lion's Mane mushroom is known to stimulate NGF production in the body. PQQ (identified in 2003 as the first new vitamin discovered in 55 years) also stimulates production of NGF. Excellent sources of PQQ include Natto (fermented soybeans), Ashitaba (a Japanese herb), as well as green tea, parsley, spinach, green peppers, celery, carrots, kiwi and papaya.

Research has also shown that foods containing Omega 3, 6 and 9, as well as vitamin B12 are effective in promoting nerve function and restoration.

A study published in the September 22, 2011 issue of the journal *Neuron* details research by biologists at University of California, San Diego, who identified 70 genes that promote axon growth after injury. They were surprised at the discovery that some of the genes that promote axon growth are the same genes that regulate the release of neurotransmitters.

I believe this confirms what other studies have also shown—that stimulating nerves and the release of neurotransmitters in turn promotes axon growth and nerve healing. Understanding this mechanism helps guide us in our approach to overcoming paralysis.

This new discovery is also further confirmation that with all our advances and knowledge, we do not yet know everything about how the human body works. We do not know what the body is capable of. Only a few years ago it was thought (and is still thought by many) that neurons have little if any healing capability. Research in study after study shows that ***the body is wired to heal***—we just have to learn how to tap that healing capacity.

Many people with spinal cord injuries have healed to a certain degree by stimulating nerve growth and regeneration using the Burdenko Method. Experience has shown that bringing the component of water into the combination of techniques creates a greater chance for healing to occur. Water exercises promote increased blood supply, sensory stimulation, a relaxation response, freedom of movement, traction, and increased mobility.

Spontaneous healing is a medically recognized phenomena, an unexpected and unexplained healing that occurs in a body. It has been my experience that spontaneous healing occurs more frequently when using water as a modality for healing.

Life is movement. Without movement, it is difficult to feel vigorous and alive. Water allows those experiencing paralysis to feel more alive by experiencing their bodies moving and flowing with the water. The weightless environment allows conscious movements to come more easily than on land. These movements in water help create muscle memory and the ability to transfer skills and movements onto land. Water provides an environment which enhances the natural healing process and promotes all components of healing to occur faster and more efficiently.

Summary

- Nerve signals travel in both directions. Just as the brain sends signals to the body, the body sends signals to the brain.
- Every neural message or attempted message stimulates activity and the opportunity for healing.
- Healing occurs when a healthy oxygenated blood supply flows through injured areas. Blood supply is the most important aspect of healing.
- The continual sensation of water moving around the body stimulates nerves to create or restore pathways. Nerves are also stimulated during massage as the sensations of touch, heat, pressure, and movement are sent to the brain.
- Mental stimulation causes the body to secrete chemicals which transmit nerve signals.
- Nerve Growth Factor promotes increased nerve activity, neuron regeneration, and causes neurons to grow, heal, and lengthen branches.
- Spontaneous healing is a medically recognized phenomena, an unexpected and unexplained healing that occurs in a body. It has been my experience that spontaneous healing occurs more frequently when using water as a modality for healing.

Bob McKenna's Story

In June of 1987, at the age of 23, I fell from a fifth-story balcony. I broke my fifth and sixth cervical vertebrae (C-5 and C-6), which left me paralyzed from the neck down. Fortunately, my father, grandfather, and brother are all doctors. Since they were in the business, they were able to locate the best medical services for me. I was treated at Boston University hospital, where the doctors fused my neck bones together in a delicate operation that helped save my life. I spent the next six months in the hospital's rehabilitation unit.

I left the hospital in October. At that point, I needed a personal attendant as I could not roll over, get dressed, get out of bed, or do any preparation by myself. Just maintaining my balance was difficult. I continued outpatient rehabilitation at Boston University Hospital. My rehabilitation program consisted of doing some controlled exercises on a mat for range of motion and to gain some basic strength. My physical therapists talked about my future in terms of ramps and adjusting to life in a wheelchair. I was very frustrated and depressed and did not know what to do with the rest of my life.

My family never gave up hope and continued to search for the best way for me to continue my rehabilitation. My father learned of Dr. Burdenko's work and made arrangements for us to meet. Dr. Burdenko analyzed and evaluated my situation in a way no one had done before. He expressed an incredible interest in what my body had gone through. For the first time, unlike other rehabilitation specialists, Igor said to me when I couldn't move a muscle, "I understand that you cannot move, but I want you to visualize the movement. Think about moving it. Even if it doesn't move, I want you to bring it through the motion in your mind."

This made a lot of sense to me. I felt that there was movement within my body, even though it couldn't be seen, felt, or even picked up with biofeedback. So Igor's encouragement to visualize the motion was an incredibly powerful tool for me, and in the following months became a primary factor in my reconditioning.

Igor treated me as an athlete in training who wanted to achieve his personal best. Traditional therapists treated me like a patient, or at best a client who was labeled quadriplegic. I never liked that. I was a young man who had an injury and who wanted to recover from that injury. I did not want to be labeled by some medical term. Igor would never even consider doing something like that. He gave me an incredible amount of respect, which is what I was looking for. This was the type of person I wanted to work with.

We began work that winter. I started with some basic balance exercises on the edge of my seat, trying to strengthen my torso. We also did some floor exercises and worked with exercise tubing as a strengthening tool while performing various motions. This created some torso balance and upper-body strength which prepared me for work in the pool. Igor said it would be easier to exercise in the water, but that was hard to imagine.

In the spring of 1988, I got into the pool for the first time. Igor and I worked on developing basic balance while vertical, trying to keep my head above water. The freedom of being in the pool was absolutely exhilarating! I came alive in the water. I felt very comfortable in the pool, being supported and suspended by the water. I wasn't stiff and tight because I wasn't afraid I was going to fall. Igor told me that I was free to make my legs move in any direction. Unlike on land, in the water I had the feeling that I could move. Igor and I worked together like sparring partners for five to six days a week in the water. Igor kept me incredibly busy with homework exercises and positions that I practiced religiously three or four times a day.

It was like a dream. I actually was able to start moving with maybe just a quiver or a slight movement one way or the other. I became aware of movement in water that I was unable to instigate on land. All of this was incredibly encouraging—to actually see my body move and to take it to another level from just feeling it inside me. It really gave me a great mental outlook because the injury had been so overwhelming. To see some progress, to feel good and to have somebody like Igor so focused wanting the best for me, all of these made for a great solution.

As part of my reconditioning, Igor had me work with a massage therapist. Igor encouraged me to visualize the movement of my body as I was being massaged. As my legs were carried through a range of motion, I was instructed to concentrate as if I were instigating the movement—totally controlling it. As my muscles were being massaged, I focused on sending positive energy and messages of healing, fluidity, and nerve function.

Another important aspect of Igor's program was nutrition. When I was eating, Igor had me focus on introducing the healthiest building blocks for recovery into my body. I ate foods that were very nutritious and high in fiber. I drank water and other fluids that were nutritious and cleansing. He wanted me to eat foods as a fuel, to give my body energy to strengthen myself.

Dr. Burdenko introduced me to a new, very positive way of recovering. It was a participatory method of recovery. I was doing the work, and he was assisting me—no one worked on me without my participation. I was totally focused on my body, concentrating on doing whatever was best.

At the end of the summer, my whole outlook had changed. I felt more energy when I woke up in the morning and throughout the day. That was exhilarating! It was also inspiring to have met such a quality person as Dr. Burdenko and his professional team. I had a new feeling of energy, possibilities, and potential.

In the fall, I returned to school to obtain my degree. Igor was very encouraging. He believes that it is just as important to develop the mind as it is to develop the body. It was good for me to focus on my studies and take a break from the intensive work we did during the summer.

When the next spring came around, I had completed my college degree, and I went back to work with Dr. Burdenko. We worked in the deep end with floatation devices. We spent a great deal of time stimulating and moving my legs. Igor kept instructing me to focus on moving my legs, always visualizing putting them through the movement of running, lifting, and extending.

One day, we were doing exercises in the pool. Igor was instructing me to concentrate on visualization, and my right leg started to move in a running motion. I couldn't believe it. I started crying, I was so thrilled. Whether we had created a new way for the nerve to communicate, or whether it was persistence, or whatever it was, the leg started moving. Things just took off from there.

I would stand on the bottom, shoulder-deep in the water holding onto floatation barbells. Slowly, I would move up the incline into the shallow end, usually losing my balance and falling over. By the end of the summer, I could actually walk without barbells and stand in the shallow end. It was spectacular! I remember Igor saying then that thousands of steps in water were equal to a few steps on the land.

My family never gave up hope, but they really didn't think I would ever walk again. When they came to the pool and saw me walk in the water, they couldn't believe their eyes. It was like a miracle.

So this is how it happened working with Dr. Burdenko. It was through being healthy, working hard, exercising regularly, stimulating the body, looking for new potential. Exercising in water was enjoyable, which made recovery possible. Weaker muscles that had atrophied could express themselves easier in the water where there was less gravity forcing the leg down or restricting it in any way. Previously, exercising on a mat in the rehab unit was miserable. I was limited in the direction that my legs might be able to move. It wasn't something I looked forward to doing every day. I would intentionally or sometimes unintentionally try to find ways of getting out of it. In water, I could see results, which was encouraging and helped to make it an enjoyable experience.

In the two years that I worked with Dr. Burdenko, I went from being confined to a wheelchair and feeling very awkward, to walking in the shallow end of a pool. To me this was a virtual recovery. Since then, I have been able to continue my rehabilitation, and today I walk on land with only the support of ankle braces and crutches. I have a fully independent life. I live by myself, work, study, and basically do everything I want. Through Igor I feel I have achieved this. With him I believe there are possibilities that even I haven't thought of yet.

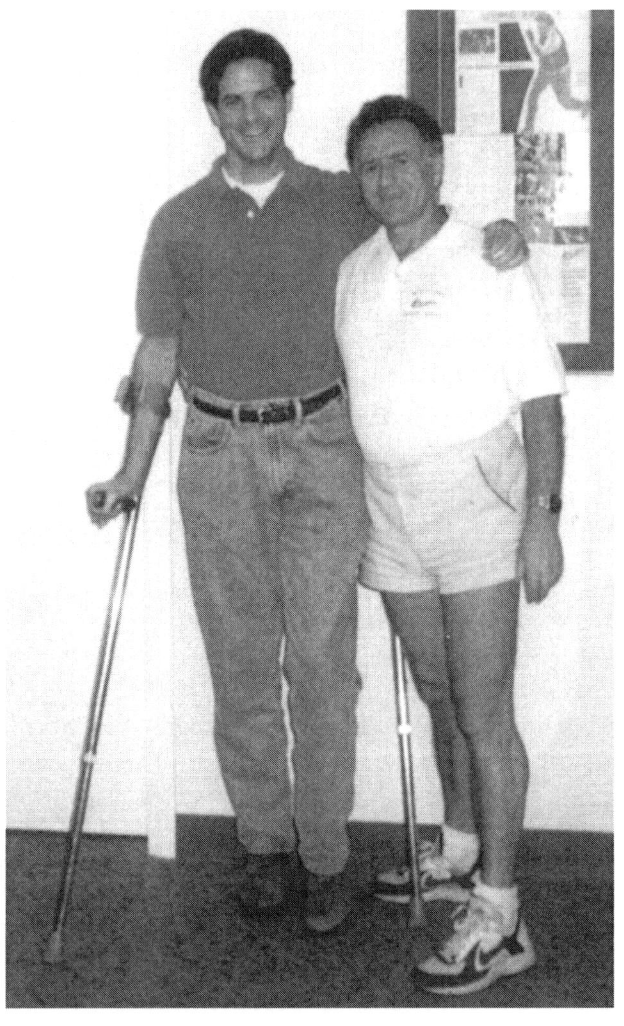

Chapter FIVE

Nutrition Therapy

This chapter is written with Nelli I. Pavlotsky, M.S., Certified Nutrition Specialist; Director, Personal Programs for Health and Productive Living; Burdenko Method Certified.

The material in this chapter reflects over two decades of experience at the Burdenko Water and Sports Therapy Institute, as well as the latest diet therapy research.

What is food? Food is energy. Food is your fuel. If you have a Mercedes, but no fuel, where can you go? Nowhere. No matter how fancy your car is, it will not go anywhere without fuel. Everyone understands this. In the same way, the kind of food you eat reflects on your energy level. Yet many people believe the way they fuel their body does not matter.

Maintaining good nutrition does not mean being on a diet. To maintain good health, you do not need a diet—you need nutritional education. A specific medical diet is useful if you are sick or recovering from an injury. However, there is a clear distinction between medical diets and using sound nutrition as an aspect of maintaining excellent health. When you understand the importance of providing your body with the essential food and fluids it needs to function efficiently, choosing what, how, and when to eat becomes an intelligent and enjoyable decision.

This chapter contains general guidelines that have proven to be effective. However, your food and liquid intake must be modified according to your goals. Consult with a professional nutritionist to help analyze your eating habits and ensure your body is getting the fuel it needs.

Maintaining proper weight can be achieved through a lifestyle of proper nutrition, developing good habits, stress management and exercising. A weight-loss diet is a short-term fix using specific foods and liquids. Most people regain weight in the months following a diet because their short-term diet did not change the habits that led to being overweight in the first place. Balanced nutrition also can help overcome the negative effects of drugs given to individuals after surgery or injury.

An assessment of your heredity, medical history, present nutrition, present habits, present exercise routine, as well as your workload and stress level, is needed before any modification can be designed.

The following principles of nutrition were successfully applied to people of all ages and varying needs.

Develop Proper Habits

Good habits to maintain:

- Eat all foods in moderation. This creates a strong supply of vitamins and minerals and everything your body needs. Eat a wide variety of foods. This helps you to get more nutrients. Many people do not eat fruits, or nuts, or vegetables. You have a great spectrum of food from which to choose, all of which have unique benefits. Eat meals with the right balance of protein, carbohydrates, and fat. These are the building blocks for your cells. You need the right amount of all of them.
- Do not overemphasize any specific type of food.
- Eat 3-4 times a day. Your digestive system will work more efficiently, and you will have enough energy from food during the day, distributed evenly. This will reflect on your energy, alertness, and mood. It is difficult to maintain a positive outlook when you are hungry.
- The biggest meal should be in the middle of the day, when you need more fuel.
- Plan your cooking, eating, and snacking. At specific times during the day, the pancreas releases digestive enzymes with the expectation of incoming food. If food is eaten, the enzymes help to digest the food. If the enzymes are released but there is no food to digest, the digestive system is pushed out of balance. The acidity of the stomach rises, which over time can lead to acid reflux, heartburn, ulcers, and gastric problems.
- Eat at regular times. Eating at inconsistent times, or overeating, creates dysfunction in your digestive system. The reason you feel tired after overeating is that your body puts vast resources into producing digestive enzymes and bile. Your organs must work overtime, taking resources from the rest of your system.
- Do not wait to be hungry. When people are hungry, they tend to overeat. Hunger can create mood swings, impact the energy levels, con-

centration, and produce stress in the digestive system. That is why it is important to have food 3-4 times per day *at the same times each day.* That altogether will back up energy performance all day long.

- Eat food warm or at room temperature. Cold foods slow down the digestive system.
- Know the quality of the food that goes into your body. Do not eat food after its expiration date. Read labels and look at ingredients, fat content, minerals, and vitamins. This helps you make the right choices and sustains healthy living.
- Keep track of your weight. Weigh yourself at least once per month. Maintain optimal weight for your height and body type, age, and activity level.
- Monitor blood pressure twice per month; check cholesterol and sugar at least twice per year. It is good to be aware of the vital signs of your system. Knowing this can help you prevent problems. For example, elevated cholesterol can be addressed before issues arise.

Habits to avoid:

- Try to avoid eating appetizers and snacks before a full meal. If you have appetizers or snacks, look at the portions. The added food should not change the whole amount of food taken during your meal. Too many appetizers or high-calorie appetizers create imbalance with the enzymes your body has secreted in preparation for the meal.
- Try to avoid eating after 7 pm. If you go to bed with a full stomach, your digestive system is still working to digest the food. That means you spend energy instead of saving energy when you sleep. This loss of energy will affect your body performance and your mindset when you wake up. That is why a lot of people who do not follow this habit need coffee in the morning. They cannot move without a boost. People should wake up full of energy. The whole night's sleep, which is so important for the human body, was wasted. Eating at night also contributes to weight gain.
- Making the right choices, knowing how to apply good habits, and how to make your mind and body function efficiently, are keys to sustaining good health. Every rule has exceptions. At a social event, enjoy yourself, but do not eat everything on the table. Do not behave like you are eating for the last time in your life. Enjoy yourself at social events with common sense. In your home, as your general habit, do not eat after 7 pm. Have self-discipline, listen to your body, learn for yourself what is good and what is not for your body. Use the knowledge you acquire in a practical manner. A lot of people say they possess the knowledge to be

healthy, but this knowledge does not mean very much unless they use it. Using what you know is the way to improve the outcome.

- Do not overeat. Overeating causes extra work for your digestive system, slows down your metabolism, and creates a habit for becoming overweight. Stop eating before you feel full. It takes time (20 minutes) for the signal from your stomach regarding feeling hungry or feeling full to be recognized by your brain.
- Avoid mixing different proteins (meat, fish, dairy) in the same meal. It slows down the digestive process. Different digestive enzymes are required to process different types of food, and these different enzymes are not available at the same time.
- Avoid strenuous exercising for one hour after a meal. Exercises will slow down the digestive system, and make it difficult for your digestive system to process the food, as the blood will be redistributed to the muscles.
- Avoid ice water and iced drinks. Cold drinks contract the digestive system and slow down the digestive process.
- Avoid heating foods in microwaves. Microwaves penetrate food and destroy the ingredients and structure of the food.
- Limit alcohol consumption.

How to Eat

Our bodies work best with a regular routine. Develop a routine: wake up, go to bed, and eat meals at the same time each day. If you do so, your body will work like a clock and increase the efficiency of your system. Your body will become accustomed to eating at the same times each day, produce the right amount of enzymes at the right time, and your digestive system will provide you with more benefits from the same food. You can survive on less food if your food is digested properly.

- As a general rule, meals should be eaten hot, warm, or at room temperature—not cold. Hot liquids should be included at the end of meals. This warms the stomach and helps nutrients be absorbed into the bloodstream more efficiently.
- It is better for those who are recovering from injury to eat several small meals (about four or five) throughout the day rather than three big meals. This keeps your energy level up throughout the day, and prevents your digestive system from being overworked. Additionally, several small meals will help satisfy your hunger since you will eat more often, even though you are not eating a large quantity.

- Eat slowly and chew your food thoroughly. Chewing your food thoroughly helps your digestive system speed the digestive process. Savoring your food also allows you to enjoy your food and your meals and feel satisfied at the end of the meal.
- Swallow in small portions. This adds more saliva to each bite. The increased moisture in swallowed food helps digest it and receive the most nutrition from your food.
- Start your day with a hot breakfast. Doing so is like warming up before exercising. It gives you enough fuel to do what you need during the day. Warm food is easier to digest and the warm feeling you start with in the morning is carried throughout your day.
- Your evening meal should be lighter than your lunch. When you sleep, all your body processes slow down. Prepare yourself to rest. A heavy evening meal means your stomach works all night. The last meal of the day should be eaten three hours before going to bed. This will benefit your deep sleep.
- Wash your hands with soap and warm water.
- Make sure your fruits and vegetables are fresh and clean. Wash them with warm water before eating.
- When preparing foods, be aware of cleanliness and sanitation. Keep hair from falling into your food. This is not only good manners, it is a health issue. Do not prepare food if your nails are dirty.
- Be aware of the packaging your food comes in. Do not buy more food than you can consume. Try not to store food in large quantities. Try not to have food in cans. Canned food often contains a lot of preservatives, sugar, sodium, and heavy syrup.
- Prefer glass over plastic and metal containers. Food that has been processed does not have as much nutrients and value. Consider natural foods. Read labels. Make sure the food has been stored properly. Be interested in finding good brands of fruit, vegetable, and dairy products. Try to use local produce.
- Remove skin from fish and poultry. Skin is a filter—it contains many toxins. It is also a high source of fats.
- Focus on your food while eating—do not read or watch television. Keep your mind and body functioning together. You have one process to focus on eating. You should acknowledge the color of the food. The taste. The amount. The temperature. There are so many things to process. Eat the way you exercise or brush your teeth—have a consistent pace. Concentrate. The meal should be a pleasant, focused experience, free of arguments, business, or tension.

- If you get hungry between meals, eat fresh or dried fruits and vegetables. When you are hungry, you usually do not smile, and it is easy to develop a negative attitude.
- People who exercise and compete should have special knowledge of food nutrition. Their nutritional needs are not typical, because they use so many calories for their training and performance. The sprinter should eat differently than the long-distance runner. A gymnast should eat differently than a weight lifter. They all need a different amount of calories, and a different volume of food and water.

Proper Digestion

In addition to food quality, we must be concerned about proper digestion, absorption and elimination. Food passes through a number of stages before its nutrients can nourish and repair your cells and organs. Each stage is critical—even a slight breakdown along the way can result in incomplete nutrition, toxic overload, or compromised health. We are not just what we eat, we are what we digest and absorb!

Proper digestion depends on good bacteria. A healthy intestine is one that maintains a critical balance of bacteria. Stress, medications, excessive alcohol use, and meals high in fat, meat, and sugar may endanger the fine balance of intestinal bacteria, resulting in weakened digestive and immune systems. Inadequate food and rest, exposure to environmental toxins, antibacterial drugs, chlorine and fluoride in drinking water, and undue use of antacids and antibiotics may alter the balance of the gastrointestinal (GI) tract and promote an intestinal environment in which pathogenic bacteria and yeast can flourish.

Consumers are becoming aware of the value of supplemental enzymes and beneficial bacteria (probiotics). Worldwide, this natural approach has been used for many years. Millions of people in many countries take probiotics as a proactive way to maintain good health.

Research has shown that a healthy lifestyle and dietary supplements with probiotics can help balance the body's supply of friendly intestinal bacteria. The highest quality probiotic supplements contain enough live cultures and starter nutrients to establish a healthy population of friendly bacteria. A balanced digestive system alleviates much of the stress on your immune system, which can lead to an overall healthier you!

The word probiotic literally means "for life." Our vast internal ecosystem, which contains billions of living microorganisms called intestinal flora, dramatically influence the body's metabolism, physical health and mental well-being. Sufficient beneficial bacteria can help prevent negative influences such as free radicals, pathogens and undigested fats and proteins from penetrating the intestinal wall and entering the blood stream. Better digestion creates vitality and increases quality of life.

Friendly bacteria, or probiotics, have many important roles, including:
- Enhancing absorption of nutrients
- Producing vitamins
- Supporting immunity
- Promoting healthy peristalsis and elimination
- Maintaining proper acid/alkaline (pH) intestinal balance

Stimulating Your Digestive Tract

Eat plenty of roughage (fiber) to stimulate your bowel movements in order to eliminate the toxins from your system. Fresh and dried fruits and vegetables are good sources of fiber. Unprocessed grains work like sandpaper to clean the lining of your stomach and intestines.

The accumulation of food within your body depresses body functions. Can you run on a full stomach? Right after a full meal you feel that you cannot.

Having bowel movements at least once per day prevents the accumulation of toxins in your body. Maintaining a routine of bowel movements at the same time each day helps the digestive system function smoothly.

To stimulate digestion, contract and relax your abdominal muscles in a wavelike motion. This will result in peristalsis, the contraction of muscles which propels food through the digestive tract. Shaking your body (discussed in Chapter 2) also stimulates digestion.

Certain foods will also help stimulate peristalsis. Juicing half a beet and/or a handful of parsley along with several carrots is an excellent and natural way to clean your system.

Even if you feel you are not ready to have a bowel movement, sit on the toilet at the same time each day. Coming to a certain environment provokes certain behavior. If you go to the bathroom at the same time daily, you teach your body a routine which helps to stimulate bowel movements. Try it. After some time, your body will respond.

A healthy digestive system also reflects on your mind and mood. Unhealthy eating habits and digestion can contribute to or be one of the causes of depression. After a satisfying meal, you might have one mood. When you are hungry, you have another. If you overeat, you have yet another mood. Healthy eating habits and regular bowel movements will help to achieve a stable mood and prevent mood swings.

Many people these days eat irregularly and have a bowel movement once every two or three days. I recommend a healthy, regular eating schedule with bowel movements at least once a day. Twice a day is even better. With practice, it can be done, and your body will function more efficiently and your mood will improve and stabilize. Regular bowel movements also help avoid headaches.

Choose a good diet therapist with the same diligence you use to choose a good physician. Honor your body, and supply it with the proper building blocks it needs to be healthy. Eating intelligently is not stressful the way dieting often is. Once you begin eating nutritionally, you will notice that life becomes enjoyable. Good nutrition should be a lifetime commitment. Your body deserves the best! It is just as important to eat the right foods and drink the proper liquids as it is to exercise the mind and body. Proper nutrition is part of whole body conditioning.

For your body to work most efficiently, the food in your meals must be varied, balanced, and eaten in moderate quantities. It is important to keep all the food groups in mind when planning your meals. Every day, your diet should include something from each of these groups: breads and grains; fruits and vegetables; milk and dairy products; meats, poultry, and fish. You should eat at least five different fruits and vegetables every day.

Guidelines on what to eat:

- Squeeze fresh lemon juice on salads, fish, meats, and poultry to help digest fat, prevent bacterial growth, and for a good taste.
- Eat one to two cloves of raw garlic twice per week to disinfect your digestive tract and prevent illness.
- Eat watermelon, cucumbers, and celery to stimulate kidney function and urination. These foods help the body hold and absorb water, making it easier for kidney function and performance.
- Substitute table sugar with honey (which is also an antiseptic), 100% maple syrup, and unsweetened dried fruits in moderation.
- Eat orange, green and yellow fruits. The beta-carotene and fructose will help balance your energy levels.
- Eat calcium-containing products such as cottage cheese and yogurt, to help maintain bone density and prevent osteoporosis.
- Buy quality fresh, frozen, or dried foods from reputable sources.
- Plan your menu to include foods with plenty of vitamins, amino acids and minerals. Try to structure your food intake by planning in advance. Consume a variety of it.

Enzymes are needed as catalysts for every bodily process. Without enzymes, our bodies could not function. Likewise, enzymes could not function without vitamins. Vitamins ("vita" means life) are called coenzymes. We do not need them in megadoses, but we need the whole spectrum of them every day. Food should be your primary source of vitamins, minerals and amino acids; however, for those who do not take in adequate nutrients from their meals, supplementation is a viable means of obtaining the vitamins and minerals necessary for health and recovery.

Of particular importance to those recovering from nerve damage are the vitamins and minerals, responsible for nerve functions: vitamins B_1, B_3, B_5, B_6, and B_{12}, and the minerals calcium, phosphorus, and copper. See Table 5.1 below for a list of some of the vitamins and minerals vital to nerve function.

Table 5.1. Vitamins and Minerals Responsible for Nerve Functions

Nutrient	Food Sources
Vitamin B_1 (thiamin)	Pork, fortified grains and cereals, seafood.
Vitamin B_3 (niacin or nicotinic acid)	Poultry and seafood, seeds and nuts, or potatoes, fortified whole grains and cereals.
Vitamin B_5 (pantothenic acid)	Almost all plant and animal foods. Also manufactured by intestinal bacteria.
Vitamin B_6 (pyridoxine]	Meats, fish, and poultry, grains and cereals, spinach, sweet potatoes, white potatoes, bananas, prunes, watermelon.
Vitamin B_{12} (Cobalamin)	Meat and poultry (esp. calf's liver, venison, lean beef, lamb), seafood (esp. sardines, snapper, salmon, scallops, shrimp, halibut), cheese (esp. Swiss, Mozzarella, Parmesan), eggs. Plant sources have inconsistent and unreliable quantities, but tofu, tempeh, and sea vegetables tend to be more reliable.
Calcium	Milk and milk products, canned salmon (with bones), oysters, tofu, broccoli, kale.
Phosphorus	Dairy products and egg yolks; meat, poultry, and fish; legumes, caviar, edamame, sprouts, Brussels sprouts, broccoli.

Copper	Lobster, organ meats, nuts, dried peas, beans, prunes, barley, lima beans, Spirulina (seaweed).

Fats

There is a lot of media hype about maintaining a low-fat diet. One should not eat fat in excess. However, be careful not to eliminate fat from your meals entirely. Fat serves a purpose, and should not be eliminated completely, but taken in moderation.

Many people have come to believe they must avoid all fat, even from healthy sources such as almonds. This is the wrong message. You need some fat. The best thing to remember—your diet should include a balance between fats, carbohydrates, and proteins. You cannot have a diet with only protein, or only carbohydrates, or no protein, or no carbohydrates. It will bring your body out of balance, and create a lot of harm in the long term.

Your body requires a proper amount of fat for many reasons, including the following:

- It surrounds your internal organs and acts as a protective cushion.
- It helps regulate and maintain body temperature (like insulation in your house).
- It is required by your hormonal system.
- It is a source of energy.

Recommended Menu

The following is an example of a menu for one day:

Breakfast: Hot cereal with dried fruits or honey, herbal tea.

Lunch: Split-pea soup, scallops with rice and salad, tea; berries for dessert.

Afternoon Snack: Fresh strawberries, toast, herbal tea.

Supper: Cottage cheese, whole-wheat crackers with jam, tea.

Liquid Intake

Your body is 80 percent liquid. It needs an ongoing supply of fluids for metabolism and digestion, as well as for the life and function of your body's cells. However, it is my belief that too much liquid can be harmful to your heart and puts a strain on the kidneys. Adjust your liquid intake for climate conditions and for increased exercise activity.

When you do not take in enough liquid, the balance of your biochemical reactions shifts and disturbs the biochemistry of your body, causing everything to shrink. (Picture flowers wilting without water or grass without rain). Additionally, without liquids to carry away the by-products of digestion, your body will accumulate toxins. Drink plenty of fluids to stimulate urination and wash these toxins away. However, monitor your liquid intake carefully to maintain the fine natural balance your body requires.

Guidelines for developing good liquid intake habits:

- Eat soup daily. Try having soup with your lunch. Soup will help replenish fluids in your body, and it is easy for the body to digest. Soup is full of vitamins and minerals, and is warm, which helps the digestive process. The best liquid intake is from food.
- Always have hot water or tea after each meal. It coats all the food in your stomach and promotes healthy digestion.
- Drink hot liquids at least 3-4 times a day. Hot liquids help to dissolve fats, soften the food in your system, and speed up the digestive process. Good choices include tea, soup, and hot water.
- It is recommended that the average healthy individual drink 6-8 glasses of liquids per day. This should be adjusted based on physical activity, weight, climate, temperature, season, and humidity. Healthy liquid intake can be from food, such as soup, fruits, and vegetables, or by drinking liquids directly, such as tea and fresh juice.
- Drink water that is clean and pure.
- Be sure to read the labels of your drinks. Be aware of the ingredients and try to avoid drinks with caffeine, sodium, high amounts of sugar or sugar substitutes.
- If drinking from a container, try to use glass instead of plastic or metal.
- Limit coffee intake, including decaffeinated. Coffee can leech vitamins and minerals from your system. Depending on coffee for energy is not the best way to feel energized.
- Drink *fresh* fruit juices as sources of fluids and vitamins. Try to implement juicing at home.
- Reduce your liquid intake two to four hours before you go to bed so that you do not interrupt your sleep with bathroom trips.
- Limit intake of alcoholic beverages. Excessive alcohol adversely affects your liver and your brain.

I cannot stress enough the importance of good nutrition. After an injury, everything changes: your mobility, lifestyle, and habits. Your nutrition should change accordingly. The quality of your food and the way it is prepared matters, as does the time of day you eat, the way you eat, portion sizes, and eating habits, and should be re-evaluated and adjusted. With the proper eating habits, you can speed up your healing process, help maintain proper weight, prevent mood swings, keep wastes and toxins from accumulating in your body, and return to a good state of health.

Summary

Good habits to maintain:

- Eat all foods in moderation
- Eat a wide variety of foods
- Eat well balanced meals
- Do not overemphasize any specific type of food
- Eat 3-4 times a day.
- Your biggest meal should be in the middle of the day
- Plan your cooking, eating and snacking. Do not wait to be hungry
- Eat at regular times
- Eat food warm or at room temperature
- Know the quality of the food that goes into your body. Read food labels (ingredients, expiration date, etc.)
- Keep track of your weight. Weigh yourself at least once per month
- Monitor blood pressure twice per month; check cholesterol and sugar at least twice per year

Habits to avoid:

- Try to avoid eating appetizers and snacks before a full meal
- Try to avoid eating after 7 pm
- Every rule has exceptions. At a social event, enjoy yourself, but do not eat everything on the table
- Do not overeat
- Avoid mixing different proteins (meat, fish, dairy) in the same meal. It slows down the digestive process.
- Avoid strenuous exercising for one hour after a meal
- Avoid ice water and iced drinks
- Avoid heating foods in microwaves
- Limit alcohol consumption

How to eat:

- As a general rule, meals should be eaten hot, warm, or at room temperature—not cold
- Hot liquids should be included at the end of each meals

- Those who are recovering from injury should eat 4-5 small meals throughout the day rather than three big meals
- Eat slowly and chew your food thoroughly
- Swallow in small portions
- Start your day with a hot breakfast
- Your evening meal should be lighter than your lunch
- The last meal of the day should be eaten three to four hours before going to bed
- Wash your hands with soap and warm water
- Wash your fruits and vegetables with warm water
- Be aware of cleanliness and sanitation during food preparation
- Prefer glass over plastic and metal containers
- Remove skin from fish and poultry
- Focus on your food while eating
- Snack on fresh or dried fruits and vegetables if hungry between meals

What to eat:

- Squeeze fresh lemon juice on salads, fish, meats, and poultry
- Eat one to two cloves of raw garlic twice per week
- Eat watermelon, cucumbers, and celery
- Substitute table sugar with honey, 100% maple syrup, and unsweetened dried fruits in moderation
- Eat orange, green and yellow fruits and vegetables
- Eat calcium-containing products, such as cottage cheese and yogurt
- Buy quality fresh, frozen, or dried foods from reputable sources
- Plan your menu to include foods with plenty of vitamins, amino acids and minerals

Guidelines for developing good liquid intake habits:

- Eat soup daily. Try having soup with your lunch.
- Always have hot water or tea after each meal.
- Drink hot liquids 3-4 times a day (tea, hot water)
- Drink 6-8 glasses of liquid per day
- Drink water that is clean and pure
- Read labels. Avoid drinks with caffeine, sodium sugar, and sugar substitutes.
- Drink from a glass container
- Limit coffee intake, including decaffeinated
- Drink *fresh* fruit juices
- Reduce liquid intake two to four hours before going to bed
- Limit intake of alcoholic beverages
-

General recommendation when injured:

People often gain weight after injury due to decreased mobility.
Eat smaller portions; decrease fat intake; finish the meal when you are full.

Nelli Pavlotsky, M.S., C.N.S. has extensive experience in biology, biochemistry, nutrition and diet science. She has spent more than a decade conducting research in the Hematology/Oncology department at Boston University Medical School. Ms. Pavlotsky has dedicated her career to research on food, vitamins, food supplements and diets. She has designed customized diets for a wide range of people such as: high performance athletes, dancers, and individuals with life threatening health problems. She has also worked with a variety of ages including children and elderly. Nelli Pavlotsky presents lectures on lifestyle optimization and nutrition in hospitals, various clinical settings and at national and international conferences.

Mark Magid's Story

My name is Mark Magid. I'm 66 years old and have been suffering with MS since 1982. I sought out and tried countless methods and treatments, official medicines and alternative. Unfortunately, nothing helped me with my symptoms.

In 2010 I had been losing weight and my symptoms were increasing. I was losing my ability to move. I visited a neurologist who confirmed my condition and referred me to the hospital nutritionist.

The nutritionist gave me a diet to follow. I felt like the guidelines I was given were general recommendations that were not specific to my problems. But I followed the recommendations. They did not help, and I continued to lose weight.

That summer, I was introduced to Nelli Pavlotsky. Nelli began working with me with a clear plan and comprehensive approach to achieve my goals. She changed my diet, added appropriate supplements and specific exercises with gradually increasing difficulty. Her approach included adding specific herbs to my diet and following macrobiotic principles. She specified what to eat, how much to eat, and when to eat. She worked with me to create a lifestyle that included a regular routine of activities and atmosphere in such a clear and comfortable way that helped me live my everyday life.

Most people don't realize that it is extremely difficult for people with MS to gain weight or even maintain weight. Yet two months after beginning my work with Nelli, I gained 10 pounds and was back to my usual weight. To this day I maintain this weight. I increased muscle strength, reduced fatigue and depression, and improved bladder and bowel control. Our work together also helped me develop a positive attitude and increase my social activities.

I am grateful to Nelli and believe the methods I experienced can help many people.

Chapter SIX

The Healing Journey

This chapter is written by Vladimir Goltsov, Holistic Healing Therapist

INNER HEALTH AND STATE OF MIND

Injuries can change everything—our thoughts, our beliefs, our hopes about the future, our awareness of the nature of those around us. What is it about injuries that bring us to a place of deep contemplation?

Many people feel isolated after an injury. Many simply do not know what to do. Do we listen to that still small voice within us that we are not really sure even exists? Do we give up our beliefs, hopes, and intuition, and let the beliefs of others guide us?

When I left my second physical therapy appointment, I felt like I had left a medieval torture chamber. My breathing was so heavy and fast I was practically hyperventilating.

The car accident six weeks prior had left all four limbs broken and joints crushed. After surgeries and a six-week hospital stay, it was time for the next step—getting everything working again. My joints were frozen—my knees could hardly bend, my right ankle and toes could not move at all, my right elbow could hardly bend, my left arm could not twist, and my left hand and wrist could barely move. There was significant bone and nerve loss. My left knee and right ankle were in extreme pain at the slightest touch. The doctor's prognosis, which I would not be aware of for another year, was that if I was very lucky, I might walk in two years, but I would always need crutches. He believed the likely scenario was that I would be in a wheelchair for the rest of my life.

Self Portrait, by Vladimir Goltsov

The physical therapist was gentle during my first session. The second session and subsequently, she did what she thought she needed to get my limbs moving again. She worked with me the way she was trained to—a bit of massage to an injured area, some stretching, then brute force.

How do you bend a frozen knee? Force it. How do you move a frozen kneecap, ankle, or elbow? Force them. It was agonizing, despite being on high doses of oxycontin, a powerful narcotic painkiller. It was not until I was introduced to the Burdenko Method that I became aware that brute force was not the only way to regain motion in joints.

After the session, I wheeled my wheelchair outside and found a place I could be alone. I calmed myself down, still breathing deeply, and unable to remove the cringe from my face. *Is this the future I have ahead of me? This is nothing short of torture. Does it have to be so painful? Is there any other way?*

What on earth did I do to deserve this? So would begin my journey of regaining use of my limbs, walking again, and trying to regain what I had lost.

Over the course of my recovery—I learned. How do I minimize pain? How do I maximize my healing? How do I deal with the stress of my environment, with my own thoughts, and with my physical helplessness? How do I deal with negativity around me and within me, and make my needs known, even when people trained and experienced tell me I must bow to their will or never improve? And what do I do with this constant feeling that I just want to curl up and die?

It is my deepest desire that this chapter may provide you with resources, thoughts, and ideas that might offer hope, excitement, and a daring zeal to heal in a way that works for you.

To hell with circumstances; I create opportunities.

– Bruce Lee, actor & martial artist

Hope

I deeply believe hope is one of the most important factors in recovery. Hope for something greater. Hope for something better. Hold hope in the deepest parts of your being that something, somehow, somewhere, will change for the better.

It is possible to come through this experience emotionally stronger, with wisdom and insight into yourself and others, rather than broken or hardened. It is possible to heal to a greater extent than western medicine may predict.

For six weeks following my accident, in my hospital room, I hoped. I hoped to walk again, to run again, to play sports again. I hoped simply for the ability to move enough to write an email to friends and colleagues. I hoped for simple things like being able to wash myself and go to the bathroom without assistance and a bedpan. I wondered if I would ever be with a woman again and hoped everything still worked. I hoped, prayed, gave up hope many times, and found hope again.

I learned the importance of being patient with myself and with the healing process. I learned to savor the moments of hope, vision, and insight when they occurred, as they do not always last. The memory of the hope and vision carried me when I could not feel the feeling.

In many shamanic societies, if you came to a medicine person complaining of being disheartened, dispirited, or depressed, they would ask one of four questions. When did you stop dancing? When did you stop singing? When did you stop being enchanted by stories? When did you stop finding comfort in the sweet territory of silence?

– Angeles Arrien, cultural anthropologist

Desire to Heal

I believe the desire to heal is one of the most important factors in recovery. Our beliefs can and do affect reality. Desiring to improve and never giving up hope directly affects the speed and extent of recovery.

Desire to heal. Truly desire to improve. Visualize in your mind a picture of yourself healed, happy, and pain-free. Visualize yourself with every quality you desire for yourself. Visualization is an integral part of the Burdenko Method and a part of ancient wisdom since the beginning of time.

I want to ask you a personal question, just between the two of us: *What do you want?*

I am not interested in your prognosis and I am not interested in what other people think. *What do you want?*

Sometimes people privately desire to receive the attention that comes with an injury. Sometimes people privately give up, go along with whatever doctors say, but know in their hearts that they will not change the current situation. Sometimes people privately like the change in their bodies.

What do you truly believe and desire for yourself and your future? This intention and inner desire guides your recovery.

I would like to request something of you. Just between us. I ask of you: *surrender yourself to the higher wisdom of your body and soul. Allow this higher wisdom to help you.* It helped me, and I believe it saved my life.

For a short concentrated time each day, I allowed myself to be truly open to desiring full health and allowing higher wisdom to help me. Even when I was having difficulty for most of the day, I did my best to allow myself, if even for 10 seconds each day, to truly be open to unlimited healing potential.

From the depths of my being to the depths of yours—in your most private moments, allow your deepest belief system to reflect the highest vision of possibility for yourself.

Imagination is your greatest gift. Do not be afraid to use it. Imagine yourself as being okay right now. Totally okay. Imagine yourself as Whole, Complete, and Perfect. With nothing to change, nothing to "improve." Imagine your heart as being open again, your life as if it were starting over in the most important ways. Can you imagine this? Then you have just created Tomorrow.

– Neale Donald Walsch, author & spiritual teacher

Love

I truly believe love is one of the most important factors in recovery. Love is more than an emotion—it is a state of being. Love can literally change the functioning of every system in the body. The experience of love sends all sorts of signals throughout the body and creates secretions in the brain that override the brain's usual state of being, reduce pain, and literally super-charge the body's healing response and capability.

I speak of pure, full, and complete love from the heart. Thinking of someone or something helps many people to move into this state and stay in it. Yet the love I speak of is not only love for another, but the feeling of pure love in the heart that overrides all other thoughts and emotions. Can you remember the last time you felt this way?

Allow yourself to experience a complete state of love, if only for a few moments, where your body, your ego, and the world melt away and nothing exists but love. Dr. Burdenko says, "Love is a state of music in your soul."

Find ways that help you remember and return to this state. For me, playing particular lines of a song from the Rent Soundtrack in my head helped remind me of pure love and bring me into that state while lying in a hospital bed with turmoil all around me. I breathed deeply, and allowed the memory of the music to bring me to a place of peace where the world and my ego melted away, and nothing existed but love.

What reminders work for you? Perhaps a song, a poem, a situation, a person, a particular memory like your wedding, graduation, honeymoon, making love, or the birth of a child? Allow yourself to fill with love from within. It changed my world; I hope it can change yours.

If tears flow, they may be a sign that you are breaking through inner barriers. Allow them a place, and let them flow if they come.

Your task is not to seek for love, but merely to seek and find all the barriers within yourself that you have built against it.

– Rumi, 13th century Sufi poet

Friendship and Relationship

Friendship and relationship is extraordinarily important to recovery. It is important not to be alone. It is important to reach out to friends and loved ones. We all need to be alone sometimes, but be aware of the trap of isolating yourself and not being in touch with those dear to you.

Call your friends and loved ones. Maintain, nourish, and create relationships that support you. Often, injuries allow the opportunity to reevaluate and change many aspects of life. Allow your injury to be a catalyst for the creation of new relationships or new kinds of relationships that you want to have in your life.

Dr. Burdenko says friendship is a beautiful instrument whose music you should hear for the rest of your life. When you have friends, you never feel lonely, you always feel support, you live your life not only for yourself. When you have friends, you are rich.

Always make time for your friends and loved ones, communicate and share your most valuable thoughts and ideas with each other. No one should ever be so busy they do not make time for people they love.

> Promise me you'll always remember: You're braver than you believe, and stronger than you seem, and smarter than you think!
>
> **– Christopher Robin to Pooh**

Passion

There was a point during my rehabilitation where I was giving up. I had quickly become known in the hospital as the guy with endless energy and positivity, but the pain and negativity around me and the realization that I may never walk again was getting to me. I wondered why I was trying so hard. I wondered why I was enduring so much. Why bother? Why not just insist on more pain medication and never leave my bed? After a week-long downward spiral, my body began to feel worse, my pain increased, and I could feel my healing process slow if not stop altogether.

It hit me that I had to stay positive. I absolutely had to. I did not have a choice—if I wanted to heal, I had to raise my energy level, smile, be positive, and will my body to heal. I listened to a fair amount of relaxing music, but I became aware that I needed something to jump-start my energy levels, motivate me to a frame of mind of achievement, of body building, of motivation, of pushing my body past all limits.

A particular memory kept popping into my head around this time. I had seen the movie *Rocky IV* in the theater when I was a child with my brother and older cousin who took us. Eight years old at the time, I convinced my cousin that my parents always bought a medium popcorn for each of us at the movies, when in fact we were lucky to get a small. I quite enjoyed that day.

I smiled each time I remembered that experience and movie. That evening, I searched Youtube for clips of *Rocky IV*, put on headphones and cranked the volume while watching various scenes. I watched the training montage, various parts of the fight, and became energized seeing Rocky get hit so much and keep coming back stronger each time.

Before the final round, Rocky's coach shouted at him, trying to motivate a tired man fighting a larger, stronger, seemingly invincible opponent:

"*All your strength, all your power, all your love, everything you've got! … This is your whole life here! DO IT NOW. NOW!*"

The powerful clip brought tears to my eyes and woke up something deep inside me. *What I do now affects the rest of my life. This is my whole life. I need to give it every last ounce of strength I've got.*

My emotions riled up and strength flowed through me as I tapped reserves hidden deep inside of me. I downloaded songs from *Rocky* to my MP3 player and listened to them all day long throughout rehabilitation. When I began to feel down, I remembered those powerful words, "This is your whole life here! This is your whole life here!"

I believe it is extraordinarily important to find something that moves us. We need a way to wake the passion, life, and hunger within us.

We need to find a way to express ourselves, whether through prose or poetry, song, or playing an instrument, to find a reason to laugh, to be excited, to let who you are shine. We must also be contemplative when we need to, and grieve when we need to.

> It doesn't interest me how old you are
> I want to know if you will risk looking like a fool
> for love
> for your dreams
> for the adventure of being alive.
>
> **– Excerpt from "The Invitation"**
> **by Oriah, teacher & author**

Act Like a Healthy Person

Deep in meditation early in the morning three days after my accident, lying in a hospital bed, hardly able to move, the following thought came to me. I share it here with you:

Act like a healthy person. Don't act like a sick person. Don't move like a sick person. Don't make noises like a sick person. Don't get into the mindset of a sick person. You are a healthy person.

If you're in pain, move slowly, but move like a healthy person. If you need to make a noise, make it, but make noise like a healthy person. If you need to feel down or complain, then do so, but like a healthy person. When you speak, make sure the voice you're speaking with is that of a healthy person. You're healthy. Act and speak and move like a healthy person.

I listened to the voice inside. As best I could, I spoke with the voice of a healthy person. I moved slowly but as smoothly and as pain-free as possible, and strained like an athlete rather than moaning like a sick person when I tried to sit up. Friends and family who spoke with me on the phone said they could not believe that I sounded strong and healthy. I learned that my voice, thoughts, and movements not only reflect my state of being, but help create it.

Everything is energy and that's all there is to it. Match the frequency of the reality you want and you cannot help but get that reality. It can be no other way. This is not philosophy. This is physics.

– Albert Einstein

Honoring Your Journey, and Letting Go

About a year after my accident, I began having a recurring dream. In the dream, I was in another accident. *A car had hit the side of my car. My hips were broken. Paramedics wanted to get me to a hospital. I yelled at the paramedics. "I do not consent! I DO NOT CONSENT!" I didn't want to be moved. I refused to go through the pain of recovery and physical therapy all over again. I wouldn't do it. I didn't care about the consequences.*

Then I'd wake up in a cold sweat, shaking.

I need to honor my journey, I thought, each time after the dream. After several recurrences of the dream, I went to a park, looked at the trees and sky, listened to the birds, and thought about everything I had been through.

Thank you, I said, with deep respect for my experiences. I thought about everything that had happened, the difficult times and the good ones; those experiences that caused me pain and those that made me a stronger person. I opened my heart and gave thanks, knowing that the intense unbearable pain portion of this journey had passed. I gave respect to a future whose events I could not know; knowing only that if and when I need more strength, I would have it in that moment, but not before.

I cannot know what the future holds, and living in the past does not change that. Honoring the past, while moving forward and looking at the situation around me, helps me live my life in a way that helps honor who I am, where I have been, and where I am going.

I honored my journey in this way a number of times, each time delving to a deeper level, and releasing the past to the past. The recurring dream stopped. Every few months when it returns, I remember that I need to honor my experiences, and let them go.

> There is no need to honor the body. There is no need to honor the mind. What is needed is distance. Once there is a distance between you and the body, and you and the mind, that is the end of suffering.
>
> **– Sadhguru Jaggi Vasudev, Indian yogi and mystic**

Depression... Are Your Inner Thoughts Consistent with Your Outer World?

A year after my accident, I was still doing physical therapy. Every movement hurt and every time I closed my eyes I would be in my car experiencing the crash over and over again, the sound of metal crushing and glass breaking as loud as a train wreck all around me. I could not concentrate. I could not think straight. My physical body was not recovered, and neither were my emotions.

I went to a mountain retreat for a weekend meditation to try and clear my head. On the second day, deep in meditation, the sweet scent of sage in the air, I began to see a vision.

I saw a man of Native American descent, an old master. He was sitting alone by a smoking fire, slowly mixing some sort of salve.

I began to hear words.

Your soul is infinite. Take care of your body. Keep your body healthy. Find a way.

The reason you are depressed is that the desires and visions from deep within your soul are not congruent with the reality before you. Allow your soul to shine. Allow yourself to do that which you desire, even given the realities of this world. Allow yourself to shine. Find a way.

Your soul is infinite. You identify with your infinite soul more than your limited body, and that is why you are confused. Your outer reality doesn't make sense given your inner world. But your body is fragile. And that is the reality you face before you. Do not shy away from anything and everything that may help your body. Take care of it. That you feel great in one moment does not mean you won't feel down the next. That you feel like you're in a bottomless pit sometimes does not mean you'll feel that way forever.

Take care of yourself. Do not shy away from supplements, diet changes, listening to when your body wants to sleep, when it wants to be creative, and when it wants contemplative silence. That you can will yourself forward does not make you stronger. True strength lies within, in a soul imbibed with patience, ancient wisdom, and understanding that there are times to push and times to recharge. Do not wait until you are depleted to recharge. Do you wait until your car engine shuts off from lack of fuel before refilling your tank? Recharge regularly. Make it fun. You will come to enjoy the silence.

When You Just Want to Curl Up and Die

A few days after my accident, I woke up early one morning in my hospital bed with a vision, something like a waking dream.

I saw myself standing in an open space, with a circle on the ground next to me. I saw myself jumping into the circle. I heard a voice say, *Jump into life. Make a commitment, every day, to jump into life.*

I thought for a moment. *I'm not sure I can make that kind of commitment*, I answered.

The voice spoke again. *Every morning, when you wake up, make a commitment to jump into life. The commitment you are making is to commit to life for those five seconds when you are visualizing yourself jumping into life and standing there for a moment. What you believe the rest of your day is for you to decide. Can you commit, for five seconds, every day, to jump into life? It will affect the level of your healing tremendously.*

I thought about it. I was not sure I cared how much I healed. But I did not want to be bed-ridden for the rest of my life. In that moment, for that reason only, I said, *Yes*. And I did so, every morning. Even when I hated everyone and everything and I was angry at the world and God, I put it all aside for those five seconds, and jumped into life.

WORKING WITH TRAUMA AND PAIN

I was in excruciating pain after my second surgery, two weeks after the accident. I complained of pain several times throughout the afternoon and evening, and was simply told by the nurse to press the button for the morphine drip. I did, but the pain continued to increase throughout the day. I meditated, did breathing exercises, and gave myself energy healing treatments throughout the day. These lessened the pain tremendously and I fell asleep in the evening.

I woke up in the middle of the night with debilitating lightning bolt shooting pain. I pressed the button to call the nurse, hoping she'd come quickly and becoming aware that tears were coming out of my eyes faster than falling raindrops, although I wasn't crying. It was my body's response to the pain. The nurse came. This time, I didn't complain of pain. It was no longer time to ask for help. It was time for action. "Something's wrong. Call a doctor," I said.

"What do you mean? What's wrong?"

I was breathing powerful, fast, deep breaths. "I'm about to pass out from the pain," I said. "Look at all these tears. I'm not crying, my body is reacting to pain. Something's wrong. Call a doctor." Tears continued out of my eyes like a rainstorm.

"Have you been pressing the morphine button?"

"Yes!" I said, continuing to breathe fast and audibly, wiping the waterfall of tears from my face.

She went to the morphine machine, looked at the screen and pushed a few buttons. "It should be dispensing. Everything's set correctly." She quickly pressed more buttons on the machine. "Wait, this says you haven't received a dose since 2 pm."

She pushed the drip button and looked back at the screen. "Something's wrong. It's not working." Her eyes widened and her mouth dropped as the realization of the situation became clear—I had just had major surgery that included drilling plates into my bones, and was without any painkillers for 14 hours.

She began franticly pushing buttons on the machine. "I'm resetting it," she said. She stopped pushing buttons and looked at the screen, waiting. After a few moments, she pressed the drip button, then looked at me. "Better?" She asked after several seconds.

I felt instant relief. "Yes," I said. "Thank you."

The same woman who spent the evening telling me to stop complaining and deal with the pain was now looking at me with wide compassionate eyes, realizing my complaints were due to a complete lack of painkillers after surgery. She was overworked and stern with patients who complained, yet she was a kind woman. Once she realized what was going on, her heart opened and she did everything she could.

I think most people are well meaning, but are busy, make mistakes, do not always know when pain requires attention, and of course cannot feel what you feel.

Those of us who experienced injury experience not only the injury itself, but also the physical and emotional trauma of the injury and the recovery. Many of us experience feelings of invasion if our bodies are cut open during surgery. Many of us are mistreated or treated less than gently at times when we are unable to help ourselves.

Many people believe that the body remembers experiencing physical pain and trauma even if the mind was sedated or unconscious at the time.

So what do we do?

Throughout your healing process, remember:

- ***Allow your inner wisdom to guide you.*** Allow your inner wisdom to guide your physical healing and the release of trauma.
- Find a heart-centered way of communicating your needs. Take care of yourself in every way that works for you. Do anything and everything you can to provide yourself with help and relief.
- Find your inner voice rather than passively accepting what others create for you, or withdrawing due to external circumstances.
- Allow the advice of others to guide you, but do not allow the beliefs of others to override your inner wisdom. Learning to distinguish your inner wisdom from background thoughts may take time and practice.

One of the great learning experiences from the situation above was that I learned that I could reduce pain in my own body in a way that was so powerful, it equaled that of a morphine drip. Only when I fell asleep did the pain return in full force.

Six months after this experience, in April 2011, a study was published in the Journal of Neuroscience which concluded that an hour of meditation produces pain relief more powerful than morphine. My experience was no longer anecdotal. It was a scientific conclusion. I believe we are only beginning to discover the power of the body to heal itself.

The techniques outlined below may help guide you with specific steps to reduce pain, elevate your mood, increase your body's healing response and capability, and access your own inner healing wisdom. I have found them extremely helpful through personal and professional experience.

> Don't fear failure. — Not failure, but low aim, is the crime.
> In great attempts it is glorious even to fail.
>
> **– Bruce Lee, actor & martial artist**

Water Therapy

This entire book is about water therapy, and it seems superfluous to mention it here, yet I would like to reiterate when specifically discussing pain, depression, and healing: immersing oneself in water reduces pain, reduces swelling, increases energy levels, and helps create a positive mood. It also increases blood circulation which improves your body's ability to heal exponentially.

Most people take painkillers to reduce pain. At the Burdenko Institute, people are advised to go into the water. This is not a common direction yet. But it works. Anyone with an injury, from brain injury to a fracture on their little toe, can benefit from the healing and pain-relieving properties of water therapy. It has the potential to help a great deal if you know what to do, when to do it, and how to do it.

Our principle is to never give up. If you do not have water therapy professionals who can help you, educate yourself, or travel to a professional. After sustaining an injury, you need your life back. Look to find everything and everyone available to make it through this stage of rehabilitation. Find a team of professionals who can help you.

That's why there are so many stories are included in this book to exemplify what is possible with a comprehensive approach to overcome injuries.

Going Outdoors

During my stay at the inpatient rehab hospital, I felt more sluggish and depressed with each passing day. Not only was my situation and environment difficult, but due to physical limitations and being wheelchair-bound, my body hardly moved. I decided I had to move. Even if I could hardly move my limbs or joints, I needed to find a way to experience movement, get outside, breathe fresh air and feel sunlight on my skin.

I wheeled myself to the parking lot and pushed my not-quite-healed arms to the limit, racing my wheelchair as fast as it would go around the lot. Feeling the wind on my face, my heart pumping hard within my chest, my lungs expanding hard and fast, and scenery whisking by, I began to feel alive and rejuvenated.

Dr. Burdenko says, "***Life is movement.*** If you want to feel good inside, go outside. It's difficult to feel truly alive without movement."

On weekends, against doctor's orders, I left hospital grounds and went to a park nearby. Doctors insisted I needed rest, and that their mandated program was the only way to health. But I needed the outdoors. I needed to see the birds in the park, the fresh flowers, families enjoying each other's company, the children playing. The hospital, filled with sick people, their worried visitors, and well-meaning but tired staff, was not nearly as rejuvenating or reviving.

The outdoors provide many opportunities to stimulate the mind, body, emotions and spirit. Fresh air provides more oxygen to fuel to heal the body. The plethora of stimulation—colors, sights, sounds, smells, and continually changing environment—is energizing and helps resist depression, stagnation, and slowing of the metabolism that may occur with continual bed rest and time spent indoors.

Sunlight provides the body with the resources to produce Vitamin D. Vitamin D is required for the functioning of the body, and is essential for bone health and healing. It is also vital for cell growth, immune system function, inflammation relief, and a positive mood. Vitamin D deficiency is associated with a variety of ailments, including fatigue, chronic pain, arthritis, and osteoporosis.

When fair-skinned people sunbathe mid-day sun in summer, they produce about 20,000 IU of Vitamin D in 30 minutes, the equivalent of taking 50 Vitamin D tablets of 400 IU each. Many people believe that our bodies produce so much so quickly because our need for Vitamin D is much greater than generally believed.

In general, the more a person weighs, the darker one's skin, and the greater one's age, the more sunlight is required for adequate vitamin D production.

But being outside is not just about oxygen and it is not just about Vitamin D. Being outside energizes the whole body. The brain functions differently outside. All sorts of chemical processes flow and the body secrets serotonin, dopamine, and other hormones which make you feel good, happy, and energized. These are similar to processes that occur when you make love or eat chocolate. One of the reasons junk food and drugs are so addictive is because they stimulate these same processes.

Being outside for an hour a day can change your life. This change may be so subtle you will not even realize it is happening. But you will be happier more. You will have more energy and be tired less. You will be in a better mood and be angry or upset less.

Your body was programed to be outside. Your body becomes revitalized and invigorated when you breathe fresh air, see the sky, the colors of plants and trees, feel the wind and hear the birds and sounds of the outdoors. All your senses are stimulated, and your body literally comes to life and begins working more efficiently as if a switch were flipped. You heal faster, your training becomes more effective, you are happier, and you have more energy. Dr. Burdenko says, "Going outdoors is like dating nature."

Breathing Techniques — please refer to www.StrelnikovaBreathingExercises.com

Meditation

Meditation can help stimulate the healing process, relieve pain, stress, and provide many other benefits to your system. This chapter contains within it a number of meditations and visualizations. Chapter two also contains a section on meditation.

Meditation has been a path to wisdom, healing, and even enlightenment since the dawn of time. Modern science is beginning to understand some of the secrets of this ancient technology, now concluding that meditation actually physically alters the brain.

A study in 2006 by researchers at Harvard, Yale, and MIT concluded that meditation changes the physical structure of the brain. They found that areas of the brain that process sensory input and attention are thicker in those who meditate. While certain areas of the brain typically thin as people age, researchers found that those areas are actually thicker in older meditators than their younger counterparts.

A study published in June 2011 in NeuroImage concluded that meditation affects the pathways of the entire brain, not just specific areas, and has "the potential to change the physical structure of the brain at large."

Many other studies have shown that meditation stimulates joy and happiness, promotes healing and overall health, reduces stress, increases focus, attention span, and memory, increases blood flow, enhances the immune system, increases production of brain chemicals that help resist depression and promote creativity, and a host of other physical, emotional, and spiritual benefits. Dr. Burdenko stresses the importance of meditation in the Burdenko Method.

> Meditation brings wisdom; lack of meditation leaves ignorance.
> Know well what leads you forward and what holds you back,
> and choose the path that leads to wisdom.
>
> **– Gautama Siddharta**
> Founder of Buddhism, 563-483 B.C.

Herbal Medicine and Natural Remedies

The healing properties of plants have been used for medicinal purposes for at least 10,000 years. Many modern medicines are derived from plants or plant extracts.

Herbs tend to be safe and have few if any side effects. However, please remember: *Herbs are powerful. Do not use them haphazardly. Understand that certain herbs may be contra-indicated by your condition. Mixing herbs with alcohol, prescription medications, or certain foods can be dangerous. Read labels and always consult your doctor before working with herbs. Consider visiting a practitioner of natural remedies.*

> What commercial drug dealer is going to want to prove that saw palmetto is better than his multimillion dollar drug?
>
> **- James Duke, Ph.D., scientist**
> USDA specialist in herbal medicine
> "World's Foremost Authority on Healing Herbs"

Juicing

Juicing is a practical application of herbal medicine. I first began juicing ten years ago and have since become a believer in the healing and restorative power of juicing.

Drinking fresh juice regularly delivers high doses of vitamins and minerals to your body that are easy to absorb and are vital to healing, pain reduction, and mood stabilization. This is especially important after an injury when digestion may not be optimal.

A few tips:
Drink a full glass of water after drinking a glass of juice, as fresh juice is very concentrated and potent.

"Chew" your juices. Drink them one sip at a time, very slowly. Swirl the juice around in your mouth before swallowing. Saliva aids in digestion and absorption.

Spinach and kale juice, while incredibly vitalizing, may cause constipation. When juicing spinach or kale, juice them together with several stalks of parsley and quarter to half a beet, both of which promote bowel movements.

Beet is very potent. Always mix beet juice with other juices, and do not drink more than the equivalent of half a medium-sized beet per day.

Sage is very potent. Juice only a few leaves at a time.

Some juicers cannot juice parsley—they just eject it with the pulp. If this is the case with your juicer, wrap lettuce tightly around the parsley, then put it in the juicer. In this way, the parsley should juice fully.

> If you eat whole vegetables, your body can absorb only about 30 percent of the available nutrients, whereas juicing or blenderizing allows up to 90 percent absorption.
>
> **- Russell L. Blaylock, M.D.**
> Health and Nutrition Secrets

Yoga

When I was in the hospital and unable to move, I closed my eyes and visualized doing yoga movements, at the same speed and with the same concentration as if I were making physical movements. As I slowly became able to move, I made whatever movement I could, while visualizing the entire movement in my head.

Moving—and visualizing moving—stimulates the body, nerves, and muscles, increases blood flow, and stimulates the healing process. Dr. Burdenko says that thinking about moving, and even watching sports or martial arts movies, stimulates nerves and generates micro-movements in muscles, like a call to action for the body.

Yoga originated in India as a physical, mental, and spiritual system. In the west it is mostly known for physical movements. These physical movements are specifically designed to stimulate the body and energize and spirit. There are many schools of yoga with many different philosophies, positions, and ways of moving.

A study published in the Journal of Pain Research in July 2011 concluded that yoga reduces pain, stress, and promotes a relaxation response in the body. Other studies have shown yoga to be an effective treatment for pain, depression, fatigue, and anxiety. Yoga also stimulates the organs and nervous system, increases blood flow, promotes healing and general health.

I attribute a lot of my progression to practicing these techniques. Shortly after I stood up for the first time, several months after my accident, my healer suggested that I practice the yoga "tree" pose, which requires standing on one foot.

"Are you kidding?" I said. "I can hardly stand on two feet, and only with a big specialized walker."

"Stand up with the walker," he said, "and do the best you can while ready to catch yourself with your hands. It will help strengthen and straighten your legs. It will help your knees begin moving again. Give it time. Practice every day."

I practiced every morning and night. At first, I had to catch myself from falling a split-second after I lifted one foot off the floor. Over time, I could hold the position for one second, then two, then five. I cried and laughed as tears flowed when I accomplished the amazing feat of standing on one leg for five seconds. I continued practicing, beginning to reach a close approximation of the position for 10 seconds, then 20, then 30.

Five months later, during my intake evaluation for outpatient rehab treatment, the physical therapist—who was the head of the department, and insisted on treating me himself as I had so many injuries—asked if I could stand on one foot.

"Sure," I said, and moved into the yoga tree pose—the bottom of one foot resting against the side of the other leg, and my hands together as if in prayer.

The therapist shook his head. "You're ridiculous!" He exclaimed.

"What? Why?"

"People with injuries like yours can't do that, not ever, certainly not eight months after an accident like yours. I've never seen anything like this. People can't do this 30 or 50 years after sustaining these kinds of injuries."

This was music to my ears, and a testament to the power of yoga and other methods I practiced, described herein.

Other methods of Eastern movement you may choose to consider include **Tai Chi** and **Qigong**.

Acupuncture

Acupuncture has its origins in ancient China as a healing system that stimulates the body's ability to heal itself. In western society, acupuncture is becoming an accepted method of treatment. I found it to be enormously helpful, both physically and emotionally.

Research has demonstrated acupuncture to be an effective method for providing acute and chronic pain relief, stress reduction, improving brain function, and increasing circulation. A study in July 2011 at Massachusetts General Hospital in Boston demonstrated that acupuncture is effective as a stand-alone method for treating clinical depression. It is also believed that acupuncture balances and stimulates the body's systems and promotes emotional stability.

> The data in support of acupuncture is as strong as those for many accepted Western medical therapies. There is sufficient evidence of acupuncture's value to expand its use into conventional medicine and to encourage further studies of its physiology and clinical value.
>
> **- National Institute of Health statement on acupuncture**

Energy Healing

I was a skeptic of "energy healing" until I experienced it myself when I was 20 years old. I was asking skeptical questions of a practitioner when she finally said, "Well, why don't I just show you." She breathed funny and moved her hands a bit and all of a sudden the stress and worries of my day were gone. I felt entirely relaxed and uplifted at the same time.

From that moment on, I knew I had to learn more about energy healing. I read, studied, learned, and have since received certifications in several energy healing modalities.

Various forms of energy healing have been used since ancient times for a wide range of physical and psychological ailments, as well as for maintaining general health. It is helpful for reducing pain, speeding recovery, and easing difficult emotions that may accompany accident or injury.

When I was in Jerusalem, there was a suicide bombing near my apartment in 2003. I rushed to the location and offered help. I went to people in shock who were crying and shaking uncontrollably. As I worked with them, they became calmer, breathed normally, and though the tears continued to flow, they were no longer completely overwhelmed. Seeing these results, paramedics asked me to work with people who they could not calm down or who refused help.

About a year later, in Jerusalem, a young woman who had been severely injured in a suicide bombing three years prior came to me as a client. Her physical injuries had healed, but she could not move on with her life, and wondered if she could ever be happy again. She later told me that she smiled for the first time in three years after our session, and began to feel hopeful.

Despite seeing many powerful effects on others and myself over a period of many years, I did not expect the profound results that occurred when I gave myself energy healing treatments shortly after my accident.

My blood was drawn and tested daily after my accident. For the first few days, the results were terrible. White blood cell count was way off. Red blood cell count was way off. The vitamin content of my blood was very low. Everything that could be wrong was wrong. They kept giving me blood transfusions, not because I did not have enough blood, but because my own would not sustain life.

I heard staff whispering about my blood tests and shaking their heads. I overheard a nurse whispering with a doctor about me. The nurse was showing the doctor my chart, and asked him what to do. "Keep giving him blood," he said.

"Isn't it too much?" Inquired the nurse. "He doesn't have internal bleeding, and his skin is turning yellow. His body is rejecting all this blood."

The doctor shook his head. "We don't have a choice," he said. "He won't live otherwise."

I was on oxygen and every time they tried to take me off the respirator, a machine next to me would loudly sound an alarm within minutes that my blood-oxygen levels were dangerously low.

Four days after my accident, I felt strong enough to give myself energy healing treatments, and felt that doing so as soon as possible after my injuries was very important. I gave myself energy healing treatments almost all day.

As usual, my blood was drawn the following morning. That afternoon, a nurse came to me holding a clipboard with a big smile. "Greg!" She said, excitedly. "You have the blood test of an astronaut!"

"What?"

"You have the blood test of an astronaut!" She repeated. "Everything's perfect! Look at this," she pointed at the paper on the clipboard. "Red blood cells, perfect. White blood cells, perfect." She continued down the list. "Vitamin levels, all perfect. Everything's perfect!"

She looked at me with a smile, shook her head, and walked off. The following day they took me off oxygen, and my blood oxygen stayed at a healthy level.

I had been studying and practicing energy healing for about 10 years at that point, and had seen many incredible transformations, physical and emotional. But I had never before seen a correlation like this.

Throughout my healing process, in addition to working on myself, I enlisted the help of several colleagues who gave me energy healing treatments. My pain lessened and I could feel my nerves tingle during and after treatments. I could feel the speed of my recovery increase. The treatments were also incredibly helpful for clearing the emotions I was going through after such a debilitating accident.

In general, I have found that the connection with a qualified practitioner is more important than the method they practice. Feel for yourself who you have a strong connection with, and who you believe may help you. Consider having an appointment with two or three practitioners before choosing one. Find the method, and more importantly, the practitioner, that works for you.

Cold Therapeutic Laser

Forever a skeptic, I was doubtful when Dr. Burdenko told me that putting a laser to my skin would reduce pain and stimulate healing in my knee and ankle. Dr. Burdenko, always enthusiastic, told me that he had used a therapeutic laser with professional athletes and laymen, and all were surprised at the results.

I still was not sure, but willing to try. I remembered Dr. Burdenko's words—"The vertical position is a functional position. Everything therapeutic should be done while vertical if possible," and "Fresh air maximizes the therapeutic effects of whatever you're doing!" With this in mind, I opened a window and stood next to it as I applied the laser to each leg for five minutes.

I sat back down, and after 10 minutes or so, noticed that my right leg was suddenly very swollen! I was told that one of the benefits of the laser is increased blood circulation, thereby increasing healing to injured areas.

This was clearly not a placebo effect—I certainly did not will my leg to swell up. My right leg had circulation issues and the laser had very clearly and immediately raised the circulation in my leg.

I continued using the laser daily as directed. The pain in both legs decreased and my skin became warmer to the touch. My right leg became accustomed to increased circulation and stopped swelling after several treatments. Pain levels decreased and the skin was warmer to the touch. I continue to use the laser regularly, and I continue to feel the benefits.

The laser Dr. Burdenko recommends is made by Multi Radiance Medical. It is endorsed by many professional sports teams and athletes.

In Conclusion

I discuss many techniques within this chapter. I use them all and truly believe that each one contributes its unique benefits to my healing process. Explore the techniques you believe may help you. The abundance of the world is at your service. Avail yourself of everything it has to offer.

One more thing. **Educate yourself.** Learn about techniques and follow those that feel right for you and your body. Western medicine may scoff at some methods, like aromatherapy and natural medicine. Yet only thirty years ago, acupuncture and yoga were thought of as having little or no medical benefit in the West (though they have been practiced for thousands of years in the East).

One hundred sixty years ago, a Hungarian physician named Ignaz Semmelweis observed that patient mortality was vastly reduced *if doctors washed their hands*. His opinion was rejected, he was ridiculed and dismissed from his position at Vienna General Hospital because of this radical opinion.

I wonder what established medical opinions of today will be thought foolish 100 years from now? How many facts do we know that cannot be completely overturned by a new discovery? We have not yet reached a point where there is nothing more to learn. People on the cutting edge are often thought crazy until what was once crazy-talk becomes common knowledge.

Will you wait until every last medical professional is on board with a belief, or will you follow your own beliefs, education, and heart's longing to take care of yourself in every way that works for you and your body?

Dr. Burdenko:
Most of the techniques within this chapter have been a part of the human experience for millennia, but are forgotten in our modern world. Before using commercial pain killers, I am a strong believer in trying alternative medicine. It makes sense to use modern pain killers as a last resort, rather than the first option. I would like to reiterate, as I cannot stress enough, ***when there is pain, there is no healing***.

Success Stories

For 20 years after disk surgery, I lived with back pain. It was a deciding factor in many decisions I made about my life from travel and sports to parties and enjoyment of children. It even governed my mood as my family would tell you. I worked with a long series of therapists using different techniques, but nothing really worked until I found Igor Burdenko 5 years ago. He first put my crooked body in a pool and showed me the benefits of water therapy. Over the years he has taught me his method both in the pool and on land. Today I am a different person. I rarely have any pain and I can do almost anything I want. At 70 years old, I am naturally stiff in the morning and spend 20-30 minutes stretching and exercising every day. I find that my body is still improving. The Burdenko method has allowed me to continue powder skiing, ocean sailing and gardening without pain. I just returned from a 27 hour plane trip home from Africa feeling fine.

Igor Burdenko's method works because he understands that the body is a complex system that must be worked with as a whole. His method is not a simplistic set of exercises; rather it grows out of a deep understanding of the interaction of muscles and bones working together. His method is based around understanding that the body can heal itself if allowed to by following the proper program. Igor believes that the body is meant to be used and that many people become disabled because they are not active enough. To Igor each client is a special case and he has a unique ability to spot issues that need attention and then to design a program that will address the problem. Other exercise or health systems usually have relatively narrow focus on flexibility or strength while Igor looks across the spectrum of alignment, strength, balance and coordination. I have seen his techniques solve a wide variety of problems and improve everyday lives slowed down by physical issues.

Richard M Burnes, Jr
Founder and General Partner Charles River Ventures
Chairman, Boston Museum of Science

At the age of 12 my daughter was diagnosed with scoliosis. We were in the orthopedic workshop at Children's Hospital where she was being fitted for the brace that was to become a constant part of her life, and the tears were streaming down her face. Then the light came on in my head, "Igor Burdenko!"

I had worked with him years prior for my own back problems. I made them take the brace off and I called Igor immediately. "Of course I can help," he told me. "The hydrostatic pressure of warm pool water can replace the cold fiberglass of a back brace." Weekly visits with Igor and nightly exercises with me became her routine.

One year later the scoliosis had reversed, six months after that the improvement was even more remarkable. Now 21, my daughter has beautiful posture and her skiing has improved thanks to the lessons learned from the Burdenko method. I can say with complete accuracy that Igor made all the difference in my daughter's life.

Gordon Owades
Lexington, MA

Igor Burdenko took me on as a patient after a very serious injury that could have ended my career. I had very little hope and great fear that I would never return to the stage. Igor worked with me tirelessly and his passion is contagious, for the first time in over a month I smiled when I was in the water starting the slow process of recovery. Igor's generosity, expertise, insight, intelligence and exuberance brought me back to the stage and to performing at or above the level before the accident. I am indebted to Igor forever. He gave me my life as I knew it back, and even better than before.

Sarah Lamb
Prima Ballerina, Royal Ballet, London, England

In 1990, I came to Igor Burdenko to work on my flexibility and strength at what I thought was the end of my career due to knee injuries. I was not even 25 years old. Igor gave me much more than a set of exercises, he gave me an outlook that inspired hope and a second wind that helped me to earn spots on the 1990 World Team and a Silver Medal in the 1992 Olympic Winter Games.

To this day I use his methods and techniques as I train for athletic feats much lesser than the Olympics! I train young skaters (and my own children) the Burdenko Method for their careers and lives. Thanks, Igor. I still enjoy skating and working out!

Paul Wylie
1992 Olympic Silver Medalist, Men's Figure Skating.
U.S. Figure Skating Hall of Fame

Chapter SEVEN

Planning Your Program

You are not a soldier and your rehabilitation specialist is not a general. This is not the mentality I preach. It is important to find the best doctors and the best rehabilitation specialists, but the most important part is you. What kind of plan can you commit to?

It is important for people to be involved in everything they want to do. Without this mindset, they are unlikely to meet or exceed their expectations. I have had many clients over the course of my career. I have found the people who succeed in their goals are not the most educated, the most intelligent, or the wealthiest. ***The people who succeed are those who have the highest levels of commitment to the priority of their health.***

Taking care of yourself with a program of health care and physical conditioning is extremely important during rehabilitation as well as for continued well-being. When planning your program, consider it an aspect of your life that will be useful to you for many years. Moving forward without planning is like sailing on a ship on the ocean without a compass. Where will you end up? Without an intended direction, you could end up anywhere.

Your program is your plan for a new lifestyle, which will include a variety of methods for keeping your body and mind in optimal health, including deep breathing exercises, proper nutrition, a positive attitude, and exercises in water and on land.

Planning gives you a concrete path to follow. It helps you avoid mistakes and frustration by creating a path for good results. It will save time and help keep you focused. Your plan needs to be flexible and fluid, because life is very dynamic. There is a constant need to adjust to feelings, environment, pain levels, and mental condition.

Many people do not understand that one should not do physical exercise before being mentally ready—if the brain does not have a clear picture of what the body will do, it is difficult to bring about the best results. I came to the conclusion after many years of experience that the more you engage your mental strength, the greater chance you have of achieving incredible results and bringing your planning to reality.

Motivation

We don't know the limits of human performance. Allow your ambition to drive you. The mind is a very powerful tool for stimulating the body and overcoming physical limitations. After the first person achieved the 2 meter high jump, a wave of others followed. After the first person broke the 10 second 100 meter dash, a wave of others followed. After the first person broke the 4 minute mile, a wave of others followed, like an avalanche.

Were people suddenly different? Or did such an achievement simply become a real possibility in the minds of athletes? They were no longer trying to do the impossible, they were simply catching up. There are many examples in this book of real people who have recovered from seemingly unrecoverable conditions. Perhaps there is possibility for further recovery in you, too?

Some people have difficulty being motivated. Why? Because they are in disharmony with their brain function. They do not stimulate their brain. Motivation comes from stimulating brain function. There is a rule, before you move, think. But when it comes to reality, not all people follow that principle, they move before they think, and that is the wrong message.

A lot of people give up because they do not see immediate results. For a seed to become a flower takes time. Be patient and envision the wonderful seed you plant in the ground as a flower.

Many people tell me that exercises are hard. My reply is, "Tell me, what is easy?" There are so many excuses that people put in front of them. They train themselves not to overcome, but to give up. All of life is a risk. Crossing the street is a risk. Consider risking trying in order to improve your life. The risk is worth the possible rewards that await you.

I believe the biggest loss in many people's lives is that they do not have the drive to try new things with a positive attitude so they can achieve something new, while being curious and playful with the experience.

When I advise clients to exercise an hour every day, many people tell me, "This is impossible, I'm so busy." My message is to have priorities in your life. Exercise should be like eating, sleeping, and working. You cannot live without sleeping. Understand that it is difficult to overcome injuries and live a productive life without an exercise routine every day. A regular exercise routine will diminish the stress of everyday life in modern society, and give you more energy for a healthy, productive life. It will create a completely different flavor to your well-being.

What is your motivation? It is very common for people's primary motivation to be the accumulation of wealth. The only thing that motivates them is the money they could have. Often the result is they have accumulated wealth but they try one drug after another, move from one doctor to another, trying treatment after treatment, after they have disregarded their bodies in the pursuit of this goal. They achieve wealth, but struggle with poor health.

I had a client with tremendous amounts of money. He passed away at 50 years young from a heart attack. He never lived to see his grandchildren. He accumulated millions, but could not spend them. Money will come when you are healthy. It is very hard to work when you are sick. It is very hard to enjoy the money you have earned when you are sick.

I believe one's motivations and priorities should include sustaining and achieving good health. These motivations will bring an understanding that life is more productive and more fulfilled than one focused on the accumulation of wealth alone. One's motivation should be participation in the festival of life. Life itself is the priority. Then one can reach all goals.

What is your motivation? Do you go forward toward the life you desire?

Creating Your Schedule

Plan to build up to one hour of exercises six days per week, and have a clear picture of what you will do the rest of the day. I recommend building up to 20-30 minutes in water and 20-30 minutes of exercises on land daily.

The most important aspect of your schedule is to create something that you will follow—a schedule is real if you follow it. Create something you want to follow and have the motivation to follow.

When first starting your routine, you may want to proceed to the water after warming up on land. When you are in better condition and able to do so without pain, add land exercises after the warm-up, then proceed to the water. On the days you do not work out in water, be sure to do land exercises.

It is generally best to begin your workout on land if you are able to do so, and finish in water. It is good to finish in water as it cools you down and helps relieve stress. However, if you are not able to perform land exercises without pain, complete your entire workout in water. Many people work out only in water for significant periods of time before adding land exercises to their routine. If you are not able to go into water, complete your entire workout on land.

Difficulty at the beginning of your program should not stop you. Nothing in life is easy. Life is like an obstacle course, but much better. Keep trying, and you will overcome and achieve.

Additionally, **have a backup plan**. Just like you have a spare tire in your car in case one goes flat, know in your mind how you will catch up if something happens and you miss your scheduled activities. This is what it means to have a flexible schedule, and to achieve your full potential from your plan.

I see so many people who schedule time to work out, but miss it for one reason or another. The next day, something else comes up and they miss it again. The next day, they miss it again. This will not happen if you truly have the motivation to follow your plan and the flexibility to substitute or make up activities you miss.

THE PREPARATORY PHASE

Get a Physical Checkup

Before starting any rehabilitation or conditioning program, you should ask for your doctor's guidance. A physical checkup is needed to ensure there are not any medical conditions to restrict your activity. Retain your blood-pressure readings and review this information from time to time when you have your blood pressure rechecked.

Understanding the Exercises

What is exercise? Exercise is the movement of life. Exercise is the ability to move your body and follow certain patterns. Exercises are a way to train the six essential qualities that you need for everyday life and sport.

The exercises within this book are designed movements which train the body to move gracefully, efficiently, and safely. You do not need to be a rocket scientist to design exercises. There are many programs in addition to the exercises you see in this book. I came up with a program that mimics sports that can be performed in water and on land. People can mimic the movements of sports in water and on land, such as boxing, skating, swimming, volleyball, basketball, or tennis, to create exercises that engage the body's ability to move, work on the six essential qualities, and reach as many muscles as possible.

Most people are familiar with these kinds of movements and can fall back on them if they forget their routine or are not able to perform some of the exercises. This is your spare tire. The technical aspects of the movements may not be perfect, but as long as you can move without pain, these motions are terrific.

Many martial arts use animals as the basis for movements. Kung Fu models many strategies and techniques on the behavior and movements of the Tiger, Leopard, Snake and Crane.

The main goal is to ***find a way to move the body without pain***. If you have the experience of moving without pain, you will have more belief in yourself and greater ability to reach a sensitive area. It will also motivate you further, and break down self-imposed movement limitations.

Pay attention to your alignment during every workout session. Ignoring alignment is like driving but not paying attention to road signs. The signs tell you where you go. It is the same with your body. If you do not pay attention to alignment, your body will move in ways you do not want it to. You will increase risk of injury, form habits that are hard to get rid of in the future, and will not receive the full benefit from the exercises.

Set Realistic Goals

There are many different factors to consider when setting your goals, including age, extent of injury, state of health, prior experience, and time planned for practice. We are each unique. Some of us progress faster than others. Sometimes, you may fall back and not be able to accomplish the exercises you practiced a few weeks prior. This is a common occurrence in rehabilitation. The important thing is to keep at it, always moving in the right direction. This is especially true after an injury or if you have not exercised in a long time.

Make your goals attainable. For example, your first goal might be to perform twenty minutes of exercises in water without becoming exhausted. Your next goal might be to balance while sitting on a water barbell for thirty seconds without using your hands. After you achieve your goals, set new ones of greater difficulty. In this manner, you will be less likely to feel overwhelmed by the whole program.

Select the Appropriate Exercises

The exercises in this book have been separated into two categories: water and land exercises. In each category, the exercises have been grouped according to difficulty, which is the progression of the six essential qualities of the Burdenko Method. If you understand how and why we created this progression, you will be capable of creating your own routines if you desire, and it will be easy for you to choose the exercises you know will accomplish your goals.

Be creative and choose the exercises appropriate for you and your condition. Know the principles. The same exercise may focus on differing qualities depending on factors such as the intensity used, number of repetitions, resistance (if any), the distance moved, and the amount of concentration employed—all play a part in determining the use for each exercise.

The progression of exercises is from simple to complex. However, what is simple for some people may be complicated for others. I usually teach people 3-4 exercises in water and 3-4 exercises on land at a time. Try using exercises in the progression shown. If you cannot do one or more or if you feel pain, try the next one, and return to it later. Modify the order according to your own needs and abilities.

Pick exercises according to your condition, and have a clear picture of how to execute your plan. Understand that the appropriate exercises should always focus around the six essential qualities. Which qualities to focus on depends upon each unique individual. For example, if someone has good skills in strength but not coordination, he should select more exercises in the qualities that need to be developed.

The beauty of my profession is to connect every exercise with previous ones. If there is no connection, you do exercise for its own sake, rather than exercising for everyday life and sport. It is like if you are learning the alphabet, and you decide you will not learn the second letter. Even if you learn all the rest, you will not know the alphabet, because this letter is interconnected with the rest.

As you progress through the exercises, you will most likely notice a significant improvement in your physical capabilities. You may start to notice you can overcome limits and do things you may not have been able to do previously. Perhaps you have newfound ability to climb stairs, climb a hill, or walk for 15 minutes.

People generally do the exercises they remember, and the ones that feel good. People often do push-ups in every workout, because they remember them. Push-ups are excellent, but people who need coordination exercises should learn those, and bring instructions with them. Doing so will make their strength exercises more efficient, as each quality compliments the others.

Every movement includes the six essential qualities. Otherwise, we do not move right, because, for example, we do not have coordination or balance.

It is very difficult to have every quality at the same level, but this is the goal to move toward. The main goal is to develop all qualities as close as you can to their highest potential. This will help ensure harmony in your body performance.

Select the Time and Place

Consistency is important. If you know your exercise sessions will be 3 times per week at a specific time, the mind and body will come to expect that and you will receive more benefits from each session.

I encourage everybody to build up to doing exercises every day. Your body may be able to tolerate only short sessions at first, which is perfectly fine. You need to ease into a program of daily exercise. The important thing is to set aside a time to exercise, and stick to it. Create consistency.

It is common in our society for people to work many hours daily with little if any physical activity. When this is the case, life expectancy will be short, and life will be difficult due to poor health.

My strong belief is that everybody can and must exercise every day. You brush your teeth every day. People understand that if they do not brush their teeth, they will have difficulty.

I see so many people who cannot do the things they want because they are in poor shape. They cannot go for a walk, because they feel pain. They cannot travel or play with their children or grandchildren. This can be avoided. It is my belief and practical experience that daily exercise can and does make life much better and more productive.

A typical exercise session is a combination of water and land exercises, consisting of thirty minutes in water, and thirty minutes on land. The ideal situation would be to spend a part of each day in water. Minimally, if you want to be in good shape, exercise 2-3 times per week. I see great results from people committed to this. You may be more comfortable starting with exercising two or three times a week, and eventually building up to exercising six days per week.

It is important to prepare yourself and be ready for each session. Ensure you bring proper clothing, any equipment you need, and know which exercises you will be practicing.

If possible, I highly recommend finding a place for exercising where there is fresh air, plenty of light, and no music, especially loud music. Loud music tends to create distraction, lack of focus, and disassociation from what you're doing.

Whenever possible, exercise outdoors in fresh air and sunshine. It is difficult to have enough oxygen in a room crowded with people. Your body cannot metabolize Vitamin D from sunlight in a dark place. A pleasant environment will positively affect your attitude. Being outside gives you a sense of freedom and more energy. People who spend time outdoors have more energy than people who are primarily indoors.

One of my students, Scott Beiler, moved from the suburbs of Boston to the beautiful mountains of northern New Hampshire after his accident. He says, "It is exhilarating to be outside in the country on a beautiful day in the fresh air. You can feel the difference!"

If at all possible, practice your water workout in salt water where you are more buoyant. This will make your water workouts a little easier. Your body accepts this environment much better. Minerals from the water are absorbed into the skin. Outdoors there is fresh air, sunlight, breathing is easier, and there are no pool chemicals. If you are able to exercise in the ocean in a cove or bay where the water is smooth, you can transition from exercising in deep water to shallower water, and slowly work your way up onto the beach. This transition may take several weeks or several months depending upon your level of injury. The goal is to walk freely without support and regain full use of your body.

It is important to change the location of your exercises frequently: try the patio, the park, the back yard, the bedroom, the living room, in front of a window, together with family, with friends, etc. Variety will keep it interesting, as well as prevent adaptation and boredom.

People know where they will eat—there is a table. People know where they will sleep—there is a bed. But in most homes, there is no place set aside for exercise. Many people have a lot of furniture they do not need, or things they can live without. One action that will make a big difference in people's lives is to create space for exercise and equipment they use.

If you have a backyard, consider it a space for outdoor exercises for you and your family. Most people mow their lawn but never use their yard for exercising.

Even if you have a gym membership, consider places in your home you can exercise in when you cannot get to the gym. This is like having an umbrella if it rains—have it available, and you will open it if you need it.

THE EXERCISE SESSION

To make your session more efficient, I recommend dividing your workout program between water and land. Incorporate deep breathing and shaking into exercise sessions. Set aside times for deep breathing and shaking at least twice daily.

Every exercise session should consist of three distinct phases: the warm-up, the workout, and the cool-down. Most people have heard of these, but many ignore them or make excuses to skip them. They do not have time, or they forget. The warm-up and cool down are as important as the workout itself. An exercise session without the warm up or cool down is like being in the shower without soap—it is incomplete. Without the warm-up, the body will not be physiologically ready for the best possible outcome of the workout, and you will not achieve the results you expect.

Additionally, without warming up or cooling down, you will lengthen the time needed to recover from the workout, and are more likely to sustain injury. If you will not cool down and reduce stress after a workout, you will carry stress in your body and acid build-up in your muscles all day and are more likely to feel sore.

Traffic lights have three lights—red, yellow, and green. If you ignore one of these lights, you are in trouble, because all three are important. You should always pay attention to all of them. In the same way, you should always warm-up, work out, and cool down. Follow the traffic light rules and you will not get a ticket. Follow the workout rules and you will provide your body with the fullest workout possible.

It is results that count, we all know that. Yet too often people expect results while ignoring the steps that produce those results. Practicing all three phases of a workout will help achieve better and faster results, and you will feel better after your workout sessions.

Always start and end your program with deep breathing exercises and shaking.

The Warm-Up

Warming up serves several purposes: It loosens joints, limbers up muscles and helps them relax, gets blood pumping, and stimulates breathing. As the name implies, the warm-up is used to raise the temperature of the muscles and the whole body. The increased temperature is a foundation to boost your metabolism and provide energy to the body, making for a more beneficial workout.

Warming up is also a safety issue. If you work out with cold muscles, your body is not ready and your mind is not in the proper mindset. This is a recipe for injury.

A warm up generally lasts eight to ten minutes. Some people may need more time based on their experience and condition.

While warming up, be aware of your frame of mind. Visualize your body vigorous and healthy. Visualize the oxygen in your lungs being absorbed into your blood. Picture your oxygenated blood traveling through your arteries and entire body. In your mind, see your nerves and muscles using the oxygen and nutrients in your blood to heal your body. If you apply the visualization, you will feel it—you will feel the oxygen absorbed into your blood.

Begin each exercise session with a gentle warm-up routine. The warm-up consists of deep breathing, stretching, light exercises, and shaking.

Warming up in Water:
Using a combination of the deep and shallow ends, begin gently by walking and jogging in water at different speeds in different directions, turning while walking, moving from the vertical to horizontal position to laying on your side, and jogging and running in water while on your side. Use different styles of swimming as well: back stroke, breast stroke, crawl, any kind of style you can. Jump on both legs, jump on one leg. Remember this is all preparation and warm up—do not exercise vigorously. Nice and light is the purpose here. Feel yourself building up enough confidence to accomplish your plans in the main part of the workout.

Warming up on Land:
Begin walking at different speeds, jogging at different speeds, in different directions and with different ground inclinations if possible. Practice light exercises for upper and lower extremities. Stretch.

If the air temperature is warmer than the water, perform your warm-up on land. This will help your system work more efficiently before you enter the water.

If you use an indoor pool, try to perform your warm-up outside in fresh air. If you practice your water workout outdoors, and the water is warm, perform the warm-up in the water.

If the water is cold, warming up in water is difficult. When this is the case, practice the warm-up on land.

The Workout

In my professional practice, I have worked with people who exercise only in water, and those who exercise only on land. The results of **the combination of water and land exercises** have convinced me that it is the best way to work with the human body.

Combining Water and Land Exercises
I have helped a number of Olympic champions reach the podium, but only by combining workouts in water and on land. In my 50 years of experience I am convinced that this is one of the best ways for the human body to achieve incredible results.

People who challenge my assertions argue that not every Olympic champion uses a combination of water and land exercises.

To this challenge I have a response—*every single one of the Olympic athletes I worked with arrived at the Burdenko Institute with a severe injury.* Alexandre Despatie arrived limping three months before the Olympics. Nancy Kerrigan arrived with a severely injured and swollen knee just five weeks before the Olympics. Both won a silver medal after being told the Olympics were a long-shot.

Paul Wiley believed his figure skating career was over after increasing chronic knee pain and injuries. After working with the Burdenko Method, competed in the Olympics and won a silver medal. He recently told me, “I can’t imagine myself without water in my workouts.” Many others have made similar statements. Today he works as a coach, training others.

Most of my clients are not Olympic athletes, yet their achievements are no less noteworthy. A 12 year old girl diagnosed with scoliosis was told by doctors that she would need to wear a back brace for at least a year, possibly many more. Her father decided to look into alternatives. They approached the Burdenko Water and Sports Therapy Institute. We designed a program for her, and she visited us once per week while working independently with water therapy 3-4 times per week and land therapy daily. A year later, her scoliosis reversed. Today, 11 years later, she has beautiful posture and enjoys downhill skiing and traveling.

Another client, Janis Redlich, had a double-hip replacement. By using the Burdenko Method water and land therapies in her recovery and continued well-being, she maintains an active lifestyle which includes regular horseback riding. Her doctor, a respected and well known surgeon, cannot believe her high activity level. She was so impressed with her results that she became certified in the Burdenko Method. A year later she earned Master Certification in the Burdenko Method. She now helps others with hip problems.

I have worked with a number of clients experiencing back problems, pinched nerves, herniated and bulging discs, who were told by doctors that surgery was their only option. One of my clients had four bulging discs in the cervical area after a car accident. Doctors estimated surgery would give a 50% chance of recovery, with risk of complications.

She explored a number of options, and came to the Burdenko Water and Sports Therapy Institute. We designed a program for her. At first, she worked only in deep water 4-5 times per week. As she progressed without experiencing pain, we added land programs in a horizontal position in combination with water exercises. All exercises focused on strengthening the muscles, building the muscle corset surrounding her cervical spine, and working the upper body. With time, she progressed from deep water exercises to the shallow part of the pool, then to sitting, standing, and dynamic exercises on land.

A year later, she was pain-free, her body returned to proper alignment, and her discs were in place. She began performing daily activities and returned to work. Today, she is back in shape, pain free, and enjoying life.

Her doctor, chief of neurology at a major hospital and professor at Harvard Medical School, monitored her progression with regular check-ups, X-rays, and MRIs. After our client's remarkable recovery, he invited me to his office along with our client and several of his colleagues. He projected her X-rays onto the wall, showing the progression over time as she continued the water and land therapy. His colleagues were impressed with her progression, and eager to learn about non-invasive protocols they could recommend to their patients.

At 88 years young, retired engineer Bill Stern decided he would not allow the aging process to take him without a fight. He asked me to help him be stronger, more energetic, and regain the ability to keep up with his family and grandchildren. He also wanted to celebrate his 90th birthday by qualifying for the US National Senior Games.

He qualified for the games with flying colors. He then won the gold medal in the 1500 meter race, a silver medal in the 400 meter race, and a bronze medal in the 100 meter race. Today, he is 93 years young, and continues exercising every day. He is in good health, good spirits, and enjoys an excellent memory.

I am emphasizing the combination of water and land therapy so strongly because I have seen the benefits on everyone from the top athletes in the world to the average person next door, from children to elderly. Yet this is not a common method, little research exists, and many people just do not believe such results are possible.

Even among my own clients, people want to skip the water aspect of their program. It is so ingrained in modern western society to look for a quick fix, a pill, an operation, a thing we can do to make a problem disappear.

Always use a combination of water and land exercises for your main workout if possible. Be creative and find a way to practice water exercises, whether at a friend's pool, public pool, health club, the YMCA, community center, ocean, lakes, rivers, ponds.

A Comprehensive Approach

A comprehensive approach which includes water and land therapies, actively participating in one's own healing, and a number of modalities such as meditation, visualization, and deep breathing, is extremely effective. Change your routine and equipment frequently to keep things interesting and to challenge the body.

In the Burdenko Method, we use our knowledge, experience, and initiative to achieve physical, mental, and psychological advances. We create direction as to what to do, how to do it, when, and for how long. Listen to your body, establish communication between your mind and body, and use your experience to guide you.

Keep in mind that one of our goals is to recruit as many muscles in the body as possible with each exercise. Pay attention to alignment and perform each exercise at different speeds while maintaining proper alignment. Pay attention to pelvic stability. If you are vertical, your pelvis should always be under your shoulders. Your pelvis and shoulders should always be in one line.

When working with clients, I do not tell people on **which side of the body to start an exercise**. For example, if I tell someone to lift his knee, I do not say which knee. People tend to automatically start with the side of the body they are more comfortable with or that is not injured. People are able to perform a movement with an injured joint more easily if they have just performed it properly with a healthy joint. This is an efficient way to practice motions that may be difficult for an injured area. Starting a movement with an injured area produces pain and stress, and is more difficult and stressful on the heart than starting with a healthy arm or leg.

Some people believe they should start with the injured area. This will produce pain and stress, and will be much more difficult on the heart than starting with a healthy limb. I always recommend: ***begin the action on the part of the body that is not injured.***

If both limbs needed for a particular exercise are healthy and pain-free, it is generally better to start on the right side. In this way, motions begin further from the heart, causing less stress. This in turn causes challenging actions to be less dramatic and less stressful to the body. These are some physiological reasons for performing exercises in a particular way.

Once you can do an exercise well, challenge your body and mind by practicing the exercise at different speeds, in different directions, and from different starting positions. For example, you can start an exercise in a sitting position, a standing position, or facing different directions. This creates variety, makes you more alert, and engages more receptors and senses.

Rehabilitation Program

Rehabilitation is intended to restore functional ability of the body. When practicing a rehabilitation program, build up exercises to 10 repetitions at a comfortable pace. After achieving 10 repetitions, practice 3 slow, 3 medium, 3 fast, and 1 slow repetition. Shake after each set of 10.

Practice approximately 20-30 minutes in water, and 20-30 minutes on land. The total workout time for most people should be approximately 45-60 minutes per session. Practice at least 2-3 days per week, and build up to practicing 5-6 days per week.

If exercising only in water, try to start with a minimum of approximately 20-25 minutes, and build up to 30-60 minutes.

If exercising only on land, try to start with a minimum of approximately 15-20 minutes, and build up to 45-60 minutes.

The fastest way to relieve pain from injuries is to be in water as much as possible with a program designed for you. ***If you are in pain, practice a water only program.*** When you are pain-free, begin to incorporate a land program into your schedule. Follow your feelings. Some days you will exercise more or less than the recommended time, but the average should be approximately as suggested.

Each week, try to add new exercises to your routine. As you progress in your exercises, you will advance from exercises that are relatively easy to ones that are more challenging.

In order to keep your total workout time within the recommended period, lessen the number of repetitions of exercises from previous weeks. The best way to learn new exercises is to keep the foundation of previous ones. In this way, the amount of time you practice is the same, and you constantly create room for something new. This is the most efficient formula I have discovered for rehabilitation, conditioning, and training, based on results, research, and experience.

Rehabilitation does not only mean going to a physical therapist. Rehabilitation should consist of practicing exercises as much and as often as you can without pain, in water and on land. If you cannot move without pain, ask your physical therapist or medical professional to help you find what you can do.

Conditioning Program

This book is primarily about rehabilitation, but we are including information about conditioning and training so that you have a clear path after rehabilitation. It is also discussed so that people not needing rehabilitation have an approach for working with the Burdenko Method.

Conditioning is intended to maintain and build functional ability of the body for health in life and recreational sports. Be aware and in tune with your body and know your level of each of the six essential qualities.

When possible, start each exercise session on land and end in water. This pattern works very well for injury prevention, stress reduction, and enhancing performance.

Practice a conditioning program only if you are not in pain.

When practicing a conditioning program, build up exercises to 21 repetitions at a comfortable pace. When that is achieved, practice 7 slow, 7 medium, and 7 fast repetitions. Shake between each set of 7.

Practice water exercises at least 3-4 times per week, and build up to practicing 5-6 days per week, for approximately 30-45 minutes.

Practice land exercises 5-6 days per week, for approximately 30-45 minutes.

The total workout time for most people should be approximately 45-90 minutes per session.

If you feel tired or worn out on a particular day, do your entire workout session in water. This will help your body de-stress and recover. The most important thing is to listen to your body. You will not benefit if you are tired and stressed and continue to add more workload. Go to the water and practice there. The next day, return to your routine.

Conditioning exercises are intended to be everyday programs for people who want to be in shape, prevent injuries, look good, feel good, and think clearly. A conditioning program should focus on the six essential qualities of everyday life and sport, while paying special attention to developing the qualities that need work. This routine should be a part of everyday life, something people do as a part of their day, the same way they brush their teeth. Such a program is a great investment in one's physical condition, and provides the opportunity to have a healthy productive life.

Exercising as a necessary and regular part of the day is not a very common belief in many people's minds, but if they do not have that, their life is not as rich as it could be, and they are more likely to have health problems and injuries. A conditioning program is a maintenance program—it helps maintain your health.

Why do you have a maintenance program for your car? It costs a lot of money, and it takes time to go to the mechanic. Why do you do it? If you want to have a car, you must have a maintenance program. If you want to have a healthy life, you must have a conditioning program. Do it religiously, without excuses for canceling. There is always a way to exercise, whether in the morning, evening, outdoors, indoors, in a lying down position, sitting position, standing, walking. There is always a way to maintain your body's continued ability to move gracefully, efficiently, and safety.

Do not to wait until you slow down with age before you begin to preserve what you have and try to enhance your abilities. Use water and land, go outdoors, use the guidelines within this book to maintain and improve your health.

A conditioning program must always precede training.

Training Program

Training is intended to enhance the functional ability of the body for those who wish to engage in competitive sports. Training is based on conditioning. Before you begin a training program, be aware of your level of conditioning. This builds a foundation for future work, and helps avoid injuries. Success in training is very strongly related to one's level of conditioning, whether amateur or professional. Many people ignore the conditioning phase and jump straight to training. This leads to joint problems, heart problems, and injury.

A training program should focus on the qualities needed for a particular sport. For example, someone running a marathon focuses on endurance. Someone working on gymnastics focuses on flexibility and coordination.

Start each exercise session on land and end in water when possible. This pattern works very well for injury prevention, stress reduction, and enhancing performance.

Practice a training program only if you are not in pain.

When practicing a training program, build up exercises to 30 repetitions at a comfortable pace. Then practice 10 slow, 10 medium, and 10 fast repetitions. Shake between each set of 10.

Practice water exercises 6 days per week, twice per day, for approximately 30-45 minutes.

Practice land exercises 6 days per week, twice per day, for approximately 45-90 minutes.

(If training for a water sport, practice 45-90 minutes in water and 30-45 minutes on land, twice per day.)

The total workout time for most people should be approximately 90-120 minutes, twice per day.

Learn and practice. Your goal is to learn the way you learn in school or university. Master the qualities and techniques needed for your specific training program.

If you feel tired or burned out on a particular day, do your entire exercise routine in water.

The purpose of a training program is to prepare for competition. If that is not your goal, you do not need a training program. You need a conditioning program. Engaging oneself in a training program pushes and strains the body, and is a serious decision to make.

Those practicing a training program should work out twice per day. That is how I train people for the Olympics, for marathons, and other competitive events. But I do not teach a runner how to run or a figure skater how to skate. They already have a coach. I teach them how to work on the six essential qualities, while focusing on the qualities needed for their sport.

It is a common belief that the more people train, the more they are at risk for injuries. Yet proper training twice per day is like a guarantee for fewer injuries. In my personal and professional experience, I have learned that those who train properly, with discipline and a focused mind, develop the 6 essential qualities, follow principles contained herein, and give themselves time to recover, create protection from injuries.

Those who do not pay attention, do not listen to their coach's recommendations, do not warm up or cool down, are creating a recipe for injury.

Using the Synergy between Water and Land

As a general rule, whatever is difficult for you on land, do it in water. And whatever is difficult for you in water, do it on land. There is a synergy between the two environments which lifts the efficiency of human performance to another scale.

Practice land exercises in water if they are difficult or not possible to perform on land, if you experience stiffness, or have difficulty keeping alignment. Practicing land exercises in water opens the body to accomplish movements that may not be possible on land. The synergy of moving between environments where you experience gravitation and do not experience gravitation makes the healing process more efficient, and the learning process more interesting and challenging, which means people do not give up the way they might on a land-only program.

For example, if you cannot squat on land, squat in water. Start at the deep part of the shallow end. Build up to 10 squats. Then practice 3 slow, 3 medium, 3 fast, and 1 slow. Then progress to more shallow water, and again build up to 10 repetitions at this new depth level. Then practice 3 slow, 3 medium, 3 fast, and 1 slow. Continue to shallower water with this pattern. Then progress to practicing on land.

Practicing in this way also helps you to step over mental barriers. When you practice squatting (or any other exercise) in water and are able to perform the movements successfully and in alignment, it becomes easier to perform the same movement on land.

When transferring from water to land, try to mimic as much as possible the exercises that were done in water. The beauty of this is that you can say, "Oh, I know that exercise, it's the breast stroke in sitting position." Your muscles have already experienced the pattern of the exercise. Second, it is easy to remember, as you have already been doing it. Third, you have a chance to transfer your skills from water to land. This helps you progress.

Practice water exercises on land if they are difficult or not possible to perform in water. This also gives you a chance to practice movements you want to master in a totally different environment. This practice enhances overall performance in both water and land. For example, water movements are very slow compared to movements on land. When performing the same movements on land, they will be easier, and you will experience just how much progress you have made.

Anything you do on land, you can do in water. I have figure skaters do their entire routine in the water. Anything you can do in water, you can do on land. That synergy is very strong.

The water and land environments complement each other. This principle of the Burdenko Method has helped many people from many walks of life achieve the results they strive for.

Decreasing the Level of Difficulty of Your Exercises

If you are unable to perform an exercise, divide it into pieces. Try to accomplish only the actions for the arms, or only the actions for the legs. Practice them separately. Over time, you will be able to perform actions for arms, legs, and the whole body movement together.

Change the starting position. For example, if you find an exercise difficult to perform in a standing position, try it in a sitting or lying down position.

If you cannot perform an exercise, build up the skills from previous exercises, which will help you to progress.

Remember, if an exercise causes pain, stop and try a different one.

Increasing the Level of Difficulty of Your Exercises

When you increase the challenge of exercises, it is very important to have a certain mindset and reason to do it. Choose the right time. You cannot increase difficulties without doing the preliminary work or spending enough time to practice.

Gradually build up the number of repetitions to 10. The next step is to perform 10 repetitions at different speeds: 3 slow, 3 medium, 3 fast, and 1 slow. When you are able to do an exercise proficiently in this way, build up to 21 repetitions. Then perform 21 repetitions at different speeds: 7 slow, 7 medium, 7 fast. The advanced level is to build up to 30 repetitions, then to perform 30 repetitions at different speeds: 10 slow, 10 medium, 10 fast.

Remember to perform every exercise in **multiple directions**. Any exercise or movement that occurs in one direction should also be performed in the opposite direction. If you move forward, also move backward. If you move left, also move right.

The Burdenko Belt or exercise tubing can be used with nearly any exercise to add varying and dynamic resistance to movements. Exercise tubing can be anchored to a stationary object or between your hands and feet.

In water, use adjustable buoyancy barbells, half-roll, wrist cuffs, or Water Walkers. They will enhance the natural buoyancy and resistance of the water.

On land, wrist cuffs and adjustable buoyancy barbells will add a little weight and are good transition from exercising with no equipment to exercising with wrist weights. When ready, add the use of wrist and ankle weights.

Different resistances create different body responses, which help build up the 6 essential qualities. This helps create a diversity of sensory stimulation and improved results.

Perform exercises at **different starting positions**. For example, if the exercise is shown with a sitting starting position, start the exercise from a standing starting position.

Many exercises have variations that increase the challenge of the exercise.

General Recommendations:

In the beginning of each workout session, *do the exercises slowly with attention to body awareness* to help avoid mistakes. If an exercise causes pain, stop and try a different one. As you start to increase your abilities, perform exercises with gradually increasing repetitions. Start with a small number, while ensuring you are doing it correctly with proper alignment and without pain. Slowly build up to 10 repetitions. When you achieve this, start using another pattern—three 3, 3 medium, 3 fast, 1 slow. This formula will make your workout more efficient and improve your results.

Shake after each set of exercises, before starting the next exercise. If you feel tired during a particular exercise, shake after the slow repetitions, for example, before moving on to the medium repetitions. This will help invigorate your system and reduce stress.

Those who are without limitations should begin an exercise session on land and finish in water. For those who have lost mobility or are in pain, it is reversed. Start in water and move toward land, up until the point they regain mobility. Gradually move to shallow water. When you are ready, move to land exercises. If you have pain when exercising on land, continue exercising in water. This will help reduce pain levels. Try doing land exercises while horizontal or sitting, rather than in a vertical position, if you are able to do so without pain.

When you are in better shape and are able to exercise on land without pain, start on land and finish in water.

As the intensity of exercises increases, move from exercises in deep water to exercises while touching the bottom of the pool. Slowly increase your weight bearing.

I highly recommend doing these activities with a partner to make your workout more social and more fun, help you to correct mistakes, help you to be in the right position, and have optimum performance.

Many people choose to exercise in front of a mirror to help them be aware of their body alignment and movements. That is why so many dance and martial arts studios have floor to ceiling mirrors.

To **make the exercises your own**, write them down in your own words. Be sure to give them a name. Whether it is my name or yours does not matter, as long as they have a name. This creates an association in your mind and makes the exercise easier to remember. Be sure to include the starting position. Write down the actions for each exercise. Know that every exercise ends in the starting position. Write your own tips and comments for each one. This is much better than if someone writes for you.

Some people come for exercises expecting a professional trainer or therapist to tell them what to do. I am against that. I ask people to be a student. If you want to learn, you must be a student. *A student should write down in his own words what he will do, according to what the teacher asked him to perform.* It is also easier to remember when you write it out on your own, and creates an understanding of what you are writing. I have a thousand examples of people who tell me they have a list of exercises given to them, but do not understand what to do.

I encourage everyone to have a notebook where you see everything in one place: write your progress, exercises, and make comments. This creates the educational process, and you will have a very strong experience that you can use and share with others.

The Cool-Down

Cooling down is often overlooked, yet is just as important as warming up. During the cool-down period, gradually decrease your activity and let your body relax. Cooling down gently slows your heart rate, reducing stress on your heart. Stretching your muscles after a workout helps them maintain flexibility, minimize soreness, and avoid stiffness in joints. Stretching helps restore alignment, rid the body of waste materials that build up during the workout, reducing pain, tightness, and soreness.

If you are tired and do not take time to cool down, your muscles will continue feeling tired and stressed, and you will carry that feeling for the rest of the day. It is very beneficial to perform your cool-down, finishing with breathing exercises and shaking.

Try to perform exercises and movements in a slow way, not vigorously. You can also close your eyes, think positive thoughts or visualize a relaxing setting.

RELAXATION

We do not overcome injuries only through exercise. It is vitally important to rest and relax, both physically and mentally, in order to overcome injuries and give your body a chance to heal.

Physical Relaxation

Take time to apply techniques such as shaking, meditation, massage, and others mentioned throughout this book to restore your physical and mental condition.

Many people believe relaxation means laying down and not doing anything. I believe the best relaxation is being active, changing from mental to physical activity, and going from indoors to outdoors. For example, change activities from reading to taking a walk.

Relaxation may include a spectrum of different activities. Read, go to a concert, go to the movies, read an old letter that you have saved, call a friend or family member. Go outside and listen to the birds. Write and read poetry, spend time with children or grandchildren. Invite people to your home. Write a letter to an old friend. Plan your next outing or vacation.

The biggest injury to the body is stress. I believe the way to rid the body of stress is through activity. If you write a letter, you are active, you are thinking, and you are in a completely different emotional place than laying down and watching TV.

When I relax, I call friends or spend time with them. I plan something I love to do, like skiing. I read or watch a movie. I dance with my wife. Sometimes I think about activities that I dream of but have not had time to accomplish. Sometimes I go to the cemetery and visit my mother and father's grave. I go to the ocean, for a swim or just to watch the waves and see the swans flying by.

Doing something meaningful and engaging is relaxing. People who lie down and do nothing often do not feel relaxed. They feel imbalanced and that something is missing. That is why so many people cannot sit still these days. They check their phone or their email continually. They are looking for something that is engaging, satisfying, and fulfilling. It is difficult to feel satisfied by activities when there is continual interruption. Engaging fully in an activity, be it reading, writing, engaging in conversation, playing an instrument, or appreciating nature, allows fulfillment and satisfaction to fill you.

When you are not active, your body's entire metabolism slows down. It may slow down even more due to injury and loss of mobility. When you are active and engaged, the healing process is more efficient than when you do nothing.

Mental Relaxation

Mental relaxation is a tool to release stress. Mental relaxation is actually a combination of physical relaxation and resting the mind in a peaceful state. Relaxation is an event that can be planned during the day. Some people relax by finding a quiet environment, closing their eyes, and finding a contemplative state akin to meditation or prayer. This can be accomplished in water as well as on land. Some of my students practice yoga techniques and find that it helps them to relax as well.

Some people practice active mental relaxation by playing chess and checkers. You use your brain and you are focused. Mental relaxation also includes the ability to find a particular mental state at any time. For example, once you learn to find a peaceful state in a quiet place, you can find this state while skiing down a mountain or going about your everyday life.

Mental relaxation can include visualization or remembering poetry or songs that you are fond of. This can give you incredible peace of mind.

Summary

- Plan your workout in advance.
- Set realistic goals
- Select appropriate exercises
- If you are in pain, practice a water only program. Make movements in water that do not cause pain.
- Every exercise session should consist of three distinct phases: the
- warm-up, the workout, and the cool-down.

PART TWO

WATER & LAND EXERCISES

Chapter EIGHT

Water Exercises

Many people associate water exercise with swimming. We use water as a modality for healing, rehabilitation, conditioning, and training, as well as swimming and recreation. Immersion in water helps restore energy and relieve stress. Water allows for movements that are difficult or not possible on land. When people incorporate exercises in water together with exercises on land, their progress is very strong.

As discussed in Chapter 7, water exercises are not only for the water. Practicing water exercises on land enhances performance in water and land. Additionally, exercises that are difficult to perform in water may be possible on land. The water and land environments complement each other, and using both creates a synergy not available when using one environment exclusively.

SAFETY IS OUR PRIORITY

It is very important to be aware of safety issues. Always have someone with you if you cannot swim. If needed, have an assistant with you in the water. I highly recommend everyone use a floatation device.

We mainly use the vertical position when working in water. The vertical position is the functional position for humans. Wearing a floatation device will allow you to easily float vertically with your head above water, feeling weightless, and allowing you to focus on techniques, alignment, motor skills, and breathing. The vertical position also a familiar one for activity, and allows you to see better and be aware of your surroundings, increasing safety.

Some people are allergic to the chlorine in pools. Find chlorine-free pools in your area (They are becoming more common!), or find natural places such as lakes, rivers, ponds, or the ocean.

When outside in the sun, wear sunglasses and a hat to protect from the sun's glare. Of course you should never be in the water outdoors during a lightning storm.

Before starting your water-therapy program, consult with your doctor, physical therapist, or health-care practitioner. Make sure that you have no health problems that may prevent you from going into water. For your own safety, as well as the safety of others, you should not enter the water if you have any of the following conditions:

Contraindications to aquatic therapy:

- Fever or a cold
- Open sores, wounds, or stitches (Can go in water if protected with CastGuard and/or waterproof tape)
- Infection (esp. urinary tract infection)
- Skin rash or a contagious condition
- Lack of bowel or bladder control
- Uncontrolled seizures
- Absence of cough reflex
- Tracheostomy
- Deep vein thrombosis
- Excessively high or low blood pressure
- Severe cardiac conditions
- Significantly limited vital capacity
- Uncontrolled diabetes
- Kidney disease (where one cannot adjust to fluid loss)
- Severe impairment in regulating body temperature
- Autonomic dysreflexia

Precautions

- Impaired sensation
- Decreased vital capacity due to respiratory muscle weakness
- Low tolerance to temperature changes
- Postural hypotension

Source:
Aquatic therapy in the rehabilitation of athletic injuries, by J. Prins and D. Cutner.

Temperature

The temperature of water is another factor to consider. The ideal water temperature for rehabilitation is 78°F to 90°F. Warm water temperature helps relax the muscles. If you are working at a higher level of conditioning and doing aerobic workouts, it may be better if the water is a little cooler.

It is very important not to stay in water so long that you feel cold. I recommend being in water 30-45 minutes at a time. If you cannot feel when you become chilled due to paralysis or other issues, have an assistant check your skin temperature from time to time.

Time spent in water should be in proportion with one's mobility. If you lose too much heat in water and get a chill, your immune system becomes weakened and you become open to illness. Your muscles and organs contract and motor skills are slowed. Additionally, every organ in the human body has its own ideal temperature. If the heart, liver, or other organs do not have the temperature they need for ideal performance, they do not function efficiently. Their performance degrades and they become stressed. This can cause difficulties for the whole body, because everything is connected.

Being active in water helps reduce heat loss. It is important to move your body, especially in ways that you cannot move on land. For example, if you cannot walk and run on land, try to walk and run in water, both with and without touching bottom. If you cannot jump on land, try jumping in water. You will have a better chance to restore body performance, movement patterns, and physical and mental activity. If you are paralyzed and cannot physically move your body, be active by performing visualization exercises, and utilize help from an assistant.

I highly recommend wearing a bathing cap when working out in water, for two reasons. One, it reduces heat loss in the body. Two, it helps keep the swimming pool clean, because hair clogs the filters. We lose an average of 300 hairs every day.

People who have problems maintaining temperature can wear a dry suit or a wet suit to keep warm in water. Simply wearing a T-shirt may be enough to keep warm. There is always a solution if you apply your creativity.

A lot of people do not realize that hot water can be dangerous. Exercising in water over 90°F may cause overheating and create serious health issues.

If you are able to control your environment, my preference is to have the water temperature one or two degrees warmer than the air temperature. Breathing slightly cooler air stimulates body function and helps build the immune system. I highly recommend wearing water shoes or flip-flops when walking on the tiles or deck of the pool. They will keep you from losing heat and reduce your changes of slipping or contracting foot fungus.

General safety:

- Before doing any exercises, be aware to have full understanding of what you will be doing. More advanced exercises should have a foundation in previous exercises.
- When attempting new exercises that involve bending and leaning, consider having an assistant with you in case you need help.
- Pay attention to deep breathing, and do not hold your breath while exercising.
- Do not exercise immediately after a meal.
- Do not continue an exercise if it causes pain.
- Check your blood pressure from time to time to make sure you are not placing too much stress on your heart.
- Always examine your equipment for cracks or wear, and only use if it is safe to do so.
- Choose a place for exercising that has enough air and has sufficient space to move freely.

EQUIPMENT

I see the water as a gymnasium. It's hard to imagine a gym without equipment. We use exercise equipment to help achieve maximum benefit from water workouts. The main consideration in selecting equipment for water exercise is safety. Choose equipment that is appropriate for your present physical condition and easy for you to use. Your physical therapist or health-care professional may be able to help you make the right selection.

Use only equipment that floats or is secured. If the equipment sinks, retrieving it could cause difficulties or danger. Try to avoid this situation.

The Flotation Vest

One of the main pieces of equipment used in water is a flotation vest or belt specifically designed for exercising in water. There are a variety of styles on the market offering varying degrees of buoyancy. First and foremost, it must keep you afloat, ensuring you are safe in the water (but remember it is not a life preserver—it is designed for exercise). Secondly, it will help support your body in a vertical position while exercising, an essential part of the Burdenko Method.

The flotation device should be checked regularly. Make sure there are no cracks in the flotation material, and ensure that the straps and fasteners are not worn out. Do not use a flotation device that is too small or too large. Ensure a proper fit. Adjust the straps and fasteners so that it fits snugly without being too tight.

A good wet vest distributes buoyancy evenly around the body, increasing stability (see Figure 8.1). A flotation vest also helps retain body heat.

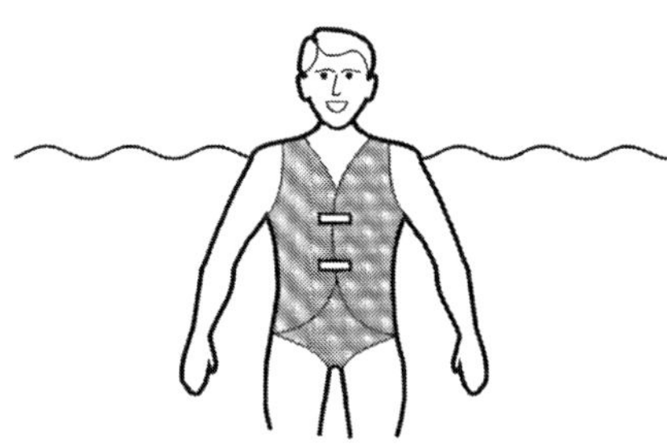

Figure 8.1 The flotation vest.

It is very important to have the right amount of buoyancy. Too much buoyancy will cause you to float too high, and you will have less control in water. Not enough buoyancy will cause contraction of muscles and fatigue as you work to keep above water. The right buoyancy is when your shoulders are level with the surface of the water. If you need extra buoyancy, use additional buoyancy devices, for example a vest and a belt.

I recommend using the Hydrofit Wet Vest II. Its unique features provide buoyancy and support with a minimal amount of interference, allowing unrestricted movement in water.

The Flotation Belt

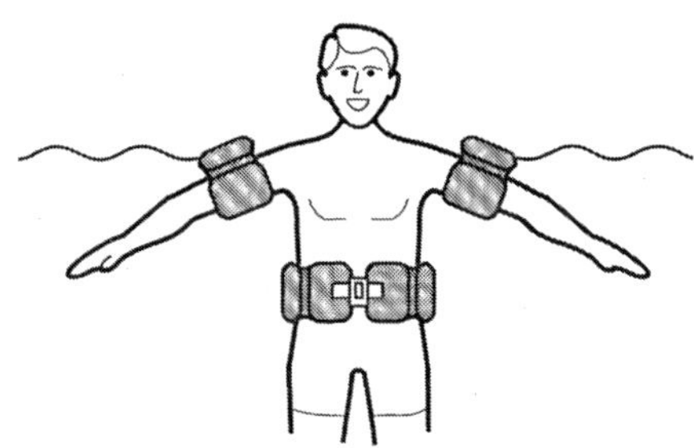

Figure 8.2
The flotation belt and cuffs.

As your rehabilitation advances, you may prefer to use a flotation belt, because your mobility has improved, you are stronger, and you will not need the amount of support a vest provides. When choosing a belt, be sure that it distributes buoyancy around the whole body, rather than only around the back, allowing you to maintain a vertical position in the water. A good example is the Hydro-Fit Belt (see Figure 8.2).

Buoyancy and Resistance Cuffs

Cuffs enhance the natural buoyancy and resistance of water. They can be used around the wrists or ankles. Some brands, such as Hydro-Fit, make cuffs with a modular design, consisting of a series of flotation pockets fastened together. Flotation material can be added or removed from each pocket to adjust the buoyancy. They can also be worn as a belt (see Figure 8.2).

Wet Vest Air Collar

I use an inflatable cervical collar for clients with head trauma, neck and spinal injuries. It works as a temporary brace, providing support for the cervical area. It can also be used at home or in an airplane when traveling.

Burdenko Board with Straps

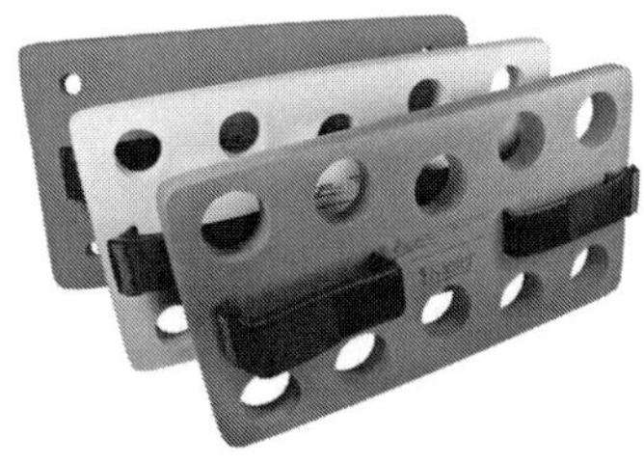

Figure 8.3 Burdenko Board.

When searching for the best equipment to use with my clients, I could not find a board that challenged the whole body, upper and lower extremities, or that offered varying levels of resistance.

The Burdenko Board has straps that allow the board to be used with feet or arms without slipping. It is available with varying resistances levels, allowing for ease of use among people of all ages and physical abilities (see Figure 8.3).

Water Walkers

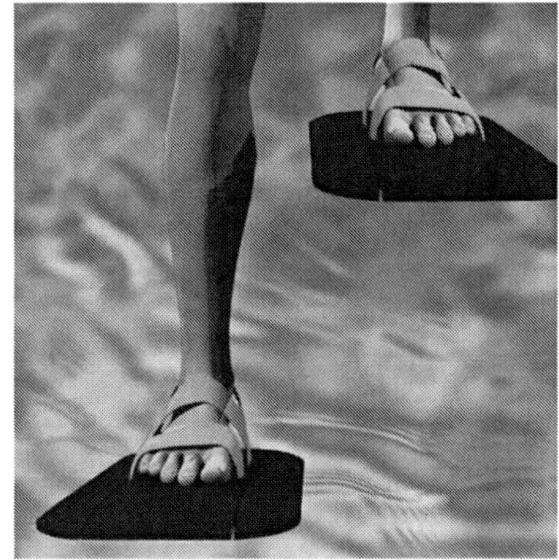

Figure 8.4 Water Walkers.

Water Walkers are winged water shoes that increase the effort required to move legs in water (see Figure 8.4). They are excellent for building cardiovascular strength, endurance, building and reconditioning leg muscles, and developing the six essential qualities for everyday life and sport .

Burdenko Water Barbells with Adjustable Buoyancy (Short and Long)

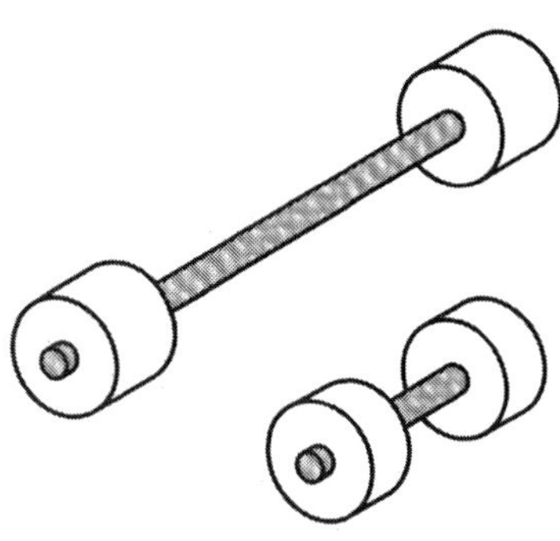

Figure 8.5 Water barbells.

Barbells are used to provide resistance, support, safety, and stability in water (see Figure 8.5). I recommend two long barbells and two short barbells for water workouts.

There are many water barbells on the market. Most are not adjustable and are plain in color. I created water barbells that are easily adjustable, and are colorful. Life should be colorful and exciting, not plain, and this should be reflected in all aspects, including our exercise equipment.

Push-Up Bars

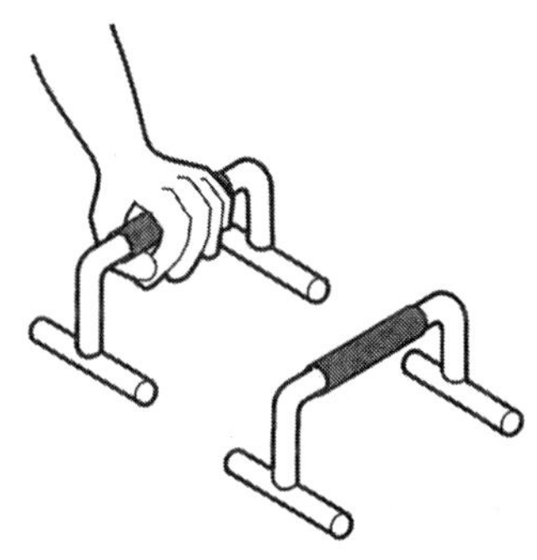

Figure 8.6 Push-up bars.

Push-up bars are useful for wheelchair users and others who have lost mobility, who may have difficulty entering the water (see Figure 8.6). They were originally designed to be used while doing pushups.

Scott Beiler says, "I use push-up bars whenever I transfer between my wheelchair and the ground. The push-up bar helps extend my arm reach, making it easier to reach the ground. When sitting on the ground, the push-up bars make it easy to lift my bottom and move. It is much easier than sliding without them."

A note of caution: Push-up bars require wrist strength. When your arm is extended at an angle to the ground and you shift your weight, the push-up bar has a tendency to tip over, so your hands and wrists must be strong enough to handle the load.

Rubber Exercise Tubing (Long and Short) "My gym in my pocket"

Exercise tubing provides resistance when stretched. It can be used in water and on land. The level of resistance is easily and quickly varied by adjusting the distance between you and the anchor point. Tubing should be adjusted for each exercise so that there is only a small amount of tension in the starting position.

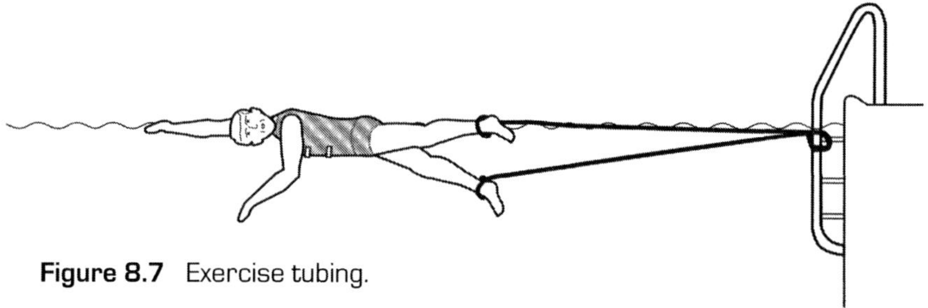

Figure 8.7 Exercise tubing.

I recommend exercise tubing that is five-sixteenths of an inch in diameter, and made from natural latex rubber that is one-sixteenth of an inch thick. To get started, you will need two 2-foot-long pieces and two 13-foot-long pieces (including the loops on each end). Tie a loop at the end of each piece of tubing large enough for your hand or foot to fit through.

For exercises that use long pieces of tubing, tie loops at each end. The loop should be just large enough for your hand to fit through and fit snugly around your wrist (see Figure 8.8). Looping the tubing around your wrist secures the tubing and prevents it from snapping in case it slips out of your hand. Be careful not to wrap the exercise tubing too tightly around your wrist.

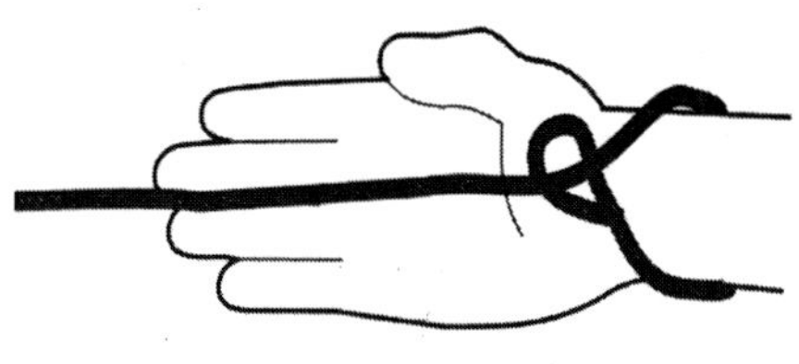

Figure 8.8
Looping tubing around hand.

For exercises in which the tubing is tied together in a circle, simply hold the tubing in the palm of your hand with your thumb on the outside. In order to prevent blisters, you may find it helpful to wear biking or rowing gloves to protect your hand but leave your fingers free.

Exercise tubing is useful in water in several ways. It can be used to add resistance and increase the difficulty of exercises. Exercise tubing is also extremely useful if attached from the arms to the legs. Arm movements will then move paralyzed or injured legs. These leg movements help stimulate nerves and muscle tissue.

I find exercise tubing to be more practical compared to the colored bands often used in physical therapy and in clubs. Exercise tubing is cheaper, very versatile, easier to grip, and easier to tie and untie loops.

Exercise tubing will wear out with use, particularly in a chlorine pool. Always inspect tubing and replace it when it develops cracks or shows any sign of wear. It will wear out faster if kept in sunlight or a dry place. Store it in a bag in a dark place.

Burdenko Belt
"My gym on my body"

I designed the Burdenko Belt in order to find a way to reach as many of the body's 650 muscles as possible with each movement.

The Burdenko Belt also provides anatomically designed posture and back support. It also provides resistance for upper and lower extremities and all muscles in the human body. It does not restrict activities and can be used in water and on land. By providing assistance and resistance, it works your flexors and extensors, and balances the muscles.

The belt enhances dynamic movements because life is dynamic, and it creates further possibilities for developing the 6 essential qualities for everyday life and sport.

It can be used with every exercise in water and on land. It can be used during everyday activities, whether walking your dog or cleaning your house. I have clients who walk to and from work wearing the belt. It can be put under clothing and worn when running errands. I have children who wear it during school activities. I have athletes who wear it during every activity.

Adjustable Rings above the Water

Figure 8.9 Adjustable rings.

Adjustable rings suspended from the ceiling can be raised and lowered to different heights above and below the water (see Figure 8.9). They are very useful for keeping the body extended and rigid, and for developing upper-body strength. The rings can be used for pushups and pull-ups from a horizontal position and chin-ups from a vertical position.

As you advance in your recovery, try standing with your feet in the rings underwater and perform forward, backward, and sideways splits. The higher the rings are raised out of the water, the more effort it will take to perform the exercises.

Water Workout Station

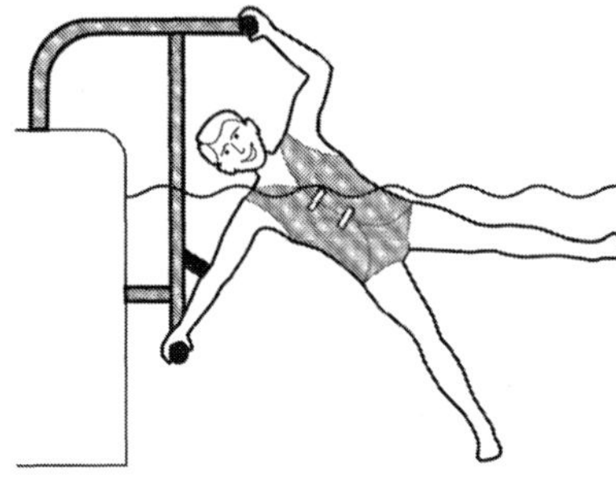

Figure 8.10 Water workout station.

A Water Workout Station can provide a gym setting in water. Aquatrend makes a portable unit that hangs over the edge of a pool. Installation requires only two small holes on the deck; it does not damage the pool, and can easily be removed. It consists of a stainless-steel framework with grips for the hands and feet (see Figure 8.10). It also has a platform that swings down below the surface for sitting and performing exercises. The station can be used for a variety of activities, including pull-ups, lateral raises, abdominal crunches, leg curls, and many more.

The Pool Lift

Figure 8.11 The pool lift.

A pool lift may be necessary for people who have lost the mobility to transfer in and out of the pool. There are electric, hand-operated, and water-powered models. A lift may allow the user to be raised and lowered while seated or lying down, depending upon his or her physical condition (see Figure 8.11). Some units can be operated by the user; others require an attendant.

JACUZZI

We use a Jacuzzi as another environment for restoring health, stimulating healing, building positive emotions, and relaxation. Be aware that the Jacuzzi is at the right temperature, and stay no longer than 10-15 minutes.

I highly recommend transferring from the Jacuzzi to cold water, and from cold water to the Jacuzzi. This builds up your immune system, and also causes your capillaries expand and shrink. I call this "gymnastics for capillaries." It increases circulation and improves blood supply for the whole body. Skin is the largest organ in the human body—taking care of it provides a multitude of benefits for the whole body. Always finish with cold water.

There are advantages and disadvantages associated with the use of Jacuzzis. The hot bubbling water relaxes muscles and helps increase circulation. This may also feel good if you become cold while exercising in the pool.

However, too much heat may make you feel faint, and the increased circulation may raise your blood pressure. Listen to your body. Everyone has different temperature thresholds. A general guideline for use is 15 minutes every other day. Those who are paralyzed should always check their skin temperature or have it checked when in a Jacuzzi to ensure they are not overheated.

If you find a Jacuzzi to your liking, consult your physical therapist or health-care professional. Have your blood pressure checked periodically before and after you use the Jacuzzi to see how your heart responds to the heat.

GETTING INTO AND OUT OF THE WATER

Scott Biehler:

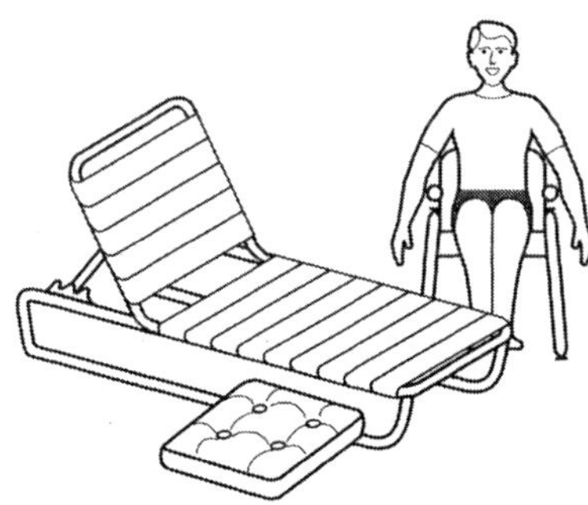

Figure 8.12 Transferring from the wheelchair to the floor–starting position.

Transferring oneself from a wheelchair to the water may present challenges. Water exercises can be performed anywhere there is water: in a lake or river, the ocean, a pond, or of course a pool. Outdoors, you can transfer out of your chair onto the ground or sand and then move down to the water. I generally transfer in stages. First, I transfer myself to a lower beach chair, then down to the sand. I make my way along the sand using push-up bars to lift my bottom as I slide over and move along.

Most facilities designed for water therapy have a pool with a special lift for the handicapped. You transfer from your wheelchair to the seat of the lift, while an assistant lowers you gently into the water.

If you do not have access to a lift, this should not restrict you from getting in and out of water. The technique you use will depend upon your physical capabilities. The following is the technique that Dr. Burdenko designed for me. (Note: I will describe the actions transferring to my right side. From time to time, alternate sides if possible to balance muscle usage.)

Before entering the water, put on your flotation vest or belt. Position yourself at the corner of the pool. Slide forward, letting the lower portion of your legs down into the water.

Place a pool lounge chair on the right side of the wheelchair. If you do not have a lounge chair, use a stool or low chair, so the height of the seat is about halfway between the floor and the wheelchair seat. To the right of the lounge chair, place a seat cushion on the floor. Position the wheelchair against the lounge chair at a 45-degree angle (see Figure 8.12). This makes it easier to slide your bottom out of the wheelchair without rubbing against the wheel on the side. (My wheelchair has removable leg rests. Before positioning the wheelchair at an angle, I remove the right wheelchair leg rest. Then I put my right foot on top of my left foot so it does not drag on the ground.)

Remove the right armrest from your wheelchair. Slide your buttocks to the edge of the wheelchair seat. Swing your right leg to the front of the lounge chair. With your left hand, grip onto the wheelchair armrest for support. Lean to the right, and put your right hand down onto the lounge chair. Pushing with both arms, slide sideways down into the lounge chair. Swing your left leg in front of the lounge chair. Then swing both legs to the right in front of the seat cushion. Scoot your bottom to the right edge of the lounge chair. Place your left hand down onto the lounge chair next to your buttocks. Lean over and place your right hand onto the far edge of the seat cushion. (If you have difficulty reaching down to the cushion, use a push-up bar to extend your reach.) Pushing up with both arms, slide sideways down onto the seat cushion (see Figure 8.13).

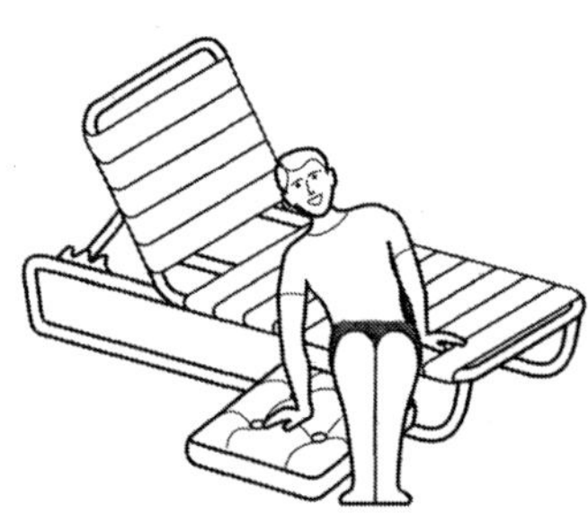

Figure 8.13 Transferring from lounge chair to floor.

Using a push-up bar in each hand to raise your bottom up off the floor, transfer over to the corner of the pool. This may take several moves. Slide your legs over with each move (see Figure 8.14).

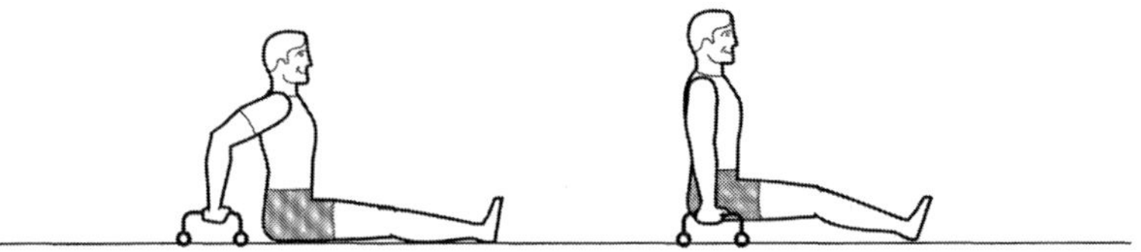

Figure 8.14 Moving along the floor using push-up bars.

With your right hand, hold onto the right edge of the pool. With your left hand, hold onto the edge of the pool. Lean forward, moving your hands out along the edges of the pool. Push your arms down and raise your bottom up and out over the water Slowly lower yourself into the pool (see Figure 8.15).

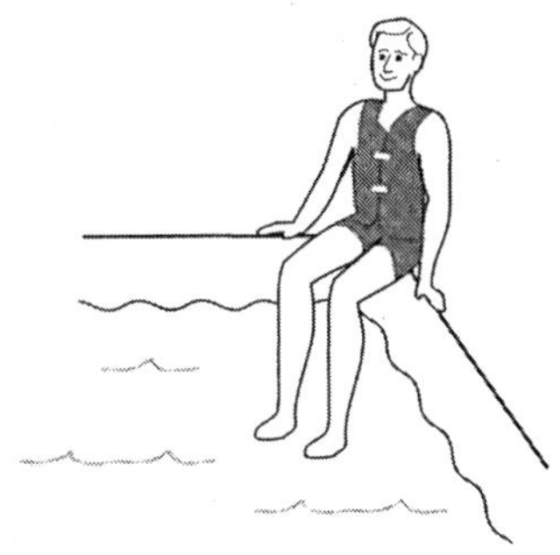

Figure 8.15 Entering the pool.

The technique for getting out of the pool is the same process in reverse. Back up into the corner, facing into the pool. Bend your elbows up high and place your hands on either edge of the pool. Push your arms down, leaning slightly forward, and raise your bottom up out of the water and onto the edge. Then scoot back onto the seat cushion. Remove your flotation vest and dry off. If this technique does not work for you, be creative! There is always a way to get into the water.

When Practicing Exercises, Remember:

- Think before you move
- Always warm up and always cool down
- Perform exercises at multiple speeds: slow, medium, fast
- Perform every exercise in multiple directions
- Do not exercise if you feel pain

Water Exercises

BARBELL EXERCISES

1. Upright Push-Pulls
2. Prone Push-Pulls
3. Forward Stretch
4. Side Stretch
5. Horizontal Stretch
6. Stand up From Lying on Back
7. Push Down with a Single Barbell
8. Parallel Barbell Push Downs
9. Angels in the Snow
10. Stretch-Outs with Short Barbells
11. Arm Swings with Short Barbells
12. Jumping Jacks
13. Breaststroke on Back with Barbell
14. The American Crawl
15. Walking with Barbells
16. Twist with Barbells
17. Jump and Walk with Barbells
18. Sit-ups with Barbell Under the Knees
19. Barbell Sitting While Holding the Wall
20. Barbell Sitting
21. Sit and Swim
22. Upright Barbell Balancing
23. Sit up and Over
24. Knee Raises with Barbells at the Sides
25. Roll-Overs
26. Straddling the Barbell
27. Swim and Step
28. Jog in Place with Short Barbells
29. Side Swings with Short Barbells
30. Back Sway with Barbells 1
31. Back Sway with Barbells 2
32. Leg Kicks with Short Barbells
33. Short Barbell Pass
34. Barbell Boxing

EXERCISES WITH NO EQUIPMENT
(except for floatation vest)

35. Walking
36. Upright Breaststroke
37. Upright Twist and Turn
38. Pendulum
39. Side Stroke
40. Backward Leg Lifts in the Corner
41. Straight Knee Raises
42. Knee Raises to the Side
43. Circle Kick
44. Side Step
45. Horizontal Stretching at the Ladder
46. Turning Along the Wall
47. Catch Your Knee

FLOTATION BOARD EXERCISES

48. Balance With the Board
49. Vertical Board Strokes
50. Flotation Board Twist
51. Push Behind
52. Prone Pushups

CORNER EXERCISES

53. Pushups in the Corner
54. Leg Lifts from the Corner

EXERCISES WITH TUBING

55. Backward Breaststroke
56. Swim with Short Tubing
57 Tethered Swim

EXERCISES FOR CONDITIONING

58. Pronation and Supination
59. Speed Walking
60. Vertical Crawl
61. Side Running (with Long Barbells)
62. Breast Stroke (with Short Barbells)
63. Pump (with Long Barbells)
64. Standing on a Long Barbell
65. Butterfly

Water Exercise 1

Upright Push-Pulls

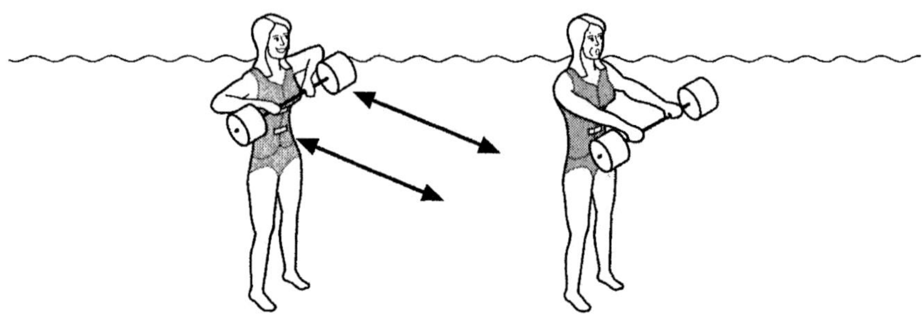

PURPOSE

To maintain vertical alignment, stretch the shoulder and back muscles and strengthen arm muscles.

EQUIPMENT

Flotation vest, one long barbell

STARTING POSITION

Float in a vertical position. Hold the barbell with both hands at shoulder width in front of your chest.

ACTION

1. Push the barbell out straight on the surface of the water. Maintain vertical alignment.
2. Return to starting position.

COMMENTS

Apply even pressure with each arm. Push and pull the barbell, using the water to create resistance. Create a rhythm with your breathing and arm movements. As you become accustomed to this exercise, push and pull vigorously. Splash the water and have fun!

Water Exercise 2

Prone Push-Pulls

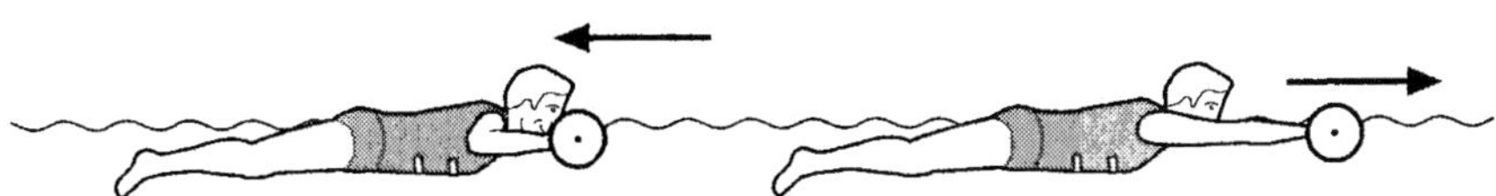

PURPOSE

To stretch the shoulder and arm muscles and work on breathing and balance.

EQUIPMENT

Flotation vest, one long barbell

STARTING POSITION

Float face down with your arms extended in front of you. Hold the barbell with both hands at shoulder width.

ACTION

1. Pull the barbell to your chest while inhaling.
2. Push the barbell out straight in front of you while exhaling.

COMMENTS

Create a rhythm with your breathing and arm movements. As you become accustomed to this exercise, push and pull vigorously, splashing the water.

VARIATION

Turn your head left and right while performing the actions.

Water Exercise 3

Forward Stretch

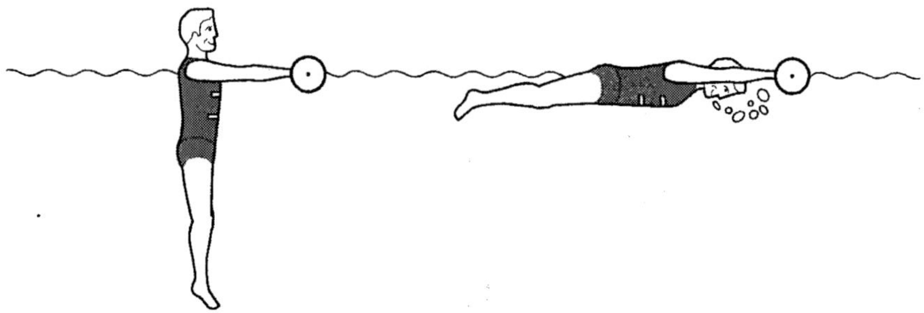

PURPOSE

To stretch the neck and shoulders, stimulate deep breathing, and strengthen the back and abdominal muscles, providing horizontal alignment.

EQUIPMENT

Flotation vest, one long barbell

STARTING POSITION

Float in a vertical position. Hold the barbell with your arms extended in front of you.

ACTION

1. Lean forward with your arms stretched out in front of you and lie face down in the water. Exhale.
2. Maintain this position for 2 to 3 seconds. Raise your head out of the water and inhale deeply. Put your head down and exhale with your face in the water.
3. Return to starting position.

COMMENTS

Tighten the muscles in your buttocks. Stretch your legs and flex your feet. When lying face down in the water with your arms stretched out in front of you, lifting your torso out of the water and returning to the vertical starting position may be difficult. At first, it may be easier to roll over on your back, then lean forward to sit up, and return to vertical position. However, keep trying to lift yourself up from the face-down position. Assist with your arms by pushing down on the barbell. Once you have mastered this, concentrate on swinging your legs down as you lean back.

Water Exercise 4

Side Stretch

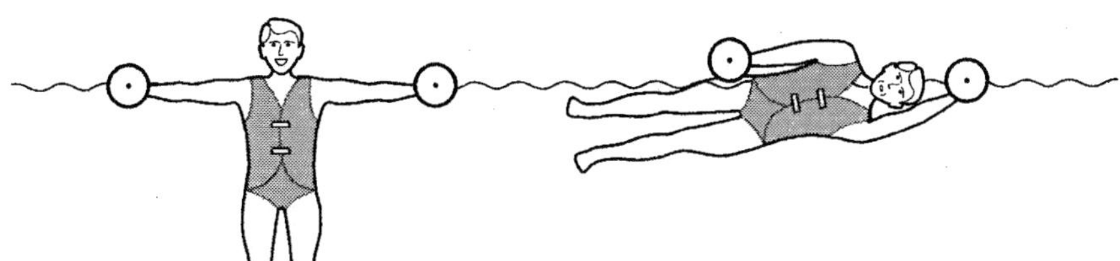

PURPOSE

To stretch the shoulder, back, and leg muscles, and improve balance and trunk control.

EQUIPMENT

Flotation vest, two long barbells

STARTING POSITION

Float in a vertical position with your arms straight out to your sides, holding a barbell in each hand.

ACTION

1. Float to your left side with your arms extended. Balance on your side for 5 to 10 seconds.
2. Return to starting position.
3. Perform the same actions on your right side.

COMMENTS

Be aware maintain a straight line with your body when in a side lying position. A firm grip on the barbells will help you maintain your balance. As you progress, stabilize your pelvis to maintain your balance and reduce your grip on the barbells, eventually letting your hands simply rest on the barbells. Breathe deeply throughout.

IF LOWER EXTREMITY FUNCTION IS LIMITED

When lying on your side, visualize your legs out straight and raised to the surface.

Water Exercise 5

Horizontal Stretch

PURPOSE

To enhance mobility and alignment by learning to change body positions in water.

EQUIPMENT

Flotation vest, two long barbells

STARTING POSITION

Float in a vertical position with your arms out to your sides holding a barbell in each hand.

ACTION

1. Lean forward and lie face down in the water. Exhale into the water.
2. Return to starting position.
3. Lean back and lie flat on your back. Exhale.
4. Return to the starting position.

COMMENTS

Initially, movement may come from your arms and shoulders. As you progress, use your abdominal, neck, and trunk muscles.

IF LOWER EXTREMITY FUNCTION IS LIMITED

When lying on your side, visualize your legs out straight and raised to the surface.

When lying flat, visualize your legs out straight, raised to the surface.

VARIATIONS

When in the horizontal position, separate your legs and bring them back together before returning to starting position.

Water Exercise 6

Stand up from Lying on Back

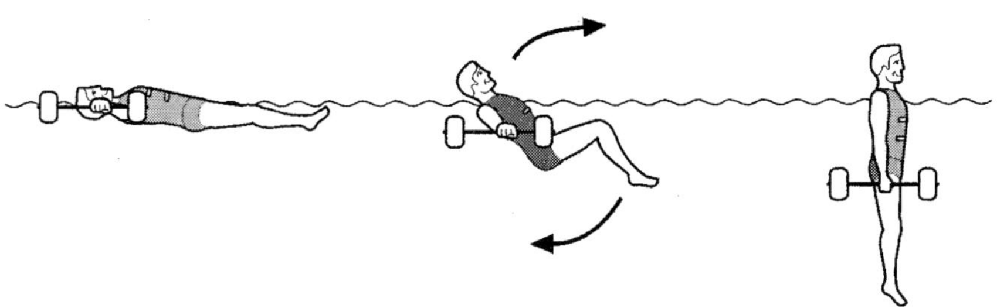

PURPOSE

To strengthen abdominal and back muscles and improve balance and alignment.

EQUIPMENT

Flotation vest, two long barbells

STARTING POSITION

Float on your back with your arms extended out to your sides, holding a barbell in each hand.

ACTION

1. Bend your knees toward your upper body, while simultaneously moving your upper body forward, gradually coming to a vertical position.
2. With your arms fully extended on the surface of the water, maintain vertical balance.
3. Return to the starting position.

COMMENTS

At first, you may need to use your arms to help push yourself forward. As you improve, rely less on your arms and more on your abdominal and back muscles.

IF LOWER EXTREMITY FUNCTION IS LIMITED

Visualize leaning forward and bringing your knees up. Contract your abdominal muscles and extend your legs down. Picture stretching your legs and flexing your feet, and feel your hamstrings tighten.

Water Exercise 7

Push Down with a Single Barbell

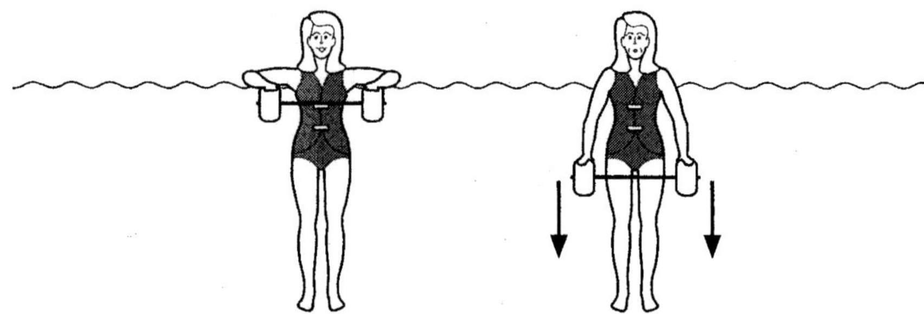

PURPOSE

To improve pelvic stability, balance, strengthen arm and shoulder muscles, and improve range of motion.

EQUIPMENT

Flotation vest, one long barbell

STARTING POSITION

Float in a vertical position. Hold the barbell at chest level, with your hands on top of the barbell floats.

ACTION

1. Push the barbell straight down. Maintain vertical alignment. Hold this position for 5 seconds.
2. Return to starting position slowly, raising the arms while maintaining balance.

VARIATIONS

1. Hold the bar instead of the floats.
2. While pushing the barbell down, separate your legs sideways. Bring them back together when returning to starting position.

Water Exercise 8

Parallel Barbell Push Downs

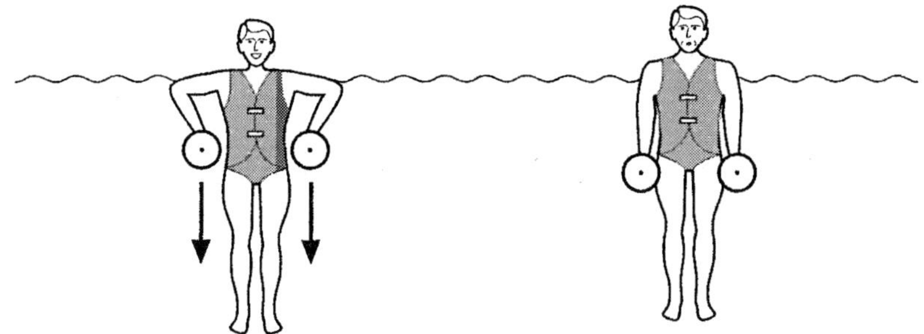

PURPOSE

To stretch shoulder and back muscles, strengthen arms, improve balance and body alignment.

EQUIPMENT

Flotation vest, two long barbells

STARTING POSITION

Float in a vertical position with your arms at your sides and elbows bent, holding a barbell in each hand.

ACTION

1. Push the barbells straight down close to your hips. Maintain body balance and alignment.
2. Return to starting position.

COMMENTS

This exercise can be performed slowly, concentrating on balance. It can also be performed pumping up and down vigorously to strengthen the muscles in the upper arms.

VARIATION

When extending arms down, spread one leg forward and the other back. Bring legs together when returning to starting position.

Water Exercise 9

Snow Angels

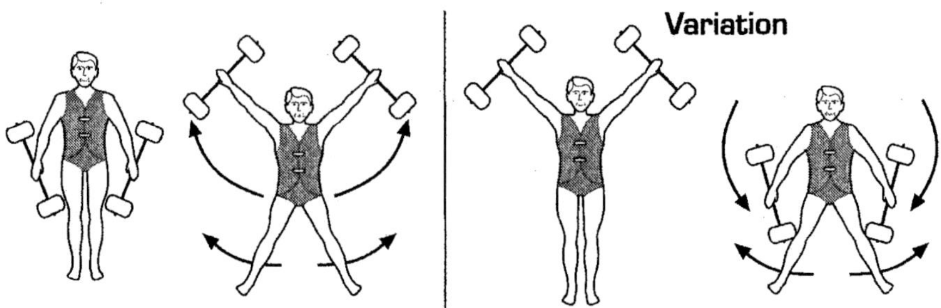

PURPOSE

To stretch shoulder and back muscles, stimulate leg muscles and lung function.

EQUIPMENT

Flotation vest, two long barbells

STARTING POSITION

Float on your back, with arms at your sides near your hips, holding a barbell in each hand.

ACTION

1. Spread your legs apart while simultaneously swinging your arms out to your sides and up above your head, while inhaling. Hold for 5 seconds.
2. Return to starting position while exhaling.

COMMENTS

Concentrate on extending your legs out straight and spreading them to the side.

IF LOWER EXTREMITY FUNCTION IS LIMITED

Remember how it felt to move your legs. Visualize your legs moving.

VARIATIONS

1. As your arms go up, bring your legs together. As you bring your arms down, spread your legs apart.
2. Perform this exercise lying horizontally, face down in the water.

Water Exercise 10

Stretch-outs with Short Barbells

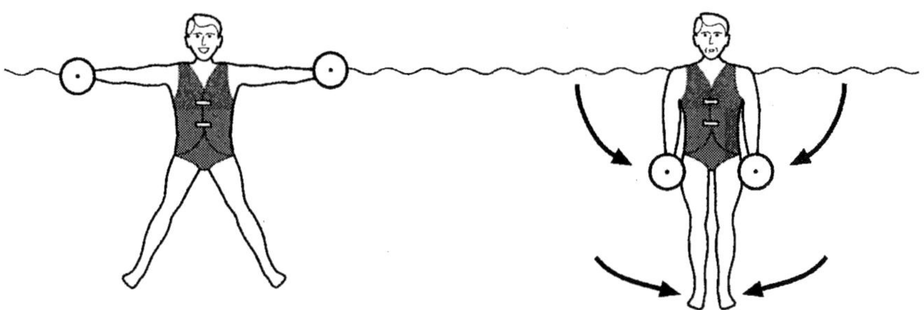

PURPOSE

To build motor skills, improve balance and coordination, strengthen arms, and stimulate legs.

EQUIPMENT

Flotation vest, two short barbells

STARTING POSITION

Float in a vertical position with your arms extended out to your sides, holding a barbell in each hand, and your legs out to the sides. Inhale.

ACTION

1. Swing your arms down to your sides, while simultaneously bringing your legs together. Exhale.
2. Return to starting position. Inhale.

COMMENTS

Hold your chin straight. Maintain your balance. Pay attention to breathing deeply.

IF LOWER EXTREMITY FUNCTION IS LIMITED

Visualize your legs moving in coordination with your arms. Picture them spreading out wide and coming in together. Think about how each muscle works to make the movements.

Water Exercise 11

Arm Swings with Short Barbells

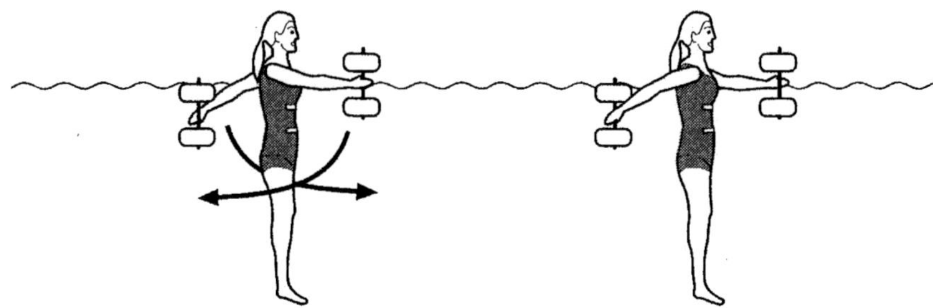

PURPOSE

To improve balance, flexibility, help build muscle mass, strength, and range of motion in shoulders and arms.

EQUIPMENT

Flotation vest, two short barbells

STARTING POSITION

Float in a vertical position. Extend one arm out in front of you and the other arm behind you, holding a barbell vertically in each hand.

ACTION

Swing your arms forward and back as if walking.

COMMENTS

Perform this exercise vigorously, splashing. Gradually increase arm swinging range of motion.

VARIATION

Twist your wrists clockwise and counter-clockwise (pronation and supination) as you swing your arms.

Water Exercise 12

Jumping Jacks

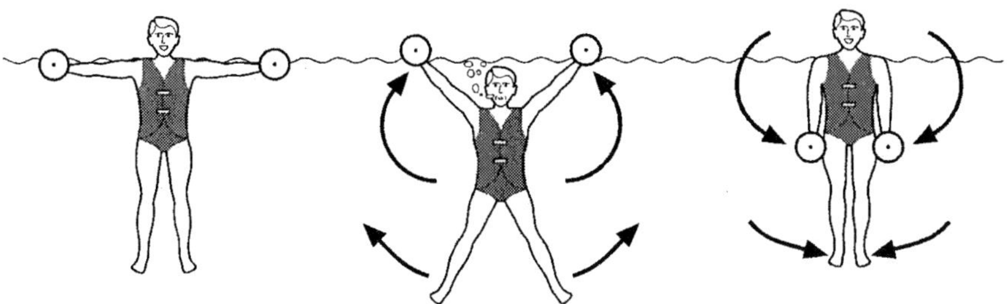

PURPOSE

To improve balance, coordination, strength, and flexibility. To coordinate and strengthen arms and legs.

EQUIPMENT

Flotation vest, two long barbells

STARTING POSITION

Float in a vertical position with your arms straight out to your sides, with a barbell in each hand.

ACTION

1. Swing your arms out and up, while inhaling deeply. Your body will temporarily dip farther into the water. As it does, spread your legs apart.
2. Swing your arms back down, exhaling as you come up. Bring your legs together.

IF LOWER EXTREMITY FUNCTION IS LIMITED

Visualize your arms and legs moving in coordination. Concentrate on sending the signal from your brain, and picture it traveling down through the nerves, stimulating the muscles in your legs.

COMMENTS

Perform these movements while maintaining a vertical position. Get into a rhythm of coordination with your arms and legs. Pay special attention to breathing and coordination.

Water Exercise 13

Breaststroke on Back with Barbell

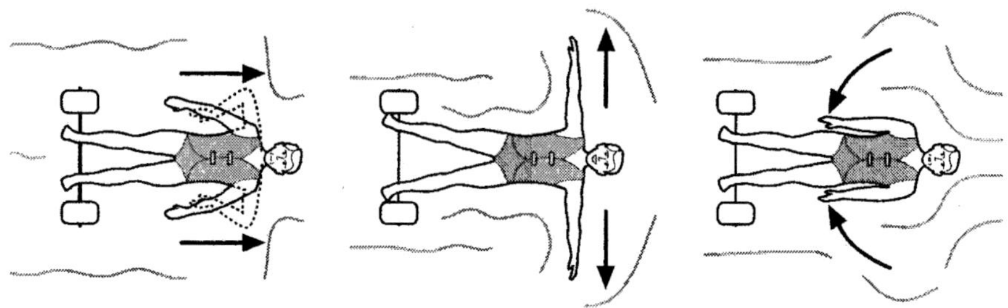

PURPOSE

To stimulate and strengthen upper and lower extremity function, and improve pelvic stability.

EQUIPMENT

Floatation vest, two long barbells

STARTING POSITION

Float on your back with your legs spread apart, pushing outward and creating pressure on the floats of the barbell under your feet. Position your arms straight at your sides.

ACTION

1. Bend your elbows and bring your arms up alongside your body.
2. Extend your arms straight out to the sides.
3. Cup your hands and swing your arms down to sides.

IF LOWER EXTREMITY FUNCTION IS LIMITED

Visualize yourself lying on the surface of the water on your back. Even if you may not feel anything, picture your ankles working in your mind, with your heels holding the barbell in position and your feet pressed against the foam.

COMMENTS

Keep your body straight and pelvis in one line with your legs, shoulders and spine. Concentrate on holding the barbell with your feet. Point your toes downward.

To position the barbell, start from a sitting position. Push the barbell under your legs and slide it down to your ankles. It is common for the barbell to slide off as you exercise.

Water Exercise 14

The American Crawl

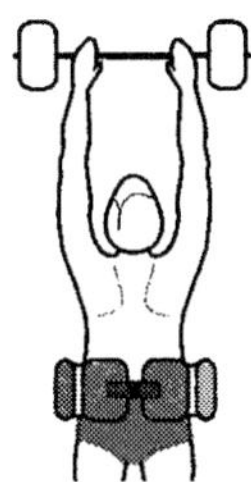 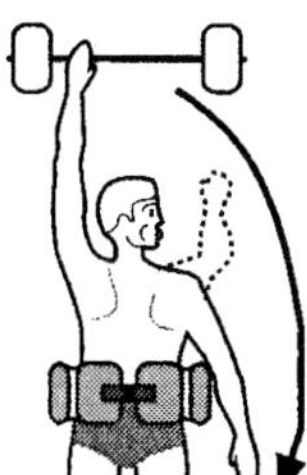 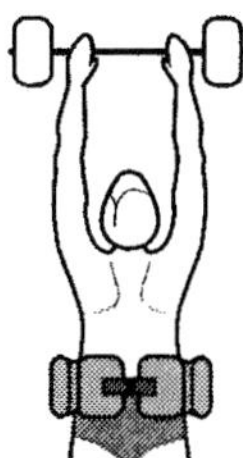 

PURPOSE

To stretch and strengthen the upper body.

EQUIPMENT

Flotation vest, one long barbell

STARTING POSITION

Float on your stomach. Hold the barbell with your arms straight out in front of you.

ACTION

1. Stroke through the water with your right arm, bringing it down to your side. Turn your head to the right and inhale.
2. Bring your right arm forward and grasp the barbell. Turn your face down into the water and exhale.
3. Repeat steps 1 and 2 using your left arm. Turn your head left to inhale.

IF LOWER EXTREMITY FUNCTION IS LIMITED

Coordinate your body position with the movement of your arms and legs. Imagine your legs kicking as your arms stroke.

COMMENTS

Concentrate on breathing and kicking your legs up and down. Get into a rhythm with your breathing and movements. Keep your ankles loose.

Water Exercise 15

Walking with Barbells

PURPOSE

To restore the pattern for walking, strengthen arms, stimulate legs, and improve arm and leg coordination.

EQUIPMENT

Flotation vest, two long barbells

STARTING POSITION

Float in a vertical position with a barbell under each armpit.

ACTION

1. Take steps as if walking on land, swinging your arms along your sides.
2. Coordinate your arm and leg movements, propelling yourself forward. As you bring your left arm forward, step with your right foot. As you bring your right arm forward, step with your left foot.

IF LOWER EXTREMITY FUNCTION IS LIMITED

Visualize walking in the water as if you were walking on land.

COMMENTS

Walk in water as if you were walking on land. Concentrate on stepping forward with one leg while pulling back on the other leg. Pay attention to the leg moving backward. This will propel you forward.

Water Exercise 16

Twist with Barbells

PURPOSE

To increase range of motion and strength in the upper body, and flex the lateral (side) muscles.

EQUIPMENT

Flotation vest, two long barbells

STARTING POSITION

Float in a vertical position with your arms extended in front of you and a barbell in each hand.

ACTION

1. Swing both arms to the left. At the same time, turn your head and your body to the right.
2. Perform the same actions in the opposite direction—swing both arms to the right while turning your head and body to the left.

COMMENTS

Proceed gently at first. As you gain more body control, perform this exercise vigorously. Splash and have fun! Keep your chin up, and practice deep breathing.

Water Exercise 17

Jump and Walk with Barbells

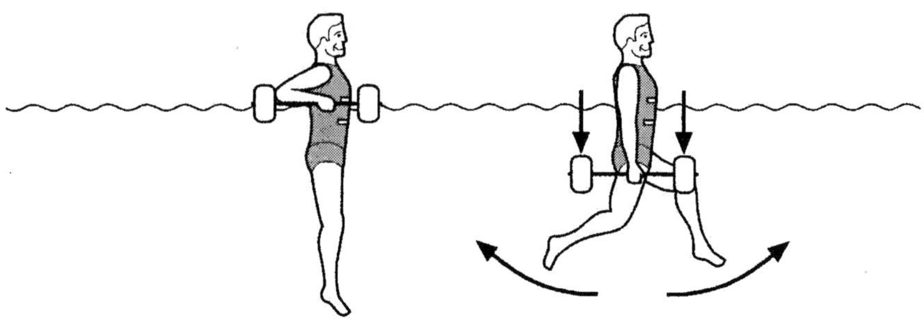

PURPOSE

To help build motor skills, stimulate leg function, improve balance, coordination, endurance, and strength.

EQUIPMENT

Flotation vest, two long barbells

STARTING POSITION

Float in a vertical position. Hold a barbell in each hand close to your armpits.

ACTION

1. Push the barbells straight down into the water. Move your left leg in front of you and your right leg behind you. Maintain your balance, staying vertical in the water.
2. Bend your elbows and return to starting position.
3. Repeat this action, switching the positions of your legs—move your right leg in front of you and your left leg behind you.

IF LOWER EXTREMITY FUNCTION IS LIMITED

Concentrate on waking up the nerves and muscles. Imagine your legs moving in the water as if you were walking.

Water Exercise 18

Sit-ups with a Barbell under the Knees

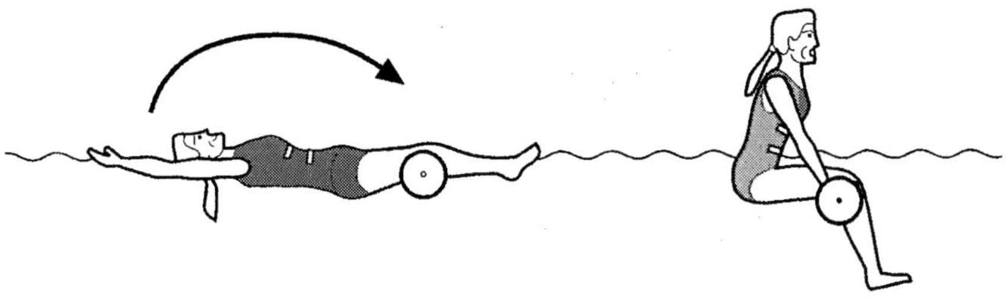

PURPOSE

To improve balance, motor skills, strengthen the spine, abdominal, and back muscles.

EQUIPMENT

Flotation vest, one long barbell

STARTING POSITION

Float on your back. Place the barbell under your knees. Extend your arms out over your head.

ACTION

1. Swing your arms around your sides to your knees, while at the same time bending your waist and leaning forward to sitting a position.
2. Sit up and hold the barbell with your hands.
3. Return to starting position.

IF LOWER EXTREMITY FUNCTION IS LIMITED

Depending upon the level of your injury, you may or may not have control of your abdominal muscles in the beginning. Use your arms for leverage, and lunge forward. As you practice this exercise, concentrate on using your abdominal muscles.

Water Exercise 19

Barbell Sitting While Holding the Wall

PURPOSE

To exercise improve balance and pelvic stability, and strengthen upper body and stomach muscles.

EQUIPMENT

Flotation vest, one long barbell

STARTING POSITION

Float in a vertical position. Hold the wall of the pool with one hand and the barbell in the other.

ACTION

1. Push the barbell below the surface and position it under your bottom.
2. Let go of the barbell. Sit upright and maintain your balance and alignment.
3. While holding the wall with one hand, turn your body to the side. Use your free hand to help position yourself and maintain balance.
4. Return to starting position.
5. Repeat this action in the other direction.

COMMENTS

You may need to use both hands to position the barbell. Then hold the wall for stability and practice balancing until the barbell stays in place. Keep your head straight and facing forward. This may seem like a simple exercise, but it requires the interaction and coordination of many muscles.

In the beginning, it may be difficult to sit on the barbell. Your arms may not be strong enough, and positioning the barbell may take some practice. The barbell may not stay in place. Keep practicing! As the weeks progress, to your surprise, the barbell will eventually stay in place.

Water Exercise 20

Barbell Sitting

PURPOSE

To improve body awareness and balance, stimulate the spine, abdominal and back muscles, and strengthen arms, wrists, back, and chest.

EQUIPMENT

Flotation vest, one long barbell

STARTING POSITION

Float in a vertical position. Hold the barbell in one hand.

ACTION

1. While sitting, push the barbell under your bottom. Use both hands to position the barbell if necessary.
2. Maintain your balance and alignment, keeping your neck and back straight.
3. Place your hands on the floats of the barbell beneath the surface and maintain balance.
4. Return to starting position.

IF LOWER EXTREMITY FUNCTION IS LIMITED

Imagine you are floating in a canoe, controlling your balance with your body position.

COMMENTS

This exercise is a lot of fun. It will take practice and patience.

Water Exercise 21

Sit and Swim

PURPOSE

To improve balance and pelvic stability and strengthen the arm, back, and chest muscles.

EQUIPMENT

Flotation vest, one long barbell

STARTING POSITION

Sit on the barbell.

ACTION

1. Mimic arm movements of the breaststroke from the sitting position. Travel forward. Stretch both arms in front of you and sweep them both back behind you under the water, while maintaining your balance.
2. Reverse this action to move backwards.

Water Exercise 22

Upright Barbell Balancing

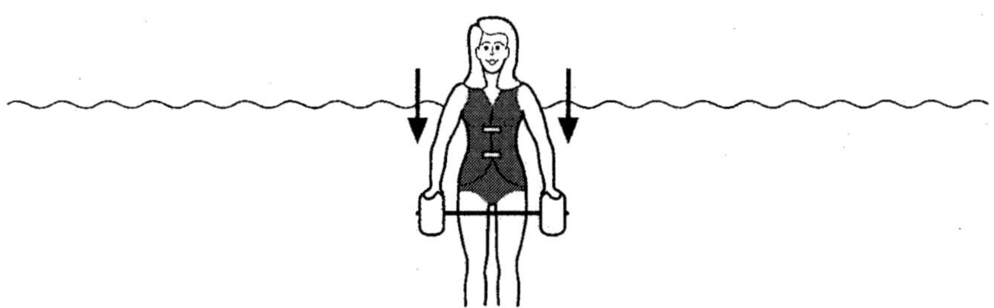

PURPOSE

To improve balance and strengthen arm, wrist, back, and abdominal muscles.

EQUIPMENT

Flotation vest, one long barbell

STARTING POSITION

Float in a vertical position. Place your hands on top of the barbell floats.

ACTION

1. Push the barbell down into the water until your arms are fully extended.
2. Hold this position, maintaining vertical balance.
3. Slowly bend your elbows and return to starting position.

COMMENTS

Maintain body awareness. Keep the barbell level—do not let it tip to either side. Raising and lowering the barbell slowly strengthens the arms, improves coordination, and helps improve balance and allows more control to complete the action. Once your arms are fully extended, concentrate on maintaining your balance. Use your torso to shift your weight and maintain balance instead of moving your arms. This will stimulate the abdominal and lower-back muscles.

Water Exercise 23

Sit up and Over

PURPOSE

To improve balance and strengthen back and abdominal muscles.

EQUIPMENT

Flotation vest, one long barbell

STARTING POSITION

Float on your back holding the barbell with both hands, arms extended over your head.

ACTION

1. Lunge forward, sit up, and move forward to lie on your stomach. Move your legs back so that your body is horizontal.
2. Hold this position.
3. Roll over and return to starting position.

IF LOWER EXTREMITY FUNCTION IS LIMITED

As you use your upper body, concentrate on moving your legs to control this movement. Picture them going down through the water together. Awaken the muscles, and strain to make your legs move. Feel your nerves tingle.

COMMENTS

Initially, you may use your arms and the barbells momentum to lunge forward. As you progress, concentrate on using your abdominal and back muscles. Rely less on the use of your arms.

Water Exercise 24

Knee Raises with Barbells at the Sides

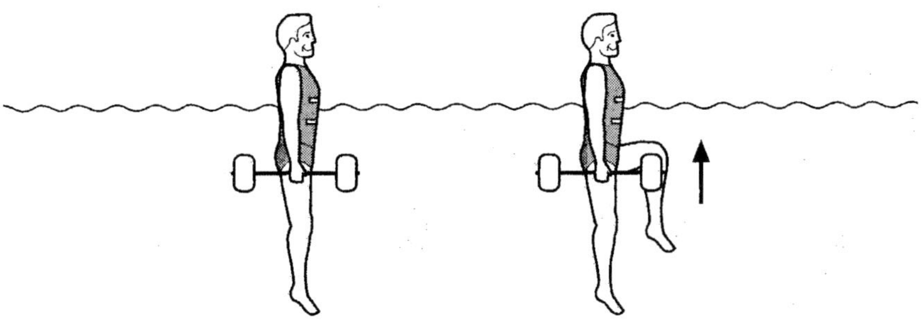

PURPOSE

To improve balance, stimulate and strengthen arms, abdominals, and lower extremities.

EQUIPMENT

Flotation vest, two long barbells

STARTING POSITION

Float in a vertical position with your arms straight down at your sides, holding the barbells. Maintain your balance and alignment.

ACTION

1. Lift your right knee up 90 degrees.
2. Bring your leg back down.
3. Repeat with your left knee.

IF LOWER EXTREMITY FUNCTION IS LIMITED

Visualize your knee rising up. Strain to move your leg, and picture the signals passing down through your nerves to the muscles. Feel it tingle.

Water Exercise 25

Roll-Overs

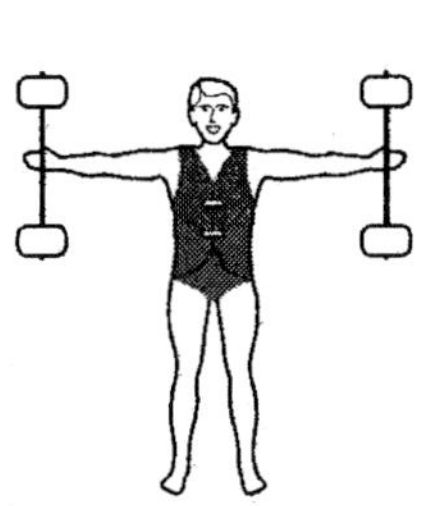

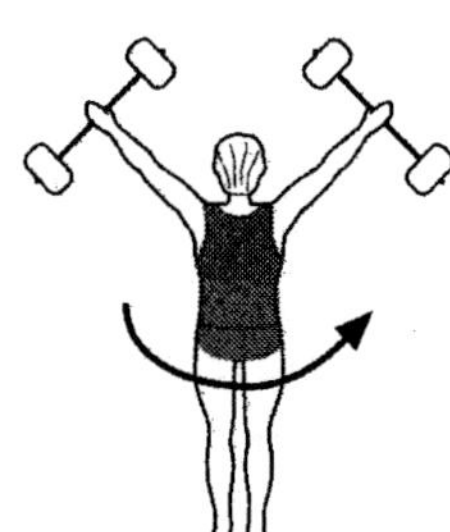

PURPOSE

To improve motor skills, stimulate and strengthen the whole body, and help improve coordination and balance.

EQUIPMENT

Flotation vest, two long barbells

STARTING POSITION

Float on your back with your arms extended to your sides, with a barbell in each hand.

ACTION

1. Roll onto your left side, turning your head and twisting your body to the left. Lift your right arm out of the water and swing it across your chest, creating momentum to help you roll over.
2. Continue to roll so that you are face down in the water.
3. Continue rolling over, turning your head and twisting your body to the left. Lift your left arm out of the water and swing it behind you.
4. Return to starting position.
5. Repeat the actions, rolling to the right.

COMMENTS

This exercise should be a vigorous movement through the water. Splash and have fun!

VARIATION

If you are unable to perform this exercise with barbells, try it without barbells. As you progress, use the barbells.

Water Exercise 26

Straddling the Barbell

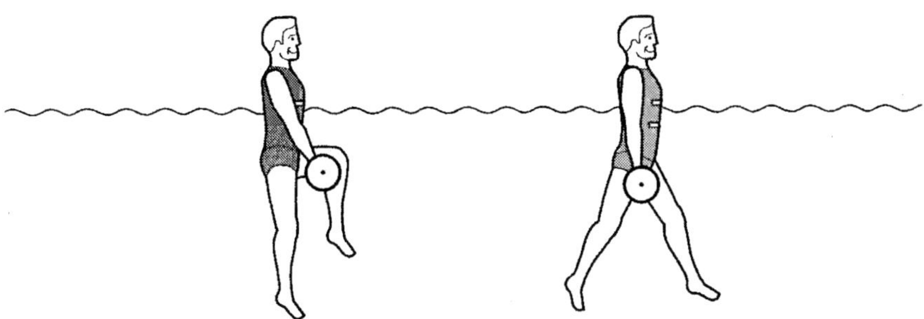

PURPOSE

To improve balance, coordination, flexibility, and improve alignment.

EQUIPMENT

Flotation vest, one long barbell

STARTING POSITION

Float in a vertical position. Place the barbell under your raised and bent right knee. Put your hands on the floats of the barbell.

ACTION

1. Push the barbell straight down, fully extending your arms, allowing your knee to straighten. Maintain your balance and alignment.
2. Return to starting position.
3. Repeat this action with the barbell under your left leg.

COMMENTS

Imagine that you are a gymnast on a pommel horse. At first it may be difficult to balance for any length of time. This exercise requires a lot of upper-body control. To help balance, fix your eyes on a stationary object in the distance. Work toward balancing for 25 to 30 seconds at a time.

Water Exercise 27

Swim and Step

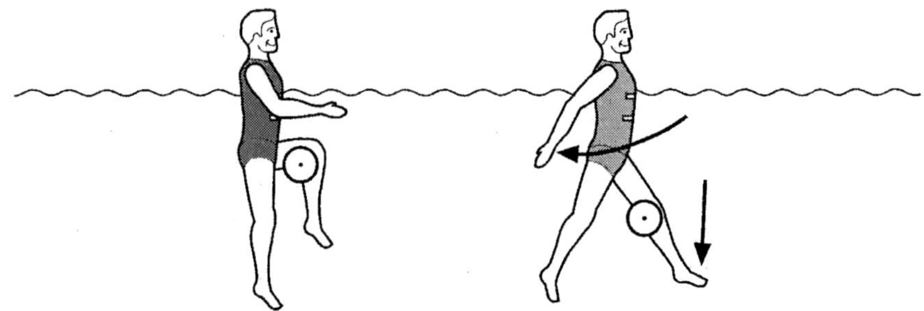

PURPOSE

To improve motor skills, balance, and stimulate leg function.

EQUIPMENT

Flotation vest, one long barbell

STARTING POSITION

Float in a vertical position. Place the barbell under your raised and bent right knee.

ACTION

1. Use the motion of a breaststroke—put both arms in front of you, cupping your hands, and sweep your arms behind you in the water.
2. As your arms are moving, push down on the barbell with your right leg, taking a step forward.
3. Let your knee float back up, and return to starting position.
4. Perform the same action with the barbell under your left knee.

IF LOWER EXTREMITY FUNCTION IS LIMITED

Imagine your leg pushing the barbell down. Visualize yourself taking a big step.

COMMENTS

Concentrate on pushing your leg down as you step and your upper body in a vertical position.

Water Exercise 28

Jog in Place with Short Barbells

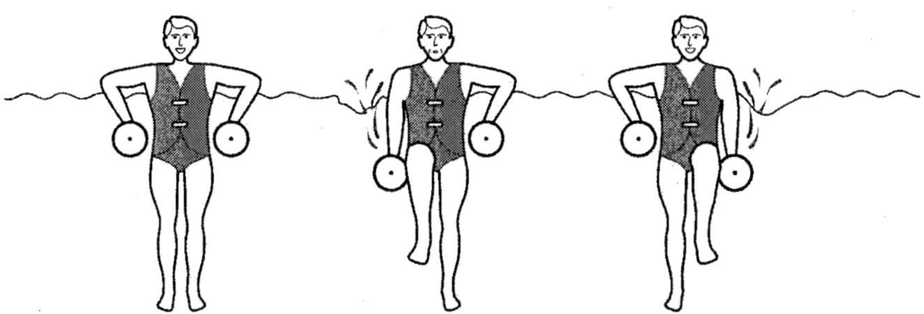

PURPOSE

To develop motor skills, improve coordination, endurance, and stimulate function in legs and arms.

EQUIPMENT

Flotation vest, two short barbells

STARTING POSITION

Float in a vertical position, holding a barbell in each hand.

ACTION

Jog in place—bring your left arm up and your right leg down, and vice versa. Coordinate your arm and leg movements.

IF LOWER EXTREMITY FUNCTION IS LIMITED

Visualize that you are jogging in place. As you strain to move your legs, concentrate on coordinating the opposite movements of your arms and legs. Picture the signals passing down through your nerves to the muscles. Feel it tingle.

Water Exercise 29

Side Swings with Short Barbells

PURPOSE

To improve balance, alignment, and strengthen the arms.

EQUIPMENT

Flotation vest, two short barbells

STARTING POSITION

Float in a vertical position with your arms extended out to your sides with a barbell in each hand.

ACTION

1. Vigorously bring one arm straight down in front and the other arm straight down behind your back. Twist your hands so the barbells are turned to a vertical position in the water.
2. Return to starting position.
3. Perform the actions with the opposite arms in front and back.

COMMENTS

Maintain body awareness; keep your balance upright. Perform this exercise over and over again at different speeds. Have fun. Splash the water.

Water Exercise 30

Back Sway with Barbells 1

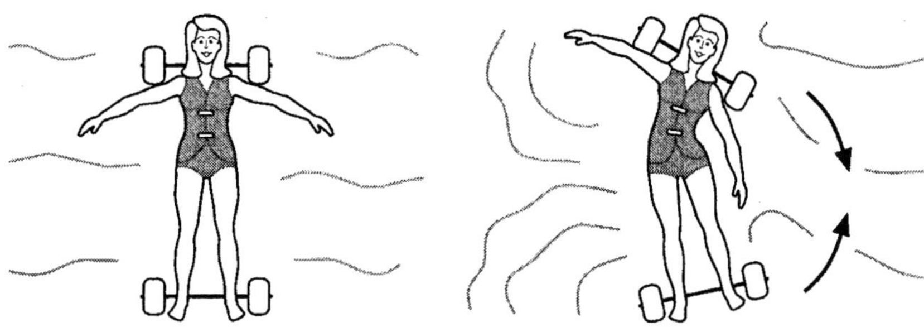

PURPOSE

To stretch upper body and lateral (side) muscles, work on pelvic stability, and stimulate the thigh muscles.

EQUIPMENT

Flotation vest, two long barbells

STARTING POSITION

Float on your back. Position one barbell under your neck and the other under your ankles. Spread your legs apart.

ACTION

1. Bend your body to the left from the side of your waist. Reach your left arm down to your hip and bring your right arm up. Swing your legs to the left. Feel the muscles stretch along your right side. Hold this position for 3 to 5 seconds.
2. Repeat this action on the right side.

COMMENTS

Concentrate on moving your legs and hips. It may take some practice to position the barbell under your ankles. Start from a sitting position and push the barbell under your legs and slide it down under your ankles.

Water Exercise 31

Back Sway with Barbells 2

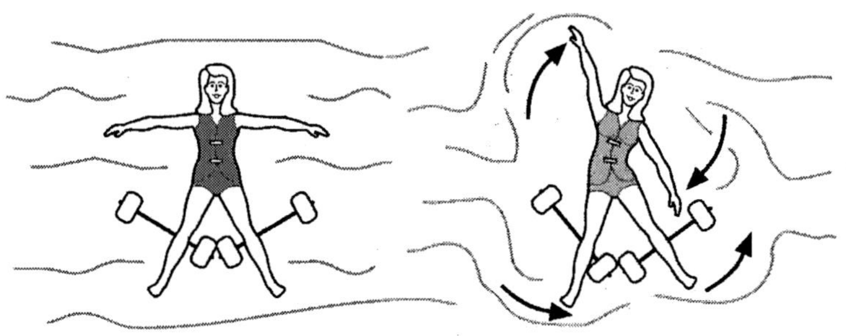

PURPOSE

To improve flexibility and coordination, and stretch upper-body and lateral (side) muscles.

EQUIPMENT

Flotation vest, two long barbells

STARTING POSITION

Float on your back with your arms held out to your sides. Place a barbell under each knee.

ACTION

1. Sway to the left. Bring your left arm down to the side, and raise your right arm out and above your shoulder. Feel the muscles stretch along your right side.
2. Reverse the direction and sway to the right.

COMMENTS

Keep your neck loose. Pay attention to your breathing and to coordinating the movement of your arms and legs.

Water Exercise 32

Leg Kicks with Short Barbells

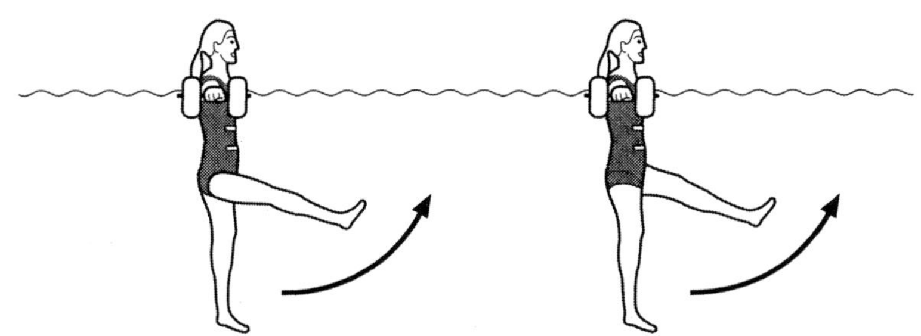

PURPOSE

Stimulates the abdominal, back, and leg muscles and challenge the trunk and spine.

EQUIPMENT

Flotation vest, two short barbells

STARTING POSITION

Float in a vertical position. Hold a barbell in each hand straight out to the sides.

ACTION

1. Bend your knee and kick your right leg forward. Extend your knee forward at the end of the kick.
2. Return to starting position.
3. Repeat with your left leg

IF LOWER EXTREMITY FUNCTION IS LIMITED

Imagine that you are playing soccer, kicking a ball high in the air. Visualize your leg coming all the way up. Strain the muscles, feel your nerves tingle.

Water Exercise 33

Short Barbell Pass

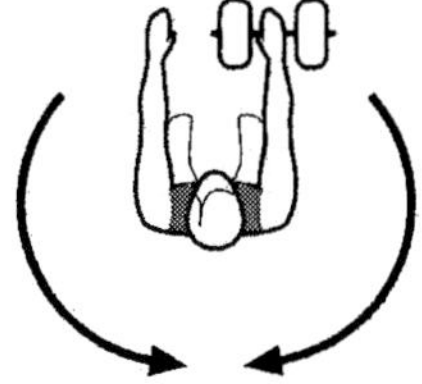

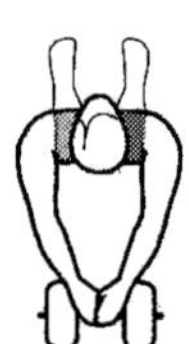

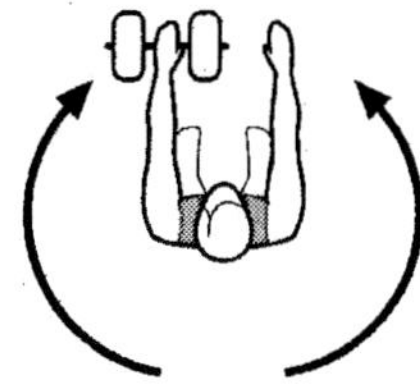

PURPOSE

To increases range of motion in the neck, arms, shoulders, and improve motor skills, balance and coordination.

EQUIPMENT

Flotation vest, one short barbell

STARTING POSITION

Float in a vertical position with your arms stretched out in front of you, holding the barbell in your right hand.

ACTION

1. Swing both arms out to the sides and reach behind your back, while turning your head to the right. Pass the barbell to your left hand.
2. Swing both arms to the front, turning your head forward. Pass the barbell to your right hand.
3. Repeat the actions moving to the left.

COMMENTS

Pay attention to keep your pelvis stable. Perform this exercise vigorously. Have fun and splash.

Water Exercise 34

Barbell Boxing

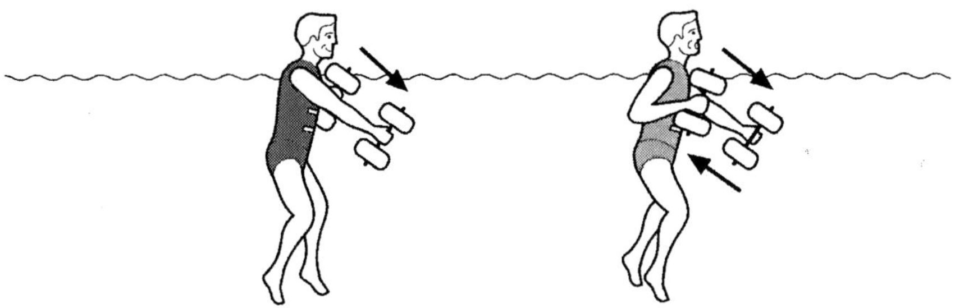

PURPOSE

To improve motor skills, coordination, flexibility, endurance, and strengthen arm and shoulder muscles.

EQUIPMENT

Flotation vest, two short barbells

STARTING POSITION

Float in a vertical position, leaning slightly forward. Hold the barbells in front of you, under the water, with your elbows bent.

ACTION

1. Punch your right arm down at an angle in the water.
2. Return your right arm to starting position while at the same time punching your left arm down.
3. Alternate arm movements, punching out with one arm while the other moves in.

COMMENTS

Exercise vigorously. Have fun and splash.

VARIATIONS

1. In the beginning, punch down at a slight angle into the water. Increase the difficulty by increasing the angle to 45 degrees.
2. Punching out to the sides and in different directions.
3. Twist your wrist inward while punching.

Water Exercise 35

Walking

PURPOSE

To develop proper techniques for walking in water, from deep to shallow. To strengthen arms, stimulate legs, and improve balance, coordination, and endurance.

EQUIPMENT

Flotation vest

STARTING POSITION

Float in a vertical position.

ACTION

With your body alignment straight, move through the water as if walking. Coordinate your arm and leg movements.

IF LOWER EXTREMITY FUNCTION IS LIMITED

Imagine you are walking. As your arms swing back and forth, visualize your legs moving. Coordinate the movements in your mind. Feel the muscles and control your steps. Concentrate on making your legs move.

Scott Biehler: "I found it extremely difficult to coordinate the opposite movements of my arms and legs (especially when I could not detect any leg movement). Prior to my accident, I walked without thinking. Now when I try to walk, I have to concentrate on coordinating the movements. This is a mental challenge as much as a physical one. Don't be discouraged. Eventually, you will feel micro-movements in your legs. This is your first step in regaining the ability to walk."

Water Exercise 36

Upright Breaststroke

PURPOSE

To develop motor skills, strengthen the upper body, and stimulate lung function.

EQUIPMENT

Flotation vest

STARTING POSITION

Float in a vertical position.

ACTION

1. Extend your arms straight out in front of you while inhaling.
2. Swing your arms out to the sides, cupping your hands to pull you through the water, while exhaling.
3. Bend your arms at the elbows, bringing your hands close together at the chest.

COMMENTS

Your body may bend forward as you move through the water. Work to maintain vertical position.

VARIATIONS

1. Perform this exercise backwards.
2. Perform frog kicks with your legs, as if swimming the breaststroke, while maintaining a vertical position.

Water Exercise 37

Upright Twist and Turn

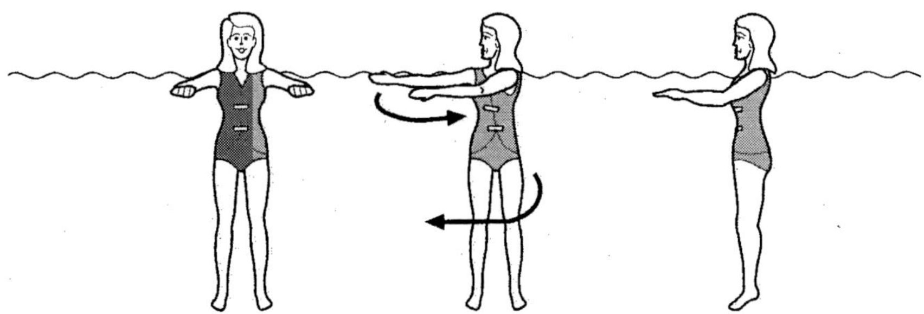

PURPOSE

To strengthen the arms and stretch the sides of the body.

EQUIPMENT

Flotation vest

STARTING POSITION

Float in a vertical position with your arms held out in front of you in a relaxed position.

ACTION

1. Lift your arms just above the water. Twist your upper body, head, and arms to the right.
2. Cup your hands and push down and back in the water as you turn your body 90 degrees to the right.
3. Repeat this exercise, turning several times until you have made a full circle.
4. Reverse the actions, turning to the left.

Water Exercise 38

Pendulum

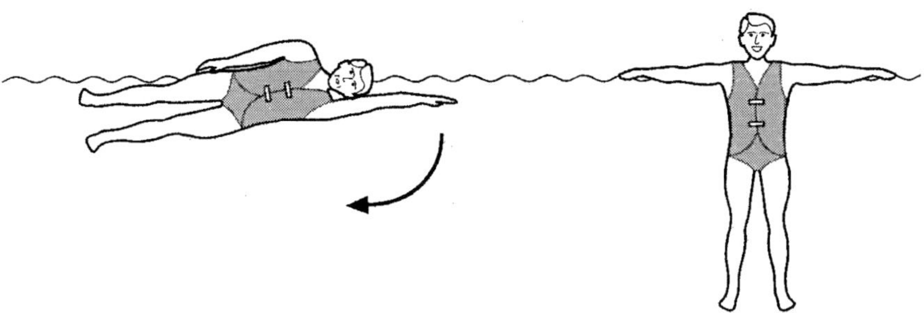

PURPOSE

To strengthen the body, improve balance, alignment, and pelvic stability.

EQUIPMENT

Flotation vest

STARTING POSITION

Float on your left side with your left arm extended past your head and your right arm resting on your side.

ACTION

1. Maintain your balance floating on your side for 3 to 5 seconds.
2. Push down forcefully with your left arm and move into a vertical position. Let your arms relax and float comfortably in the water.
3. Float onto your right side and perform the same exercise on your right.

COMMENTS

Slowly increase the time you stay balanced. At first, it may be difficult to return to vertical position. When you have mastered this exercise, you should be able to move upright quickly using your arms, legs, and body, like a pendulum.

Water Exercise 39

Side Stroke

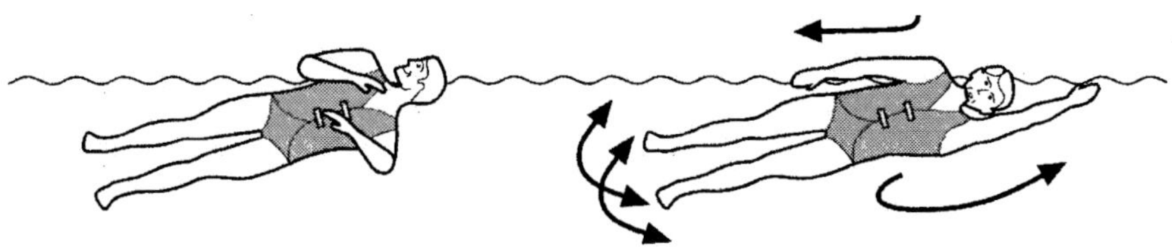

PURPOSE

To strengthen the neck, arm, and upper-body muscles and stimulate the leg muscles.

EQUIPMENT

Flotation vest

STARTING POSITION

Float on your left side with your arms bent and your hands by your chest. Inhale.

ACTION

1. Extend your left arm out straight above you, gliding it along the surface. At the same time, cup your right hand and push around and back, which will move your body forward. Simultaneously exhale.
2. Cup your left hand and pull it back to your chest, moving your body forward. At the same time, let your right hand glide back up to your chest. Simultaneously inhale.
3. After swimming some distance on your left side, alternate and do this stroke on your right side.

COMMENTS

Focus on maintaining your side-lying alignment, pelvic stability, and coordinating your movements. As you improve, concentrate on doing the scissor kick, sweeping your legs back and forth, spreading your legs wider with practice.

Water Exercise 40

Backward Leg Lifts in the Corner

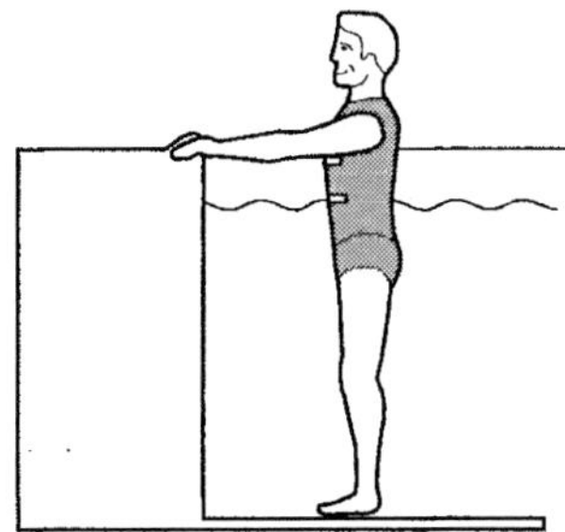

PURPOSE

To stimulate and strengthen legs, and help restore motor skills.

EQUIPMENT

Flotation vest

STARTING POSITION

Stand in the shallow end of the pool facing the corner with your arms out straight, each holding onto a side of the pool. Stand straight with your feet touching the bottom.

ACTION

1. Lean forward and stretch your right leg straight out behind you. Keep your left foot touching the bottom. Press your heel down. Hold this position for 5 to 6 seconds.
2. Return to starting position.
3. Perform the same exercise with your left leg.

IF LOWER EXTREMITY FUNCTION IS LIMITED

As you stand and raise one leg, visualize the movement of your other leg moving back. Concentrate on sending the signals from your brain through the nerves and to the leg muscles. The water will assist you to accomplish this motion.

Water Exercise 41

Straight Knee Raises

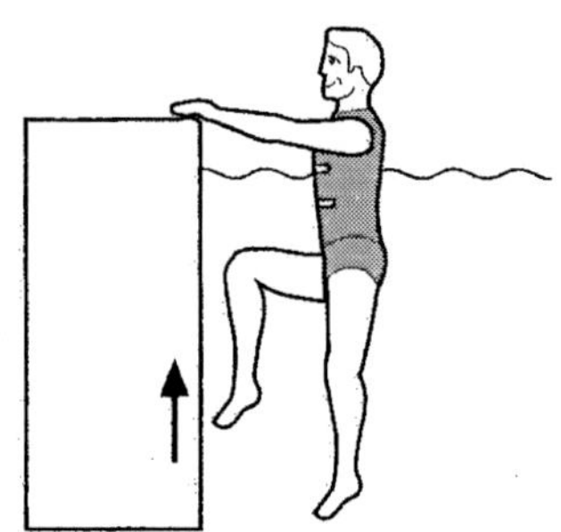

PURPOSE

To stimulate and strengthen thighs and legs, and help restore motor function.

EQUIPMENT

Flotation vest

STARTING POSITION

Stand in the shallow end, holding the corner of the pool with your arms extended in front of you.

ACTION

1. Lift your right knee up high.
2. Return to starting position.
3. Repeat with your left leg.

IF LOWER EXTREMITY FUNCTION IS LIMITED

Visualize raising your knee up high. Strain to wake up your nerves and muscles.

COMMENTS

Keep your back and chin straight. At first, it may be difficult to detect any movement.

VARIATION

Perform the same exercise in the deep end corner of the pool, without touching the bottom.

Water Exercise 42

Knee Raises to the Side

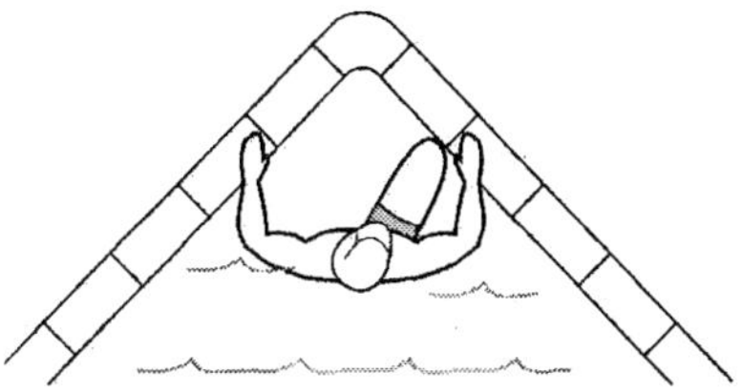
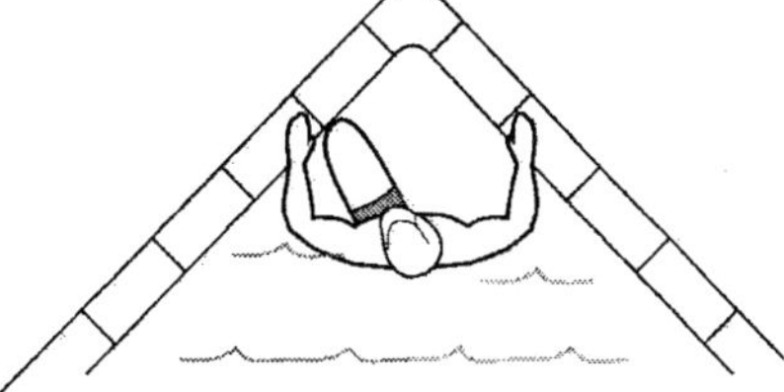

PURPOSE

To stimulate and strengthen the thighs and legs.

EQUIPMENT

Flotation vest

STARTING POSITION

Stand in the shallow end, holding the corner of the pool with your arms extended in front of you.

ACTION

1. Lift your right knee up and to the right side of the corner, and touch the wall.
2. Return to starting position.
3. Repeat with your left leg.

IF LOWER EXTREMITY FUNCTION IS LIMITED

As you strain to lift up your knee, visualize your leg rising in the water and touching the wall. Imagine what it feels like when your knee touches the wall. Picture the peripheral nerves in your knee "feeling" the wall and sending the signal back up through the spinal column to the brain.

COMMENTS

Concentrate on each leg. As you raise one, step down with the other. Contract your muscles. The water will assist your movements.

VARIATIONS

1. Lift both knees up simultaneously, and return to starting position simultaneously.

Water Exercise 43

Circle Kick

PURPOSE

To improve joint performance, develop range of motion in lower extremities, and create a synergy between joints and muscles.

EQUIPMENT

Flotation vest

STARTING POSITION

Stand on the floor of the pool at the shallow end. Hold your left foot with your right hand in front of you. Extend your left arm straight out to the side.

ACTION

1. Turn to the left. Kick your left leg out to the left while still holding it with your right hand, using your right hand to push your leg. Simultaneously cup your left hand and swing it through the water to the right, turning your body to the left.
2. Lift your left arm out of the water, and extend it straight out to your left side, returning to the starting position.
3. Repeat these actions several times until you have made a complete circle.
4. Perform the same exercise in reverse.

Water Exercise 44

Side Step

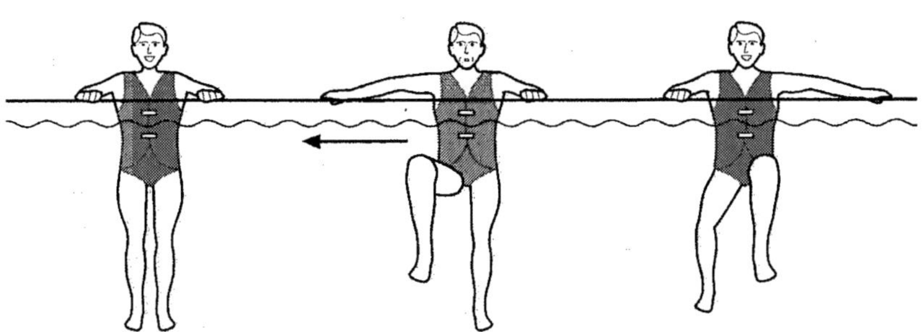

PURPOSE

To improve motor skills and strengthen lower extremities.

EQUIPMENT

Flotation vest

STARTING POSITION

Float in a vertical position facing the edge of the pool. Hold onto the edge with both arms in front of you.

ACTION

1. Lift your right knee up high, and side step to the right while swinging your right arm to the right
2. Perform the same motion with your left knee and step to the right, bringing your feet together. Simultaneously swing your left arm to the left and your right arm to your front.
3. Repeat these actions, moving along the side of the pool.
4. Repeat these exercises to the left.

IF LOWER EXTREMITY FUNCTION IS LIMITED

Visualize your legs lifting up high as you step out and move along. At first, most of your movement may be from your arms. Strain your muscles and attempt to lift your knees and move your legs.

Water Exercise 45

Horizontal Stretching at the Ladder

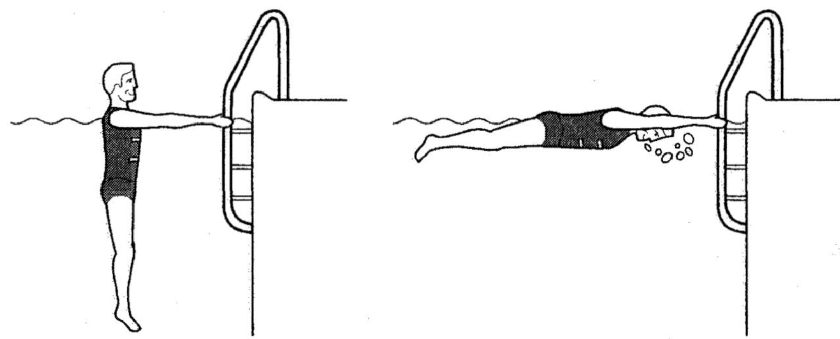

PURPOSE

To build alignment, flexibility, strength, and coordination.

EQUIPMENT

Flotation vest

STARTING POSITION

Float in a vertical position facing the ladder of the pool. Hold onto the ladder with both hands.

ACTION

1. Move into a horizontal position, kicking your legs. Hold this position, exhaling in the water, making big bubbles. Turn your head to your left or right to inhale, and exhale again in the water. Repeat 10 times.
2. Return to starting position

IF LOWER EXTREMITY FUNCTION IS LIMITED

At first, most of the movement may come from your arms. Concentrate on moving your legs. Over time, you should gradually feel the strain move down from your shoulders and into your back.

Water Exercise 46

Turning Along the Wall

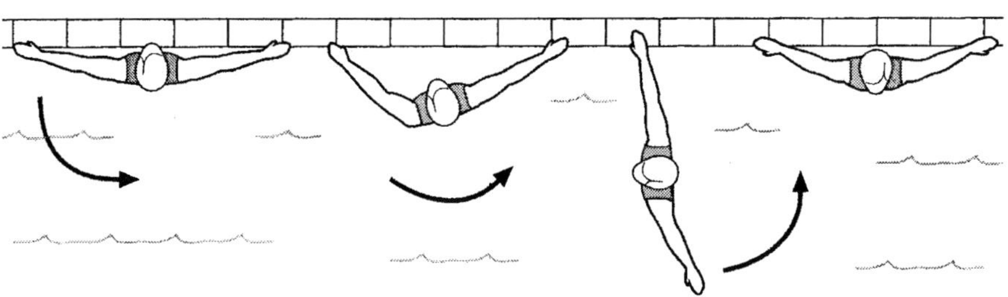

PURPOSE

To build muscles in the arms, shoulders, back, and stimulate the body to work in unison.

EQUIPMENT

Flotation vest

STARTING POSITION

Float in a vertical position. Touch your chest against the wall. Hold onto the edge of the pool with your arms extended.

ACTION

1. Push off the wall with your left arm, and bring your right arm straight out to the side of your body.
2. Return to starting position.
3. Repeat the actions to the other side.
4. Repeat the above actions, but continuing the turn, making a 180-degree turn, so that your back is touching the wall.
5. Hold onto the wall with both arms.
6. Swing your right arm out and across your chest.
7. Make another 180-degree turn, returning to starting position.
8. Repeat this exercise several times, advancing along the side of the pool.
9. Perform the actions in the other direction.

Water Exercise 47

Catch Your Knee

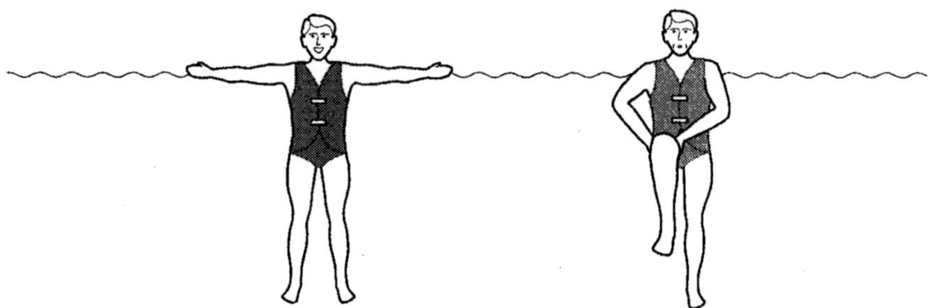

PURPOSE

To build alignment, balance and speed, and build strength in the lower extremities and back.

EQUIPMENT

Flotation vest

STARTING POSITION

Float in a vertical position with your arms floating at your sides.

ACTION

1. Raise your right knee up high. Swing your arms down into the water, grasp your hands under your thigh, and help lift your leg.
2. Hold your knee up high for 5-10 seconds.
3. Return to starting position.
4. Repeat with the left leg.

IF LOWER EXTREMITY FUNCTION IS LIMITED

This is an exercise for the mind as much as it is for the legs. Perform this exercise every time you work in the pool. Visualize your leg moving up and down without the assistance of your hands. You are training your mind to make the nerves and muscles work as you see your leg move through the water.

Water Exercise 48

Balance with the Board

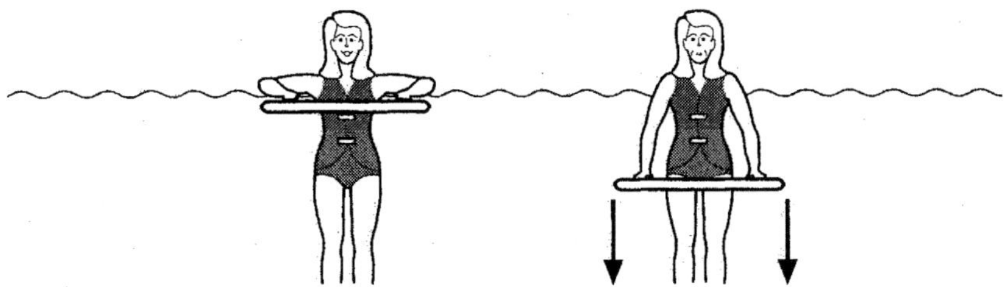

PURPOSE

To improve balance, alignment, and strengthens the arms.

EQUIPMENT

Flotation vest, flotation board

STARTING POSITION

Float in a vertical position. Place both hands on top of the board in front you.

ACTION

1. Push the board slowly under the water, extending your arms.
2. Hold this position for 5-10 seconds, maintaining your balance.
3. Bring the kickboard slowly back up to the surface.

COMMENTS

Pay attention to arms fully extending.

Water Exercise 49

Vertical Board Strokes

PURPOSE

To strengthen the upper body and help improve body awareness and alignment.

EQUIPMENT

Flotation vest, flotation board

STARTING POSITION

Float in a vertical position. Hold both ends of the board, with the board vertical at chest level.

ACTION

1. Extend the board in front on you. This will move you backwards.
2. Turn the board horizontal, flat on the surface, and pull your arms in.
3. Return to starting position and repeat the actions.
4. Perform the exercise in reverse, moving forward through the water.

COMMENTS

Maintain straight body position with your chin up. Head position is important. Breathe deeply when extending and bending your arms.

Water Exercise 50

Floatation Board Twist

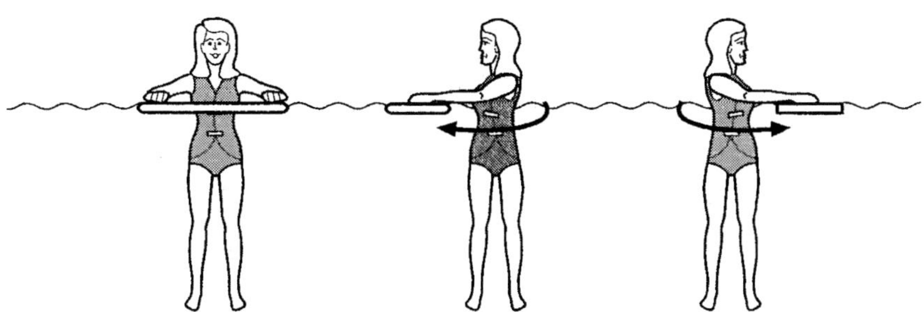

PURPOSE

To improve range of motion, balance, flexibility, and pelvis control.

EQUIPMENT

Flotation vest, flotation board

STARTING POSITION

Float in a vertical position. Hold the sides of the board with straight arms in front of you, with your hands flat on each end of the kickboard.

ACTION

1. Turn your upper body to the right, gliding the kickboard over the surface, while turning your hips and legs to the left. Pause briefly.
2. Return to starting position.
3. Repeat in the opposite direction.

IF LOWER EXTREMITY FUNCTION IS LIMITED

As you turn your upper body through the water, visualize your legs and hips turning in the opposite direction. Picture the signals from the brain going down through your nerves to move your legs.

COMMENTS

Keep your pelvis stable and legs straight.

Water Exercise 51

Push Behind

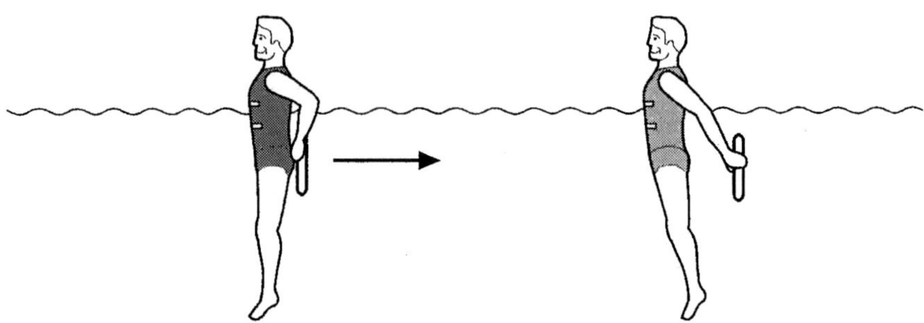

PURPOSE

To improve balance and stability, and strengthen arm, shoulder, and abdominal muscles.

EQUIPMENT

Flotation vest, flotation board

STARTING POSITION

Float in a vertical position. Place your arms behind your back, and hold the sides of the board vertically against your buttocks.

ACTION

1. Push the board away from you, extending your arms back. Hold this position for 2 to 3 seconds.
2. Return to starting position. Hold this position for 2 to 3 seconds.

COMMENTS

As you move the board, maintain your balance and vertical alignment. To help maintain your balance, focus your eyes on a spot in front of you.

VARIATION

Perform this exercise in a continual fluid motion without pausing.

Water Exercise 52

Prone Pushups

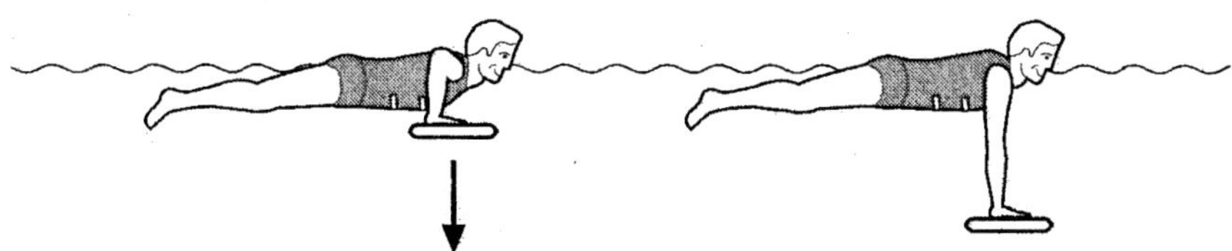

PURPOSE

To improve balance, stability, and strengthen arm and back muscles.

EQUIPMENT

Flotation vest, flotation board

STARTING POSITION

Float on your stomach. Position the board just under your chest with both hands placed flat on it.

ACTION

1. Slowly extend your arms, pushing the board down. Simultaneously exhale. Hold this position for 2 to 3 seconds.
2. Slowly retract your arms and return to starting position while inhaling.

COMMENTS

You can grasp the edges of the board with each hand for more control. As your balance and control improve, place your hands flat on top. Do not let the board wobble. Concentrate on keeping it horizontal as it moves up and down through the water. Visualize your back completely straight with your stomach in. Concentrate on your breathing.

Water Exercise 53

Pushups in the Corner

PURPOSE

To strengthen the arms and upper body, improve balance, and stimulate the legs.

EQUIPMENT

Flotation vest

STARTING POSITION

Stand facing the corner of the pool. Bend your arms at your elbows, holding onto each side.

ACTION

1. Push yourself up out of the pool. Extend your legs down straight.
2. Hold this position for 3 to 5 seconds, then return to starting position.
3. Perform the same actions with your back to the corner.

COMMENTS

Determine how many pushups you can do. Then take two-thirds of that amount and do that number of pushups two or three times. For instance, if you can do twelve pushups, do two or three sets of eight. Increase the number of repetitions as you build up strength.

Water Exercise 54

Leg Lifts from the Corner

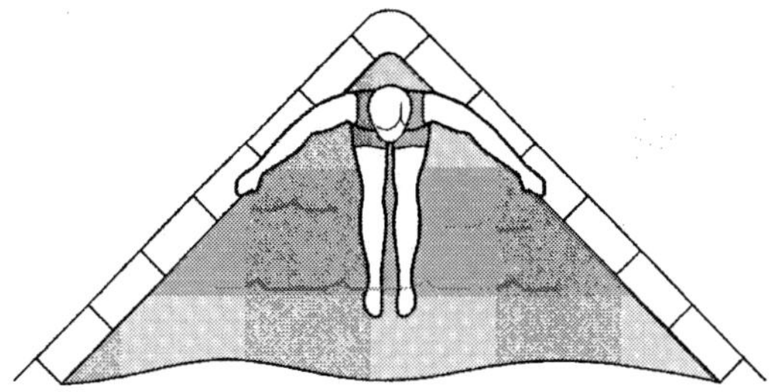

PURPOSE

To stimulate and strengthen the leg, abdominal, and lateral (side) muscles.

EQUIPMENT

Flotation vest

STARTING POSITION

Float with your back in the corner of the pool. Extend your arms out along the top edges of the pool.

ACTION

1. Bend your knees and raise them up to a 90 degree angle, while keeping your back straight.
2. Extend both your legs forward. Hold this position for 3 to 5 seconds.
3. Bend your knees and return to starting position.

IF LOWER EXTREMITY FUNCTION IS LIMITED

Visualize your legs stretching out straight. Imagine the muscles in your lower back and abdomen working together to help lift the legs and lower them. This exercise should be performed regularly, even when no movement is detected. Always picture your legs moving in your mind. At first, you may only feel the strain on your arms and upper back. As time progresses, you will feel the strain lower in your back and eventually in your legs. Don't give up.

VARIATION

Swing your legs up together, bending at the hips, keeping your knees straight.

Water Exercise 55

Backward Breaststroke

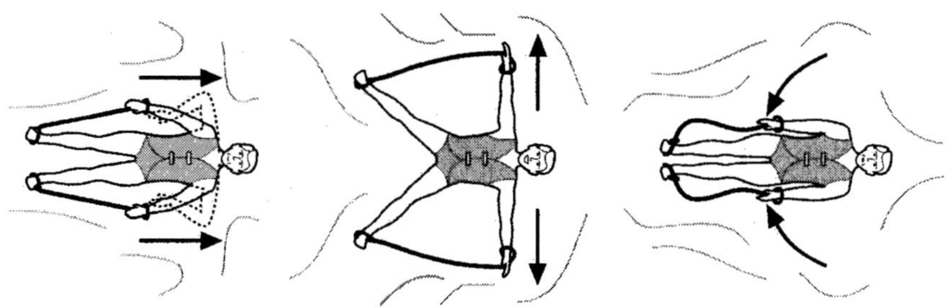

PURPOSE

To strengthen the upper body and stimulates the legs; improve mobility and motor skills.

EQUIPMENT

Flotation vest, two pieces of short exercise tubing

STARTING POSITION

Float on your back. Attach the ends of the tubing to your hands and feet. Keep your legs together and your arms down at your sides.

ACTION

1. Bring your arms straight out the sides, gliding them on the surface of the water. Simultaneously spread your legs apart while inhaling.
2. Cup your hands and return to starting position. Simultaneously exhale.

IF LOWER EXTREMITY FUNCTION IS LIMITED

In the beginning, your arms will pull your legs apart with the tubing. Picture your legs moving in your mind without the tubing. Concentrate on moving your legs. You are reeducating your body to work.

COMMENTS

Travel forward while performing the actions. Synchronize and coordinate the motion of your arms and legs.

Water Exercise 56

Swim with Short Tubing

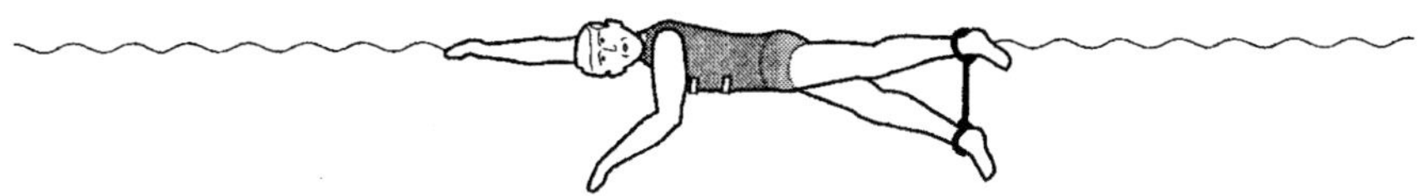

PURPOSE

To strengthen leg muscles, enhance motor skills, and build endurance and coordination.

EQUIPMENT

Flotation vest, one piece of short exercise tubing

STARTING POSITION

Float in a vertical position, with the ends of the short tubing in loops around your ankles.

ACTION

Swim the crawl stroke, focusing on your leg kicks. Stretch the tubing as you kick.

IF LOWER EXTREMITY FUNCTION IS LIMITED

Visualize your legs kicking in the water. Visualize feeling the exercise tubing and stretching it out as you move your legs. Visualize swimming in open water toward a nearby shore. At first, you may not have any leg movement. As your control improves, use the resistance of the tubing to build your muscles.

VARIATION

Perform this exercise using the backstroke, side stroke, breast stroke, and strokes of your choice.

Water Exercise 57

Tethered Swim

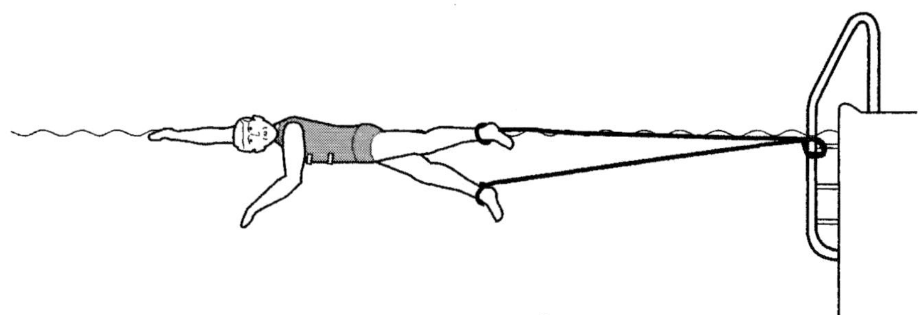

PURPOSE

To develop exceptional endurance and strength.

EQUIPMENT

Flotation vest, one piece of long exercise tubing

STARTING POSITION

Loop the exercise tubing around the pool ladder or stationary object, with the ends in loops around your ankles. Float in a horizontal position.

ACTION

Swim the stroke of your choice against the resistance, stretching the tubing.

IF LOWER EXTREMITY FUNCTION IS LIMITED

Visualize your legs kicking. In your mind, visualize swimming in a competition together with athletes on either side of you. Imagine feeling the exercise tubing and stretching it out as you move your legs. In your mind, coordinate your arm and leg movements.

COMMENTS

As you move farther away, the tubing will stretch, providing increasing resistance. Swim away from the attachment for 30 seconds to a minute.

Water Exercise 58

Pronation and Supination

PURPOSE

To develop balance, alignment, coordination, and flexibility.

EQUIPMENT

Flotation vest

STARTING POSITION

Standing or floating in a vertical position with arms extended forward.

ACTION

1. Swing arms forward while twisting palms up and down (pronation and supination).
2. Swing arms backward while twisting palms up and down (pronation and supination).

COMMENTS

Extend arms back as much as you can. Maintain body alignment and keep your head straight.

VARIATION

Walking while performing the actions.

Water Exercise 59

Speed Walking

PURPOSE

To develop coordination, endurance, and motor skills.

EQUIPMENT

Flotation vest

STARTING POSITION

Walking in water.

ACTION

Walk in the water quickly while extending each arm forward and backward.

COMMENTS

Work on coordinating legs and arms. Left leg forward—right arm forward. Maintain body alignment and pay attention to deep breathing.

Water Exercise 60

Vertical Crawl

PURPOSE

To develop balance, coordination, and flexibility.

EQUIPMENT

Flotation vest

STARTING POSITION

Walking in water.

ACTION

Mimic the crawl stroke, raising one arm at a time up and down. Simultaneously kick your legs.

COMMENTS

Maintain straight body position.

Water Exercise 61

Side Running (with Long Barbells)

PURPOSE

To develop balance, coordination, endurance, and enhance motor skills.

EQUIPMENT

Flotation vest, two long barbells

STARTING POSITION

Lay on your side. Hold your arms out straight on the surface of the water, with a barbell in each hand.

ACTION

1. While on your side, move your legs as if running. Allow your legs to turn you in a circle as you run.
2. Lay on your other side and repeat the actions.

COMMENTS

Maintain pelvic stability while in the side-lying position. Make wide strokes with your legs.

VARIATION

Run backwards.

Water Exercise 62

Breast Stroke (with Short Barbells)

PURPOSE

To develop balance, coordination, flexibility, endurance, and strength.

EQUIPMENT

Flotation vest, two short barbells

STARTING POSITION

Float in a vertical position with arms out straight on the surface of the water, with a barbell in each hand.

ACTION

1. Bend both knees.
2. Extend both legs forward, while simultaneously moving arms forward.
3. Spread your legs apart to the side, down, and together, while simultaneously spreading your arms to your sides in a breast stroke motion.
4. Repeat in the reverse direction.

COMMENTS

Maintain body awareness, pelvic stability and trunk alignment. Keep your legs straight when at the starting position.

Water Exercise 63

Pump (with Long Barbells)

PURPOSE

To develop balance, coordination, endurance, and strength.

EQUIPMENT

Flotation vest, two long barbells

STARTING POSITION

Float in a vertical position, with arms at your sides holding the barbells, and elbow bent.

ACTION

Walk forward while simultaneously extending both arms down and up.

COMMENTS

Keep your arms as close as you can to the sides of your body. Breathe deeply. Keep your body straight and look forward.

Water Exercise 64

Standing on a Long Barbell

PURPOSE

To develop balance, coordination, flexibility, and strength.

EQUIPMENT

Flotation vest, one long barbell

STARTING POSITION

Stand on the barbell, pushing your legs outward to create pressure toward the floats of the barbell. Hold your arms out at your sides.

ACTION

1. While maintaining a vertical position, bend your knees up, while moving your arms in front of you.
2. Push down on the barbell and return your arms to you sides.

COMMENTS

Keep your back and head straight. Bend your knees up 90 degrees.

Water Exercise 65

Butterfly

PURPOSE

To develop balance, coordination, endurance, strength, and enhance motor skills.

EQUIPMENT

Flotation vest

STARTING POSITION

Walking in the water

ACTION

Mimic the butterfly stroke motion with your arms, while walking in the water. (Butterfly stroke: Arms move up from the water, above your head, then swing back down to your sides, into the water.)

COMMENTS

Keep your body straight and your arms loose. Do not lock the joints in your elbows. Pay attention to your breathing, and remember to breathe deeply.

Chapter NINE

Land Exercises

Exercise should mimic and extend to everyday life. Land exercises are not only about running faster, they are about improving quality of life.

Land exercises are an integral part of the Burdenko Method. They are more efficient and most beneficial if done in combination with water exercises. When on land, you bring with you the benefits from water exercises, and when in water, you bring with you the benefits from land exercises. There's a synergy between the two environments, and this combination makes us feel better and be more functional on land.

As discussed in chapter 7, land exercises are not only for land. Practicing land exercises in water opens the body to accomplish movements that may not be possible on land. For example, if you cannot squat on land, squat in water. Progress to shallower water, then move onto land. When you successfully perform a movement in water, it is easier to work toward successfully performing it on land, because you already know it can be done.

Many of the exercises herein shown in a sitting position to exemplify that these movements are available to people of varying ability levels. *Most land exercises can be performed while lying down, sitting, standing, walking, or jogging.* Find the position your body accepts. You can be in a wheelchair, at the foot of a bed, lying down in a horizontal position, at your desk at work, or taking a walk.

SAFETY ISSUES

Consult with your doctor, physical therapist, or health-care practitioner before starting an exercise program. Ensure there are no health issues that prevent you from exercising safely.

- Before doing any exercises, be aware to have full understanding of what you will be doing. More advanced exercises should have a foundation in previous exercises.
- When attempting new exercises that involve bending and leaning, consider having an assistant with you in case you need help.
- Pay attention to deep breathing, and do not hold your breath while exercising.
- Do not exercise immediately after a meal.
- Do not continue an exercise if it causes pain.
- Check your blood pressure from time to time to make sure you are not placing too much stress on your heart.
- If exercising in a wheelchair, locate your wheelchair on level ground and do not forget to lock the brakes.
- Always examine your equipment for cracks or wear, and only use if it is safe to do so.
- Choose a place for exercising that has enough air, is not slippery, and has sufficient space to move freely.
- Temperature is very important.
- I do not recommend doing exercises when you have a fever.

EQUIPMENT

We must perform exercises both with and without equipment if we want to improve. We should always move from simple to complex. When we perform without equipment, we mimic movements with equipment, and that gives another step for improvement. Without equipment is the next step for progression. Some people start with equipment right away. That's not the best way. It creates additional stress if they do without equipment first. The combination of with and without equipment creates more variety and prevents adaptation. The body response is different with and without equipment, which altogether benefits the whole process of exercises.

With this in mind, we mimic life, and make life more diversified when we challenge our body with exercises. It adds to the flavor of life and human performance

Rubber Exercise Tubing, long and short "My gym in my pocket"

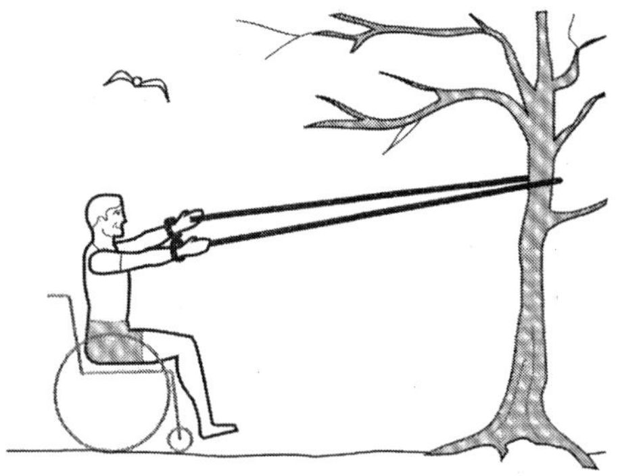

Figure 9.1 Exercising with tubing.

Exercise tubing provides resistance when stretched. It can be used in water and on land (see Figure 9.1). The level of resistance is easily and quickly varied by adjusting the distance between you and the anchor point. Tubing should be adjusted for each exercise so that there is only a small amount of tension in the starting position.

I recommend exercise tubing that is five-sixteenths of an inch in diameter, and made from natural latex rubber that is one-sixteenth of an inch thick. To get started, you will need two 2-foot-long pieces and two 13-foot-long pieces (including the loops on each end). Tie a loop at the end of each piece of tubing large enough for your hand or foot to fit through.

For exercises that use long pieces of tubing, tie loops at each end. The loop should be just large enough for your hand to fit through and fit snugly around your wrist (see Figure 9.2). Looping the tubing around your wrist secures the tubing and prevents it from snapping in case it slips out of your hand. Be careful not to wrap the exercise tubing too tightly around your wrist.

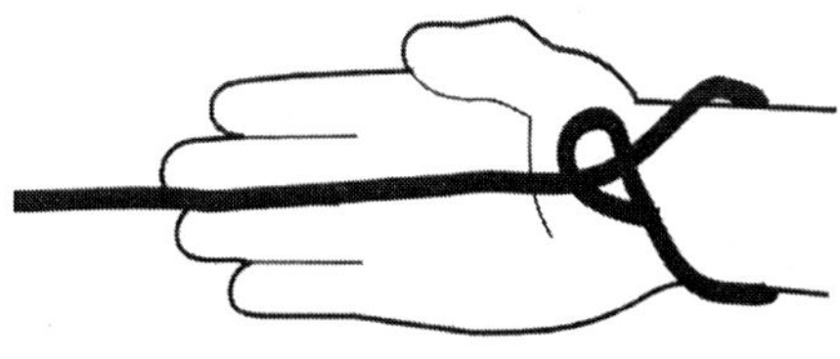

Figure 9.2
Looping tubing around hand.

For exercises in which the tubing is tied together in a circle, simply hold the tubing in the palm of your hand with your thumb on the outside. In order to prevent blisters, you may find it helpful to wear biking or rowing gloves to protect your hand but leave your fingers free.

Exercise tubing is useful in water in several ways. It can be used to add resistance and increase the difficulty of exercises. Exercise tubing is also extremely useful if attached from the arms to the legs. Arm movements will then move paralyzed or injured legs. These leg movements help stimulate nerves and muscle tissue.

I find exercise tubing to be more practical compared to the colored bands often used in physical therapy and in clubs. Exercise tubing is cheaper, very versatile, easier to grip, and easier to tie and untie loops.

Burdenko Belt "My gym on my body"

I designed the Burdenko Belt in order to find a way to reach as many of the body's 650 muscles as possible with each movement.

The Burdenko Belt also provides anatomically designed posture and back support. It also provides resistance for upper and lower extremities and all muscles in the human body. It does not restrict activities and can be used in water and on land. By providing assistance and resistance, it works your flexors and extensors, and balances the muscles.

The belt enhances dynamic movements because life is dynamic, and it creates further possibilities for developing the 6 essential qualities for everyday life and sport.

It can be used with every exercise in water and on land. It can be used during everyday activities, whether walking your dog or cleaning your house. I have clients who walk to and from work wearing the belt. It can be put under clothing and worn when running errands. I have children who wear it during school activities. I have athletes who wear it during every activity.

Figure 9.3 Exercising with the Burdenko Belt and half-roll.

Half-Roll

The half-roll is a piece of equipment made from Styrofoam that is very beneficial for posture alignment and balance. Start using the half-roll in a horizontal position, which is non-weight bearing. Progress to a sitting position, which is partial weight bearing. Then move on to a standing position, which is full weight bearing. Progress to dynamic movements. In this way, the half-roll is used to build up the body's ability. It is inexpensive, easy to carry, and safe. If your spine is sensitive to the round part of the half-roll, flip it over and use the flat part instead.

Burdenko Stick

The Burdenko Stick helps develop proprioception and hand-eye coordination, and is an excellent tool for developing the six essential qualities. It is five or six feet long and curved in the middle. This simple curve allows for variations in usage and the opportunity to easily make any exercise more or less challenging according to ability and development. One can step over the stick, jump over it, throw and catch it, hold it in both hands while moving, or any number of other exercises.

The weight can be adjusted by opening one end and adding sand or water. This increases difficulty, changes the response required from your body, and saves you from buying several sticks of different weights.

Exercise Ball

An exercise ball provides for a very efficient way to improve cardiovascular and respiratory conditioning, balance, coordination, and strengthening organ attachments. It is fun and challenging. It can be used free-standing or pushed against the wall. Choose a ball that is the right size for you. Your knees should be at a 90 degree angle when sitting on the ball.

Burdenko Water Barbells with Adjustable Buoyancy (Short and Long)

Although water barbells are designed primarily for use in water, they are also useful for adding a minimum amount of resistance when used on the land (see Figure 9.4). The light weight of these items makes them ideal for improving upper-body balance by holding them with arms extended. They provide a good transition from exercising with no equipment to exercising with wrist weights.

Figure 9.4
Water barbells.

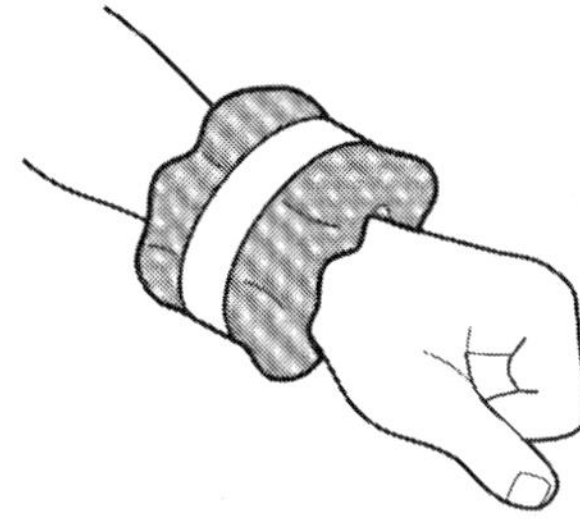

Figure 9.5
Wrist weights.

Wrist and Ankle Weights

Wrist and ankle weights (also called wrist and ankle cuffs) can be used to increase the difficulty of exercises (see Figure 9.5). As your strength improves, wrist weights can be added nearly any land exercise in this book.

SITTING POSTURE ALIGNMENT

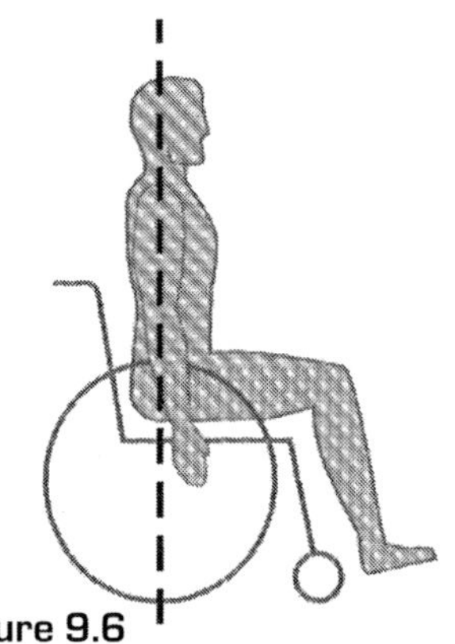

Figure 9.6
Proper posture alignment

When exercising while sitting down, ensure that you sit erect. Your pelvis should be under your shoulders (see Figure 9.6). Your spine should be long and straight, maintaining its natural curve, from your pelvis to the top of your head. Your neck should be vertical and in line with your spine, with your head facing forward. Your shoulders should be pressed back and down but relaxed. This position lifts the chest for deep breathing.

When Practicing Exercises, Remember:

- Think before you move
- Always warm up and always cool down
- Perform exercises at multiple speeds: slow, medium, fast
- Perform every exercise in multiple directions
- Do not exercise if you feel pain

Anne Barbeau's Back Story

Back pain, back ache—I'd heard these words hundreds of times, but until I had an accident when I slipped on some ice did I really understand how debilitating these ailments could be. The doctor's evaluation revealed a herniated disk and three bulging disks. Oh! How it hurt. I was unable to do anything, but lie still on my back and hope my muscles did not go into spasm. Both of my legs were eventually affected. My left leg was the most painful and the muscle on the outside of the quad was no longer functioning. I lost my reflex in my knee and the lower lateral part of the shin went numb. What to do?

Luckily, my husband Tom and I had run into Dr. Igor Burdenko in May 1992 when he was giving a clinic on the Burdenko Method in Waterville Valley, NH. Both Tom and I come from athletic backgrounds as players and coaches. So the opportunity of learning from someone of Igor's talents was attractive to both of us. Tom loved the exercises and I watched on and took notes as I was 8 months pregnant with our son. I did manage to get into the pool to do water exercises and I too was hooked. Even with a lifetime of experiences in sport and at an Olympic level, we had never come into contact with such training and rehab as the Burdenko Method. We both embarked in the program and we were thrilled with the results we were attaining. Tom began using the Burdenko Method with the athletes he coaches and became more and more involved with learning from Igor. He eventually became Master Certified in the Burdenko Method.

So in December of 2004, I had my unfortunate accident. I immediately called Igor and with my MRI's I was off to Boston to start my rehab. It did not matter that I was unable to place any weight on my left leg and that crutches helped me to slowly get around because I was still able to begin my rehabilitation in the water. I spent the next three days under Igor's watchful eye doing two workouts a day. Fortunately, I was on winter break from teaching so I could spend the time working on my recovery and learning the exercises. I week later I was able to return to work, plus, I continued my daily routine in the pool at our local Sports Center. Each day I noticed improvement. I progressed through my exercises all winter and was walking and feeling much stronger. Unluckily, in August, I sneezed in an awkward position and a second disk herniated (one of the original bulging disks).

I could not believe it, but according to the orthopedic who saw me this was not unusual. Of course, I was devastated. This time my left leg was not affected, but the right leg was from the knee down. I could not lift my foot and the side of the foot was numb. Another

MRI revealed an herniated disk, however, to the orthopedics' surprise it was another disk, not the original one. The original herniation was no longer a problem. I got into the pool two days after my injury and started again. This time my husband and I surmised that I had not done enough land movement. The Burdenko Method is both land and water based. The water reveals us from gravity and promotes healing, but we are land creatures and we need to complete our healing with land exercises.

Six weeks later, I had an appointment with a spine specialist. He looked at my MRI and explained the options for my treatment. He then examined me. Because I had religiously been doing my exercises I was able to do everything he asked me to do. He looked at me and said, "I don't know what you are doing, but keep doing it! You don't need me". I was thrilled.

I saw Igor several times after that to evaluate my progress and to continue with my recovery. I had a goal. We were working towards skiing again by spring. A good friend invited us to ski in Colorado at Copper Mt. for 4 days in March. I had never skied in Western USA so this would be a real treat.

I have been an avid skier all my life and two years without alpine and cross country skiing had been very tough. However, I knew the Burdenko Method and all my hard work would pay off. I followed Igor's instruction the letter and I was finally given the green light. What a blast!

I have since returned to most of my activities. I swim, alpine ski, cross country ski, hike, walk, kayak, drive my son to school and basketball practice teach school and swimming and garden. I continue to do my Burdenko exercises and have made them a daily part of my life. My husband and I are huge supporters of the Burdenko method as we have seen wonderful results and know it will keep us young.

Land Exercises

HALF-ROLL & BURDENKO BELT EXERCISES

1. Jumping Jets
2. Single and Double Knee Raise
3. Hurdles
4. V-Position
5. Sit-ups
6. Balance on One Leg
7. Squat
8. On and off

BURDENKO STICK EXERCISES

9. Wake-up Call
10. Billiards
11. Around the Body
12. Front Bend
13. Touch the Hill
14. Side Bend Lunges
15. Side Lifting
16. Catch and Squat

EXERCISES WITH NO EQUIPMENT

17. Arm Swings Out
18. Picking Apples
19. Push Downs
20. Shoulder Shrugs
21. Pushups
22. Neck Rolls
23. Arm Stretch Forward
24. Arm Swings Up
25. Diagonal Twist
26. Count to Eight
27. Boxing in Front
28. Boxing to the Sides
29. Body Stretch Forward
30. Stretch Around the World
31. Arm Extensions to the Side
32. Shoulder Raises

33. Arm Swings behind the Head
34. Palms Together
35. 5-Count Arm Raises
36. Arm Extensions
37. Stomach Roll
38. Tight Butt
39. Hip Moves
40. Reach Downs
41. Lower-Arm Raises
42. Diagonal Arm Circles
43. Arm Cranks
44. Arm Circles in Front
45. Arm Flutters
46. Twists
47. Push and Pull
48. Cross-Country Skiing
49. Lean Forward
50. Downhill Skiing
51. Clap Behind
52. Knee Pick-ups
53. Leg Kicks
54. Knee Lifts

WATER BARBELL EXERCISES

55. Arm Circles with Barbells
56. Barbell Lift
57. Barbell Twists
58. Barbell Grab

EXERCISES WITH TUBING

59. Curls
60. Triceps Extension
61. Arm Raise
62. Arm Circles to the Sides
63. Flying
64. Arm Circles with Tubing
65. Cross-Country Skiing with Tubing
66. Arm Stretch with Tubing
67. Pull Downs
68. Cross Your Chest
69. Hug Yourself
70. Breaststroke

Land Exercise 1

Jumping Jets

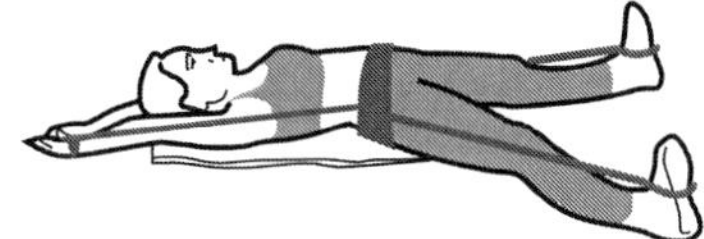

PURPOSE

To improve balance, coordination, strength, pelvic stability, and alignment.

EQUIPMENT

Half-roll, Burdenko Belt

STARTING POSITION

Lay on your back on the half roll with your legs together and arms at your sides.

ACTION

1. Move your arms in a circular motion above your head while simultaneously spreading your legs apart.
2. Move your arms in a circular motion back down to your waist, while simultaneously bringing your legs together.

COMMENTS

Touch the floor with your hands and feet. While performing the actions, stretch your ankles by point your toes downward and upward as you spread your legs apart and together.

Land Exercise 2

Single and Double Knee Raise

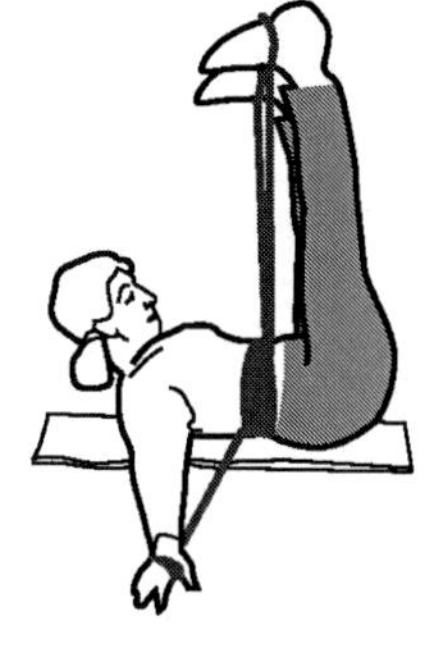

PURPOSE

To improve balance, coordination, and flexibility.

EQUIPMENT

Half-roll, Burdenko Belt

STARTING POSITION

Lay on your back on the half roll with your knees bent, feet together, and arms out to your sides at shoulders level.

ACTION

1. Bend your upper body up and forward while simultaneously raising one or both legs straight up.
2. Return to starting position

COMMENTS

While raising your legs up, point your toes down toward your head to stretch your heal, and tilt your head forward as much as you can. Keep your palms down, touching the floor.

Land Exercise 3

Hurdles

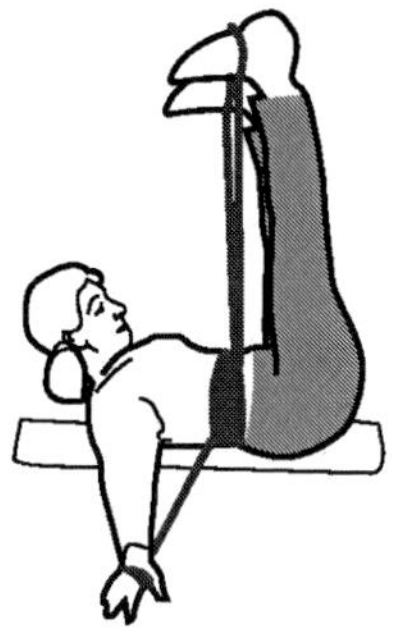

PURPOSE

To build balance, coordination, flexibility, endurance, and strength.

EQUIPMENT

Half-roll, Burdenko Belt

STARTING POSITION

Lay on your back on the half roll with legs straight and together, with both arms straight out to your sides, and palms touching the floor.

ACTION

1. Raise your right leg up while keeping it straight, while simultaneously raising your left arm and reaching toward your right foot.
2. Return to starting position.
3. Perform the actions with the opposite leg and arm.

COMMENTS

Keep your legs straight. Point your toes down toward your head to stretch your heal. Bring your torso and head forward when reaching with your hands. Coordinate arm and leg motions.

Land Exercise 4

V-Position

PURPOSE

To build abdominal muscles and flexibility.

EQUIPMENT

Half-roll, Burdenko Belt

STARTING POSITION

Sit on the end of the half roll with your arms straight behind you on the floor, knees bent, and feet close to your body.

ACTION

1. Extend one leg straight up. Hold for 2-3 seconds.
2. Extend the other leg so that both legs are straight up. Hold for 2-3 seconds.
3. Bend both legs at the knee and return to starting position.

COMMENTS

Maintain straight back position. Keep your chin straight. Point your toes down toward your head to stretch your heel.

Land Exercise 5

Sit-ups

PURPOSE

To build balance and abdominal strength.

EQUIPMENT

Half-roll, Burdenko Belt

STARTING POSITION

Sit on the end of the half roll with legs apart, hands behind your head, and elbows to the side.

ACTION

1. Extend your arms to the side, and bring them forward. At the same time, lean your body back (with arms forward).
2. Return to starting position.

COMMENTS

Keep your legs straight on the floor while performing the exercise. Lean back at different degrees. As you improve, lean further back until you are able to lie down on the half roll and return to starting position.

Land Exercise 6

Balance on One Leg

PURPOSE

To build balance, coordination, flexibility, and strength.

EQUIPMENT

Half-roll, Burdenko Belt

STARTING POSITION

Stand on the center of the half roll with one leg behind the other, and arms straight out at your sides at shoulder level.

ACTION

1. Raise your right leg with your knee bent at 90 degrees.
2. Straighten your knee so that your leg is extended and straight out (left illustration).
2. Return to starting position.
3. Raise your right leg with your knee bent at 90 degrees, then extend the leg behind you (middle illustration).
4. Return to starting position.
5. Raise your right leg with your knee bent at 90 degrees, and turn your knee to the right, and extend the leg out to your right side (right illustration).
6. Return to starting position.
7. Repeat the actions with your left leg.

COMMENTS

Do not lock the knee of your weight-bearing leg—keep it slightly bent. Point your toes toward your head to stretch your heal. Keep your head straight.

Land Exercise 7

Squat

PURPOSE

To build balance and strength.

EQUIPMENT

Half-roll, Burdenko Belt

STARTING POSITION

Stand on the half roll with one leg behind the other, with arms out at your sides.

ACTION

1. Step forward with your rear leg.
2. In one motion, bend your knees, reach to your toes with the arm opposite the leg that stepped.
3. Return to starting position.
4. Repeat the actions with the opposite leg and arm.

COMMENTS

Continue looking forward throughout the exercise. Keep the opposite arm straight out for balance. Move into the squatting position slowly.

Land Exercise 8

On and off

PURPOSE

To builds cardiovascular conditioning, balance, coordination, endurance, and strength.

EQUIPMENT

Half-roll, Burdenko Belt

STARTING POSITION

Stand on the floor with the half roll between your legs, and arms straight down.

ACTION

1. Jump onto the half roll, landing with one foot forward, the other behind. Simultaneously raise your arms straight out to your sides at shoulder level while jumping.
2. Jump off the half roll, returning to starting position.
3. Repeat the actions, switching the feet that land forward and behind.

COMMENTS

Keep knees bent and soft when jumping on and off the half roll. Keep your back straight and head up.

Land Exercise 9

Wake-up Call

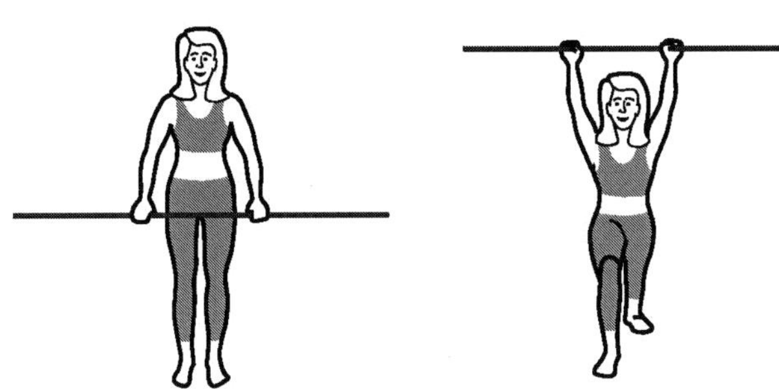

PURPOSE

To build body awareness, alignment, coordination, and flexibility.

EQUIPMENT

Burdenko Stick

STARTING POSITION

Hold the stick below waist level with both arms.

ACTION

1. Keeping your arms straight, raise the stick up above the head, while simultaneously stepping forward.
2. Return to starting position.
3. Repeat, stepping forward with the opposite leg.

COMMENTS

Pay attention to deep breathing. Keep your head and body straight. Be careful to avoid hyperextension in your back.

VARIATION

Walk while performing the actions.

Land Exercise 10

Billiards

PURPOSE

To build balance, alignment, coordination, and flexibility.

EQUIPMENT

Burdenko Stick

STARTING POSITION

Hold the stick below waist level with both arms.

ACTION

Move your arms from left to right in front of the body in a circular motion, at shoulder level.

COMMENTS

Keep your hands in place with a firm grip throughout the exercise.

VARIATIONS

1. Move your arms from left to right above your head, in addition to shoulder level.
2. Walk while performing the actions.

Land Exercise 11

Around the Body

PURPOSE

To build balance, alignment, coordination, and flexibility.

EQUIPMENT

Burdenko Stick

STARTING POSITION

Hold the stick below waist level with both arms, a little wider than shoulder width apart.

ACTION

1. Keep one arm straight while raising the other arm above your head.
2. Return to starting position.
3. Repeat the action, raising the other arm.
4. Progress to raising your arm and extending it behind your back, moving it all the way around your body in a circle.

COMMENTS

Keep your head straight and shoulders loose.

VARIATION

Walk while performing the actions.

Land Exercise 12

Front Bend

PURPOSE

To build balance and flexibility.

EQUIPMENT

Burdenko Stick

STARTING POSITION

Hold the stick with both arms wider than shoulder width apart behind your body. Ensure your palms are facing toward your body.

ACTION

1. Bend forward, while raising your arms in a circular motion behind, up, and forward, to straight in front of you at your ankles.
2. Move in the opposite direction, returning to starting position.

COMMENTS

Practice this exercise in stages. At first, practice extending your arms back and moving the stick up without moving it in front of you. As you progress, move it all the way above and in front of you.

VARIATION

Walk while performing the actions.

Land Exercise 13

Touch the Hill

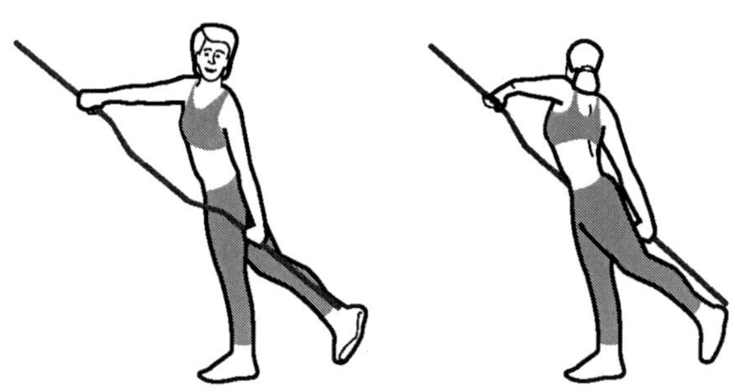

PURPOSE

To build balance, coordination, flexibility, endurance, speed and strength.

EQUIPMENT

Burdenko Stick

STARTING POSITION

Stand with your arms straight above your head, holding the stick shoulder width apart.

ACTION

1. Jump forward onto one foot while fully extending the other leg behind you, and twisting your torso to the weight bearing leg. Simultaneously touch the other heel with the end of the stick.
2. Return to starting position.
3. Repeat the action with the other leg.

COMMENTS

Land softly with knees bent. Keep your back straight.

Land Exercise 14

Side Bend Lunges

PURPOSE

To build balance and flexibility.

EQUIPMENT

Burdenko Stick

STARTING POSITION

Stand with one foot in front of you and the other behind you, with your arms straight above your head, holding the stick shoulder width apart.

ACTION

1. Bend your body toward the side of the front leg, touching the floor with the end of the stick.
2. Return to starting position.
3. Step forward so that the other leg is in front of you.
4 Repeat action on the opposite side.

COMMENTS

Make long lunges.

VARIATION

Walk while performing the actions.

Land Exercise 15

Side Lifting

PURPOSE

To build balance and flexibility.

EQUIPMENT

Burdenko Stick

STARTING POSITION

Stand with your legs shoulder width apart. Place one end of the stick on the foot, behind your ankle.

ACTION

1. Lift your leg with the stick.
2. Return to starting position.
3. Repeat with the opposite leg.

COMMENTS

Keep the leg straight out to your side. Do not lock the weight-bearing knee. Keep your head straight, looking forward.

Land Exercise 16

Catch and Squat

PURPOSE

To build balance, endurance, and speed.

EQUIPMENT

Burdenko Stick

STARTING POSITION

Squat. Hold one arm straight in front of body at shoulder level, holding the middle of the stick. Hold the other arm out behind you. Turn your head so that you are looking at the arm behind you.

ACTION

Toss the stick in the air, then quickly catch it with opposite hand. Simultaneously move the front arm back so that you are again in starting position (but with the front arm back and the back arm forward).

COMMENTS

Watch the hand behind you while catching the stick. Do not look at the stick. Create a rhythm. Squat lower when you catch the stick, and keep the stick parallel to the ground.

Land Exercise 17

Arm Swings Out

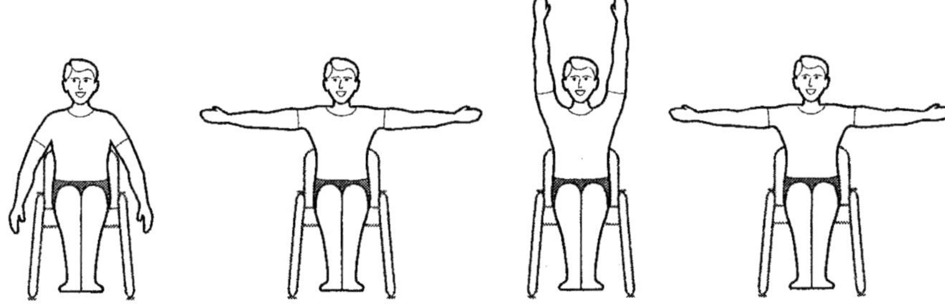

PURPOSE

To serve as a wake-up call for the body, stimulate the breathing system, and improve balance. To stretch arm and shoulder muscles and increase their range of motion.

STARTING POSITION

Sit straight or stand with arms down at your sides.

ACTION

1. Swing arms straight out to sides at shoulder level while inhaling. Pause briefly.
2. Swing arms up straight over head while exhaling. Pause briefly.
3. Swing arms out straight to sides while inhaling. Pause briefly.
4. Return to starting position while exhaling.

COMMENTS

Maintain body awareness throughout the exercise. Concentrate on maintaining balance and breathing deeply. Inhale through your nose and raise your chest, filling your lungs with air. As you exhale, purse your lips together and blow—like you would blow out a candle.

Land Exercise 18

Picking Apples

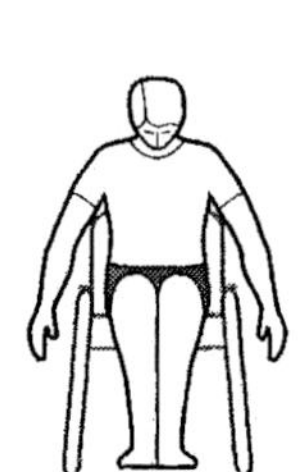

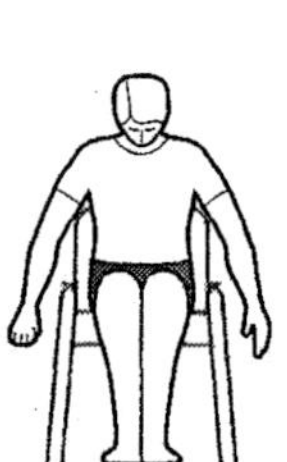

PURPOSE

To increase range of motion of the neck, shoulders, upper arms, wrists, and hands. To stretch diaphragm and rib cage muscles, and stimulate breathing. To stretch side, shoulder, and arm muscles.

STARTING POSITION

Sit straight or stand with arms down at your sides. Tilt your head down. Exhale.

ACTION

1. Bend your elbow, raise your right arm, keeping it alongside the body. Raise your arm straight over your head and stretch, spreading your fingers wide. Simultaneously tilt your head up, watching your hand, while inhaling. Hold this position for 3 to 5 seconds.
2. Bring your arm straight down. Close your hand. Simultaneously tilt your head down while exhaling.
3. Repeat with your left arm.

COMMENTS

Visualize picking apples from trees. Concentrate on deep breathing. Expand your chest as you inhale. Purse your lips and blow all the air out as you bring your arms down.

Land Exercise 19

Push Downs

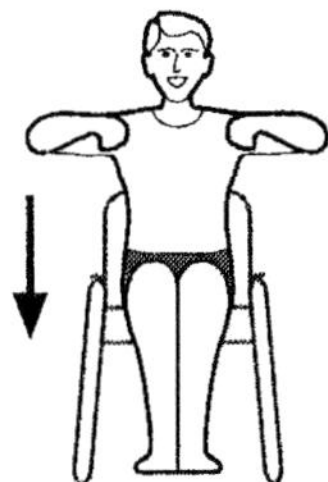
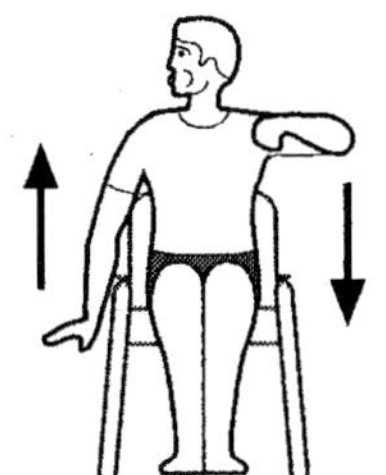
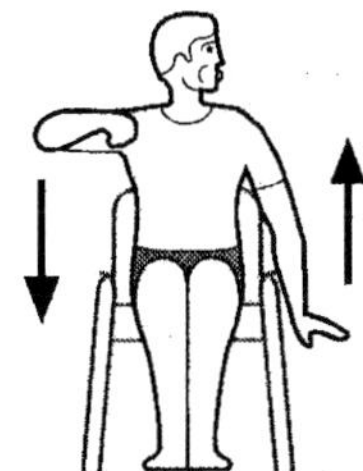

PURPOSE

To improve balance, coordination, and range of motion in the neck, shoulders, and arms.

STARTING POSITION

Sit straight or stand with arms held out at your sides at shoulder level and elbows bent. Keep your hands clenched in fists with palms down.

ACTION

1. Open your right hand and push your right arm straight down. Simultaneously turn your head to the right. Hold this position for two to three seconds.
2. Raise your right hand up to the starting position, clenching your fist.
3. Repeat with your left arm.

COMMENTS

Focus on performing this exercise precisely. As you move your arms up and down, keep your hands flat (parallel to the floor). Raise and lower them vertically in straight lines. Maintain your upper-body balance. Pay attention to your breathing and coordination.

VARIATIONS

1. As your balance and coordination improve, challenge your body by performing the arm motions simultaneously: when your right arm goes up, your left arm goes down.
2. Tighten and hold your arm muscles firm when you raise up or lower your arms.

Land Exercise 20

Shoulder Shrugs

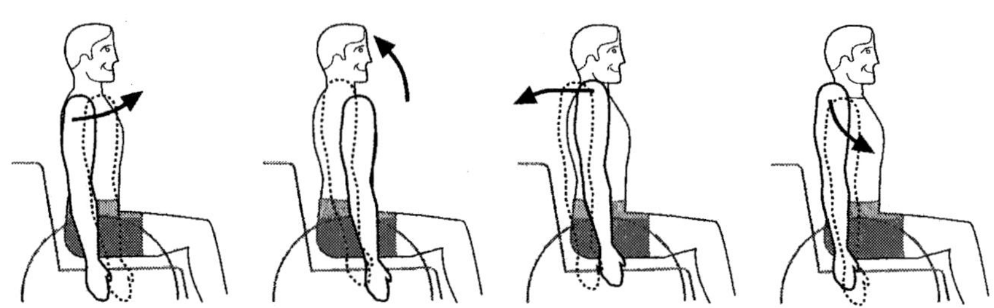

PURPOSE

To increase range of motion in the shoulders, reduce tension in the upper body and neck, lift the rib cage, and improve deep breathing.

STARTING POSITION

Sit straight or stand with your arms down at your sides.

ACTION

1. Rotate your shoulders in a forward circular motion.
2. Reverse, rotating your shoulders in a backward circular motion.

COMMENTS

Breathe deeply. Maintain body awareness. Stay straight, only moving the shoulders. Keep your arms relaxed and hanging limp at your sides.

Land Exercise 21

Pushups

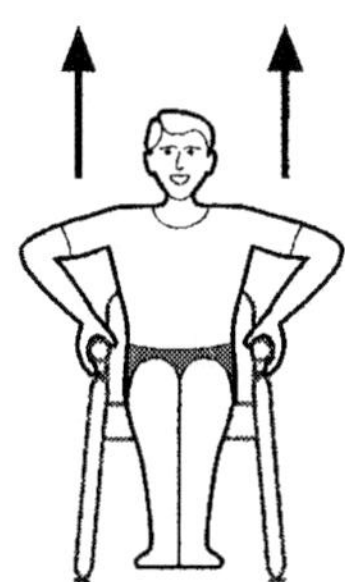

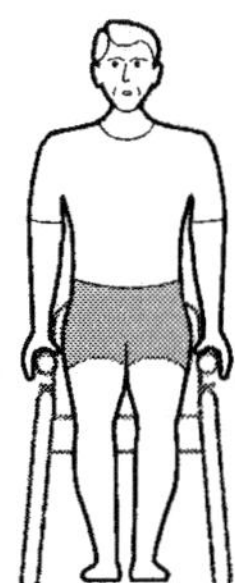

PURPOSE

To build arm and body strength.

STARTING POSITION

Sit straight in a chair with armrests. Grasp the armrests with your hands and inhale.

ACTION

1. Extend your arms, pushing your body up off the seat. Simultaneously exhale.
2. Lower your body while inhaling, until your bottom is just above (but not touching) the seat.

COMMENTS

Focus on fully extending both arms at the same time. Keep your elbows close to your body.

VARIATION

Each time you push up, turn your head in a different direction: left, right, up, down, straight ahead.

Land Exercise 22

Neck Rolls

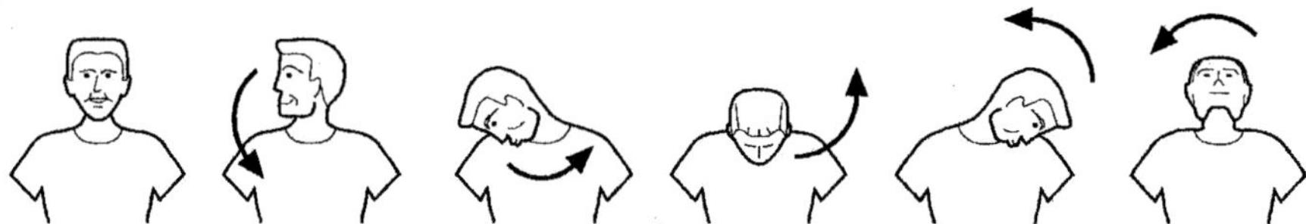

PURPOSE

To increase range of motion in the neck and stimulate breathing and equilibrium function.

STARTING POSITION

Sit straight or stand with your arms down at your sides, looking straight ahead.

ACTION

1. Inhale, taking a deep breath. Look straight ahead.
2. Exhale while turning your head all the way to the right.
3. I hale while rolling your head down and circle your neck to the left all the way around, bringing your head up.
4. Return to starting position while exhaling.
5. Perform the same actions in the opposite direction.

COMMENTS

Avoid dizziness during while performing exercise by moving slowly and being aware of your movements.

VARIATIONS

1. Instead of rolling your head down in front, roll the head back (carefully and slowly).
2. Perform this exercise with closed eyes.

Land Exercise 23

Arm Stretch Forward

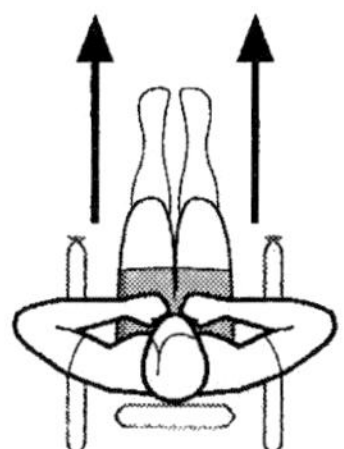

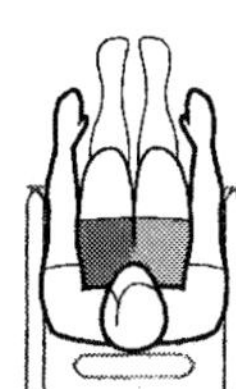

PURPOSE

To improve upper-body balance and range of motion in the shoulders, develop strength in the upper arms, and stretch muscles in the hands.

STARTING POSITION

Sit straight or stand with your arms out to your sides at shoulder level, with your elbows bent and your hands clenched in a fist in front of your chest, with your palms facing downward.

ACTION

1. Extend both arms straight out in front. Simultaneously open your hands and spread your fingers apart.
2. Return your arms to the starting position. Simultaneously clench your hands into a fist.

COMMENTS

When you perform, pay attention to maintain a straight position. If you cannot maintain your balance, only partially extend your arms.

VARIATION

As your balance improves, flex your arm muscles to build strength.

Land Exercise 24

Arm Swings Up

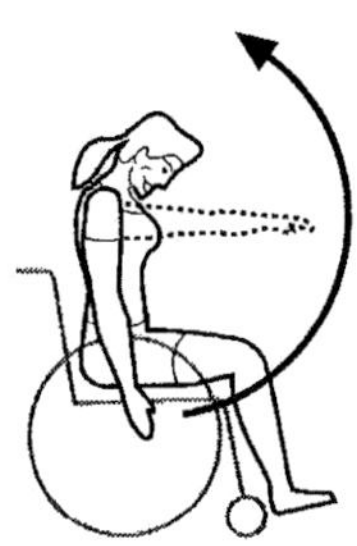
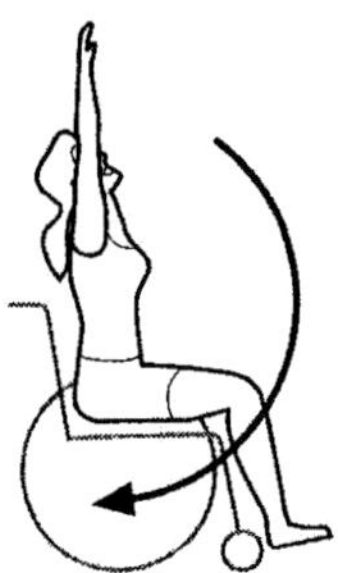
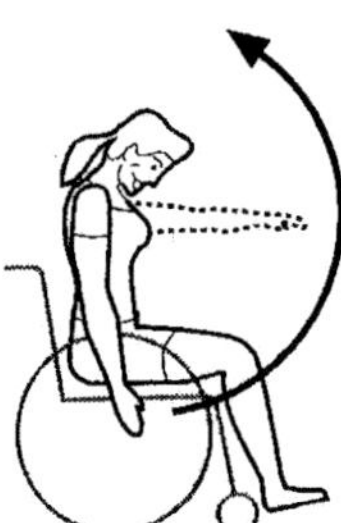

PURPOSE

To stretch the neck, shoulder, and arm muscles, and enhance motor skills.

STARTING POSITION

Sit straight or stand with your arms down at your sides and your head tilted down.

ACTION

1. Swing your right arm straight in front of you, then up over your head in one continuous motion. Follow the motion of your arm with your head, looking at your wrist. Inhale simultaneously. Hold this position for a moment.
2. Swing your arm back down. Again, follow the motion of your arm with your head. Exhale simultaneously.
3. Repeat with your left arm.

COMMENTS

Concentrate on breathing deeply. If you have difficulty maintaining balance, hold onto the chair or armrest for stability with one hand, while raising the other arm. As your strength and balance improve, let go of the armrest and let your arm hang down at your side.

Land Exercise 25

Diagonal Twist

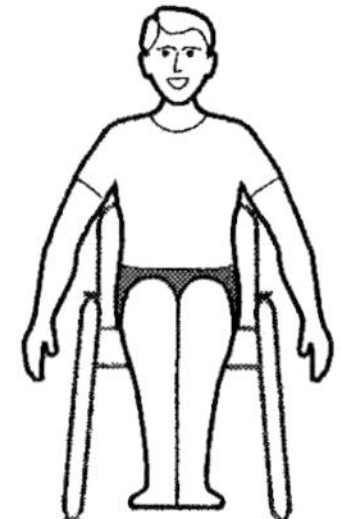

PURPOSE

To improve upper-body balance, stretch lateral (side) muscles, shoulders, rib cage muscles, and arm muscles, and increase range of motion in shoulders and arms.

STARTING POSITION

Sit straight or stand with your arms down at your sides.

ACTION

1. Extend and swing your right arm out diagonally over your left shoulder. At the same time, turn your head and twist your upper body to the left. Pause briefly.
2. Return to the starting position, simultaneously moving your arm, head, and upper body.
3. Repeat this action twisting to the right.

VARIATION

Move your arm in one continuous motion without pausing when your arm is raised.

Land Exercise 26

Count to Eight

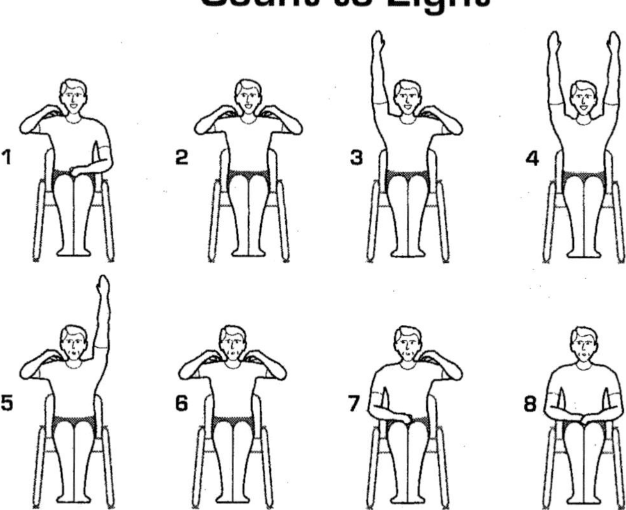

PURPOSE

To improve upper-body balance, stretch and improve range of motion in arms and shoulders, and improve coordination.

STARTING POSITION

Sit straight or stand with your hands in your lap.

ACTION

1. Raise your right arm keeping with your elbow bent out to the side, and put your right hand on your right shoulder.
2. Perform the same action with your left arm.
3. Raise your right arm up straight over your head.
4. Do the same with your left arm.
5. Lower your right arm, with your elbow out to the side, put your right hand on your right shoulder.
6. Do the same with your left arm.
7. Lower your right arm, returning it to starting position
8. Do the same with your left arm.

COMMENTS

Count out each step to yourself. Keep your chin straight. Try to keep your body straight. If your body is not stable as you perform this exercise, hold your eyes on a spot in front of you to help maintain balance.

Land Exercise 27

Boxing in Front

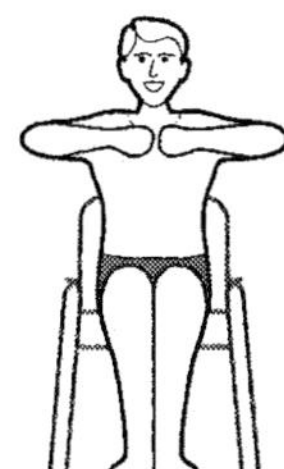 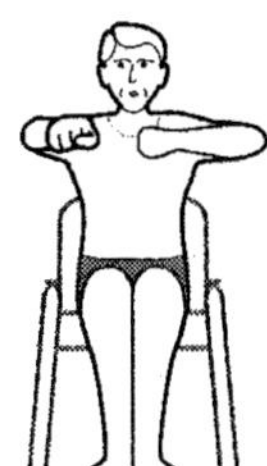 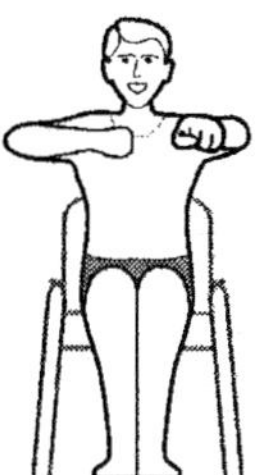

PURPOSE

To help restore motor skills and improve upper-body balance. To stretch arm and shoulder muscles, increase range of motion of the arms and wrists, and help breathing concentration.

STARTING POSITION

Sit straight or stand with your elbows bent outward at shoulder level, arms up, and hands clenched in fists. Inhale.

ACTION

1. Punch your right arm out in front of you, twisting your fist a bit inward (counterclockwise). Simultaneously exhale.
2. Return your right arm to starting position while inhaling.
3. Do the same with your left arm.
4. Continue boxing, alternating arm movements.

COMMENTS

Maintain a straight body position. Keep your elbows at shoulder level. This position lifts the diaphragm, making it easier to breathe. When you can do this exercise while maintaining stability, increase your speed.

VARIATIONS

1. As your balance and coordination improve, challenge your body by performing the arm motions simultaneously: as your right arm goes up, your left arm goes down.
2. Use different style punches: jabs, uppercuts, etc.

Land Exercise 28

Boxing to the Sides

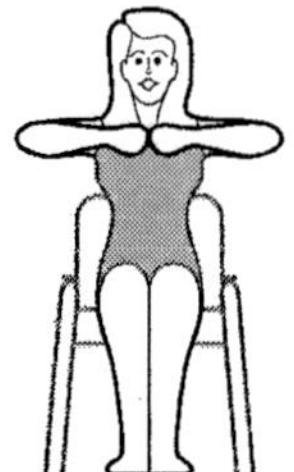
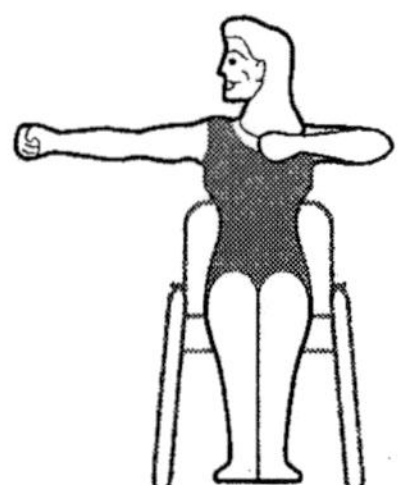
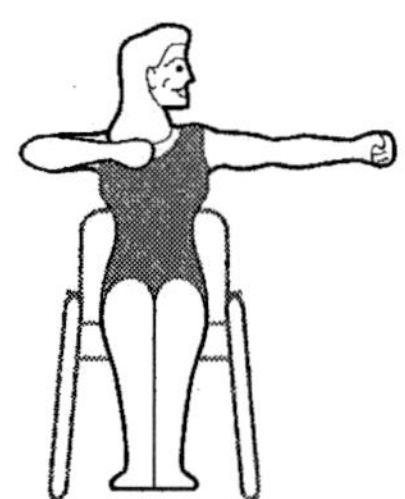

PURPOSE

To improve motor skill function and upper-body balance; stretch the side, shoulder, and arm muscles; increase range of motion of the neck, arms, and wrists; and help breathing concentration.

STARTING POSITION

Sit straight or stand with arms up and elbows out to the sides at shoulder level . Clench your hands into fists. Inhale.

ACTION

1. Punch your right arm out to the side while turning your head to the right. Simultaneously exhale.
2. Return to starting position while inhaling.
3. Repeat on the left side.

COMMENTS

Pay special attention to moving your neck without lowering your chin. Keep your head straight.

VARIATION

Combine "Boxing in Front" (Land Exercise 27) with "Boxing to the Sides," alternately punching to the front and side.

Land Exercise 29

Body Stretch Forward

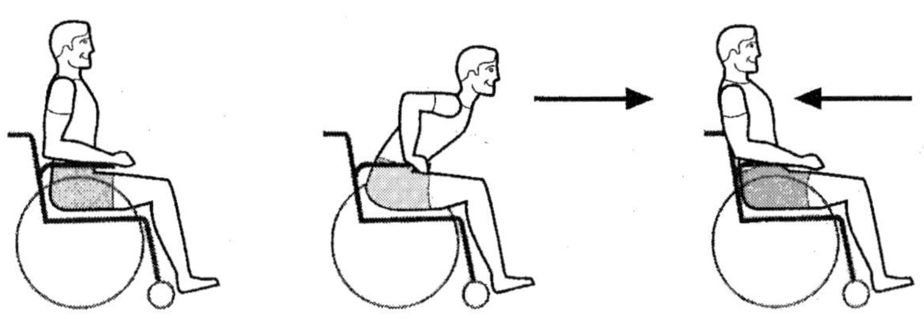

PURPOSE

To improve balance, flexibility and strength of back and upper-body muscles.

STARTING POSITION

Sit straight and hold onto the armrests of your chair. Inhale.

ACTION

1. Lean forward and stretch. Look straight ahead, keeping your chin up. Simultaneously exhale.
2. Lean back, returning to the starting position, while inhaling.

IF LOWER EXTREMITY FUNCTION IS LIMITED

Imagine that you are leaning, using only abdominal and back muscles. Reteach those muscles to work. Coordinate in your mind the motion of your body with the movements those muscles would be making. Stimulate the nerves through visualization to help the body heal itself. Pay attention to your breathing. At first, leaning will be controlled by the arms and possibly the back muscles. As strength improves, use your abdominal muscles more than your back muscles.

Land Exercise 30

Stretch around the World

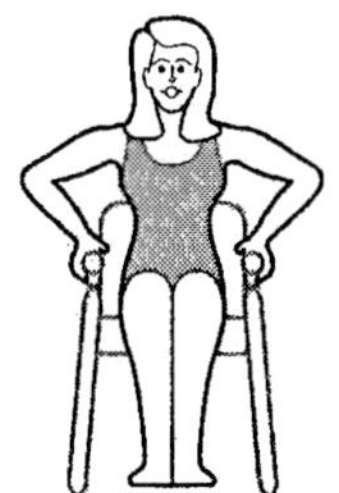
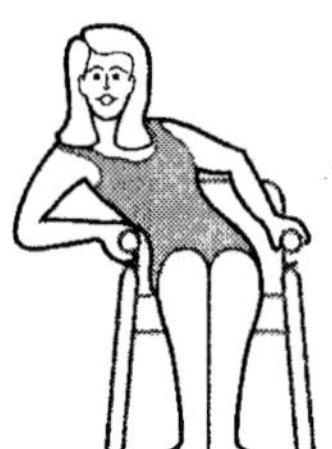
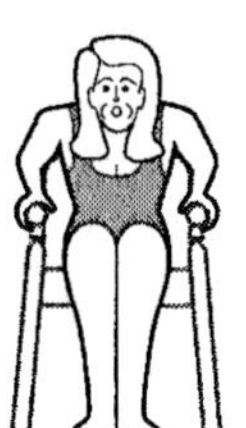
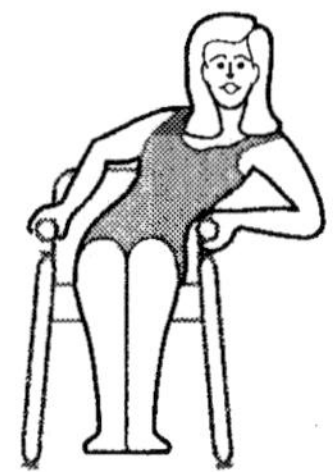

PURPOSE

To improve balance and strengthen the side, back, and front muscles.

STARTING POSITION

Sit straight and hold onto the armrests of your chair.

ACTION

1. Lean right while breathing in deeply. Continue looking straight ahead, with your chin up. Exhale.
2. Repeat the action leaning forward.
3. Repeat the action leaning left.
4. Repeat the action leaning back.

COMMENTS

Try to perform this exercise with and without the help of your arms. As you improve, increase the distance that you stretch.

VARIATIONS

1. Move your body in a continual circle motion.
2. Perform the exercise while standing.

Land Exercise 31

Arm Extensions to the Side

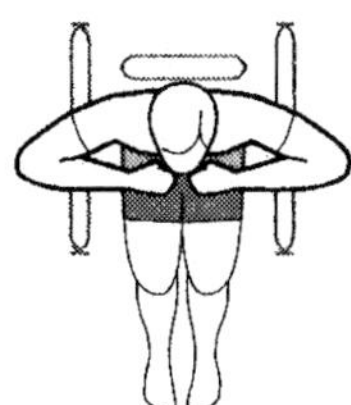
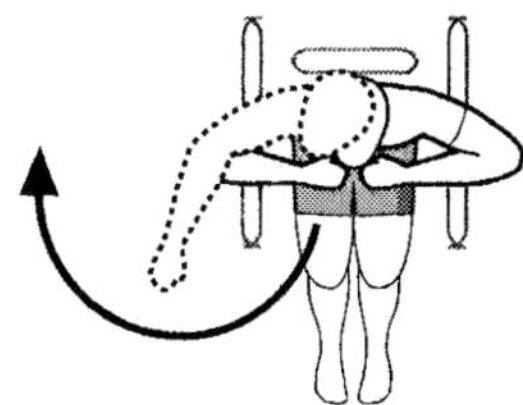
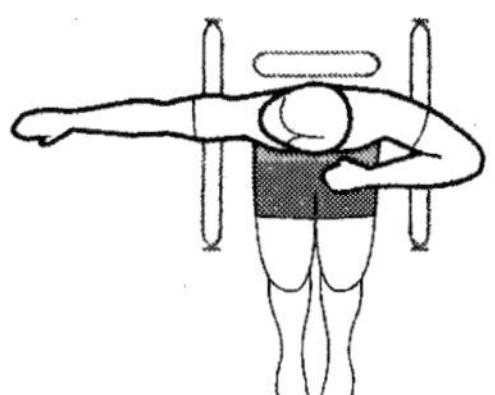

PURPOSE

To increase range of motion in the shoulders, neck, and arms. To enhance proprioception (the awareness of parts of your body in relation to each other).

STARTING POSITION

Sit straight or stand with your arms at shoulder level, elbows out to your sides at shoulder level, and hands clenched in a fist in front of your chest.

ACTION

1. Slowly swing your right arm forward, then out to the side, while opening your hand. Turn your head to the right, following the motion of your arm. Inhale simultaneously.
2. Slowly return your arm to starting position, while closing your fist. Turn your head following your arm, returning to look straight ahead. Simultaneously exhale.
3. Repeat the action with your left arm.

COMMENTS

If swinging your arm in front throws you off balance, keep your arm closer to your body as you swing it. Maintain proper body awareness. Concentrate on keeping your back straight. Keep arms straight and level. Keep elbows at shoulder level to raise your chest and increase your deep breathing.

Land Exercise 32

Shoulder Raises

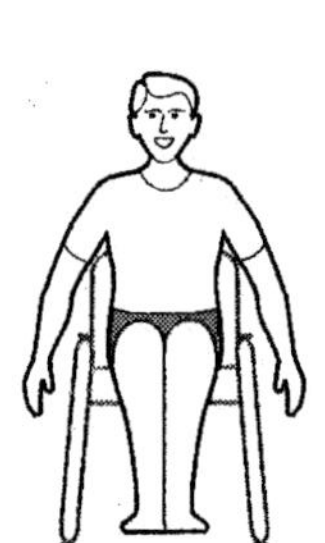
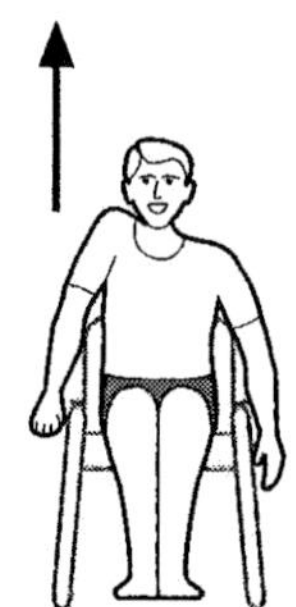
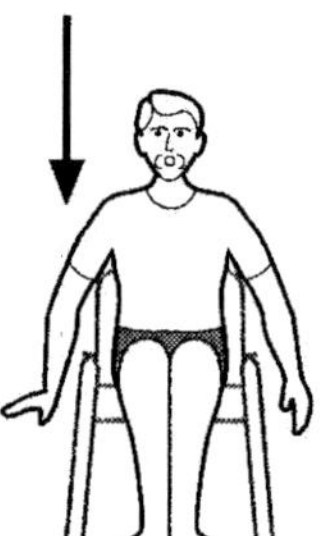

PURPOSE

To concentrate on body awareness, improve range of motion in the shoulders, and stretch the lateral (side) muscles.

STARTING POSITION

Sit straight or stand with your arms down at your sides.

ACTION

1. Raise your right shoulder straight up while closing your right hand.
2. Relax your shoulder muscles and drop your arm quickly like a dead weight, while opening your hand.
3. Perform the same actions with your left shoulder.

COMMENTS

Concentrate on body awareness. Sit up straight. Breathe deeply.

VARIATION

As an advanced exercise, move your neck up and down as your shoulder moves.

Land Exercise 33

Arm Swings behind the Head

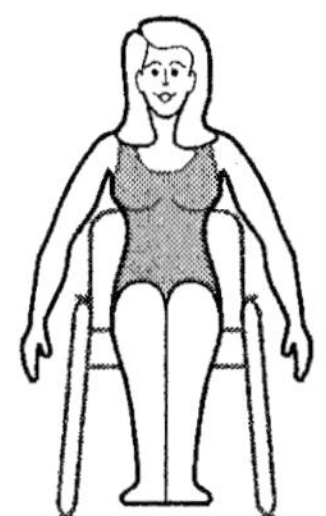
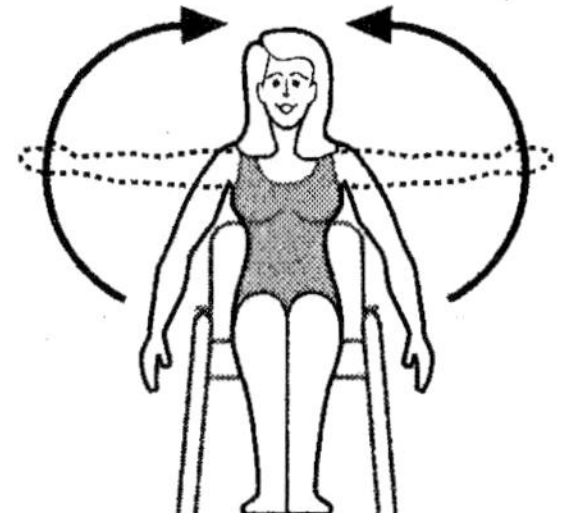
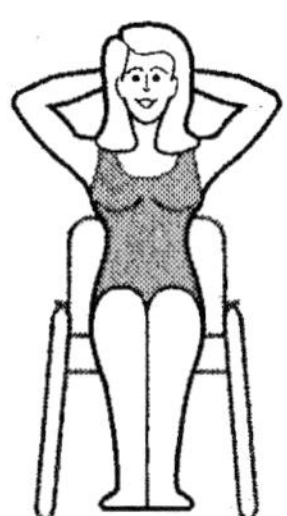

PURPOSE

To improve upper-body balance and range of motion in the shoulders. To maintain body awareness, improve coordination, and strengthen back muscles.

STARTING POSITION

Sit straight or stand with your arms down at your sides.

ACTION

1. Swing your arms straight out to your sides, then bend your elbows and place your hands behind your head. Inhale simultaneously.
2. Return to the starting position while exhaling.

COMMENTS

Move your arms slowly and coordinate movements of each arm so that they move simultaneously. Keep your back straight. Initially, it may be difficult to maintain your balance. Focus on a spot directly in front of you in the distance to help maintain balance.

VARIATION

Swing one arm at a time. This adds difficulty to balancing.

Land Exercise 34

Palms Together

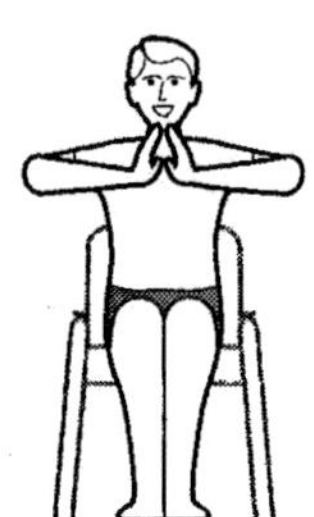

PURPOSE

To improve upper-body balance and increase range of motion in the shoulders, elbows, and wrists.

STARTING POSITION

Sit straight or stand with the palms of your hands pressed together in front of your stomach, with fingers pointing up.

ACTION

1. Raise your arms to shoulder level with palms together.
2. Raise your arms over your head, keeping palms together.
3. Return your arms to shoulder level, keeping palms together.
4. Return to starting position.

COMMENTS

Concentrate on the position of your hands. Maintain even pressure on your hands throughout the exercise.

VARIATIONS

1. Keep your fingers separated while extending your arms.
2. Separate and close your fingers while extending your arms.
3. Perform the arm movements in one continual motion.
4. Increase pressure pushing your hands against each other during the exercise.

Land Exercise 35

5-Count Arm Raises

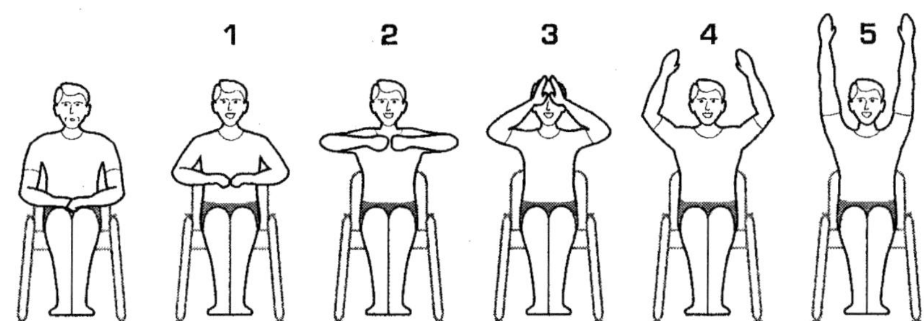

PURPOSE

To improve upper-body balance and increase range of motion in shoulders and arms.

STARTING POSITION

Sit straight or stand with your hands in your lap.

ACTION

1. Raise both arms just below chest level with elbows out to the sides and fingertips lightly touching together.
2. Raise arms just above shoulder level, keeping fingertips lightly touching.
3. Raise arms just above your head with fingertips touching together.
4. Raise arms slightly above your head with hands spread apart.
5. Raise arms straight up over your head.
6. Reverse the movement step-by-step, returning to starting position.

COMMENTS

Make each movement distinct, and hold that position for one full second. Concentrate on maintaining balance. Use your back and abdominal muscles to prevent yourself from swaying.

Land Exercise 36

Arm Extensions

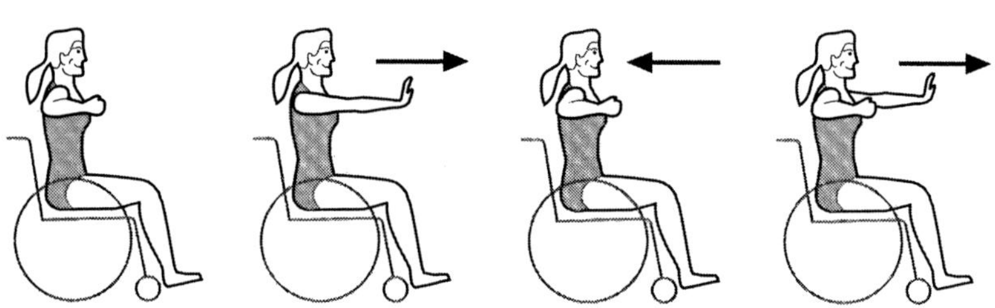

PURPOSE

To improve upper-body balance, stretch shoulder and arm muscles, and increase strength and range of motion of arms, wrists, and hands.

STARTING POSITION

Sit straight or stand with your arms up at shoulder level, with elbows bent outward and hands closed in front of your chest.

ACTION

1. Open your right hand, and slowly push your arm straight out, fully extending it. Hold this position for two to three seconds.
2. Return your hand slowly back to your chest, and close it.
3. Repeat action with your left arm.

COMMENTS

As you extend your arm, keep your hand pointing upward (as if pushing against a wall). If you have difficulty maintaining balance, only partially extend your arm.

Land Exercise 37

Stomach Roll

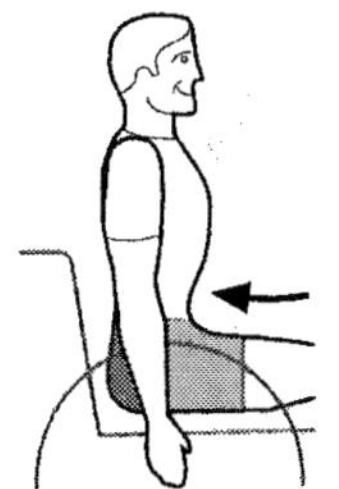
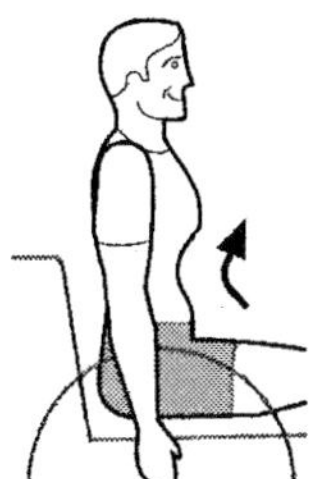
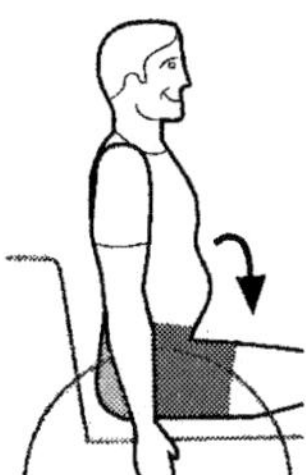
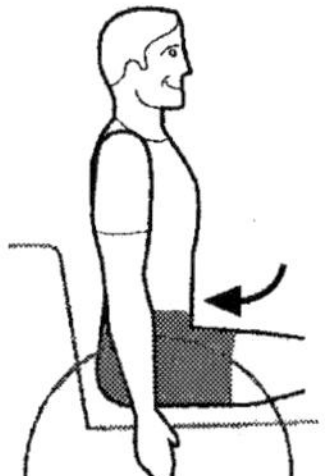

PURPOSE

To stimulate and tone abdominal muscles. To increase flexibility and strength in the diaphragm, and help stimulate peristalsis.

STARTING POSITION

Sit straight or stand.

ACTION

Roll your abdominal muscles in a continuous wavelike motion:

1. Suck your stomach in by contracting your abdominal muscles. Pull in the lower portion of your stomach first, and then pull in the top portion.
2. Push out at the top of the stomach, and then push out toward the bottom.
3. Perform two or three repetitions, then reverse the direction of the wave.

COMMENTS

This exercise is similar to a belly dancer's stomach roll. It will improve the function of your gastrointestinal system. Perform this exercise several times each day. At first, you may not have any control of your abdominal movements. Keep practicing. Eventually it will produce results.

Land Exercise 38

Tight Butt

Use your imagination

PURPOSE

To build the muscles at the base of the spine by strengthening the muscles of the buttocks (the glutei).

STARTING POSITION

Sit straight or stand.

ACTION

1. Tighten the buttocks by contracting the gluteal muscles.
2. Hold the muscles tight for five to eight seconds.
3. Relax the muscles.

COMMENTS

The gluteus maximus (the largest gluteal muscle) is one of the largest muscles in the human body. Perform sets of repetitions of this exercise several times a day, speeding up or slowing down the exercise by changing the length of time you hold the contraction. This will build the muscles and restore nerve supply for these muscles. As you gain control, hold the contraction for ten to fifteen seconds.

Land Exercise 39

Hip Moves

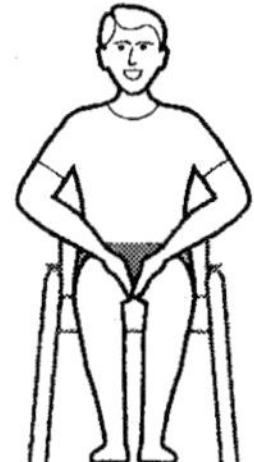
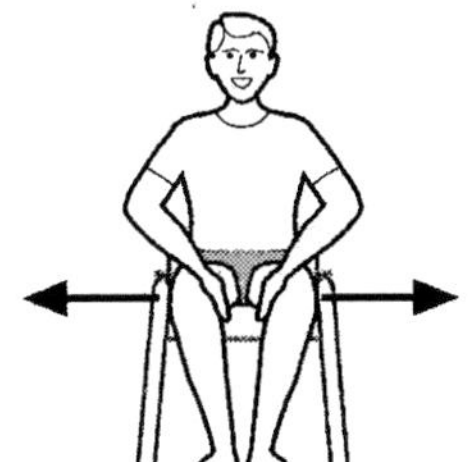
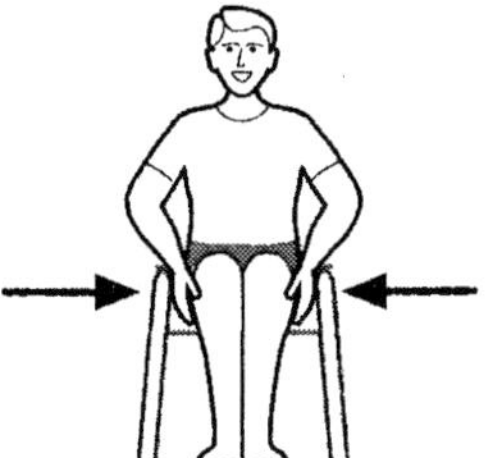

PURPOSE

This exercise is geared toward people who have lost movement in their lower extremities. It stretches the lateral (side) leg muscles (the hip abductors and hip adductors), and stimulates nerves and muscles in the upper legs.

STARTING POSITION

Sit straight with your hands between your knees.

ACTION

1. Spread your knees apart with your hands, visualizing that the action is being done by the legs and engaging as much of the leg muscles as possible. Simultaneously inhale deeply.
2. Put your hands on the outside of your knees and push your legs together so the knees touch, again engaging as much of the leg muscles as possible. Simultaneously exhale deeply.

MINDSET

Visualize your legs moving without the help of your hands. Strain to move your legs, stimulating the nerves and muscles to wake up.

VARIATION

Try placing your hands on your thighs and pushing your legs together and pulling them apart.

Land Exercise 40

Reach Downs

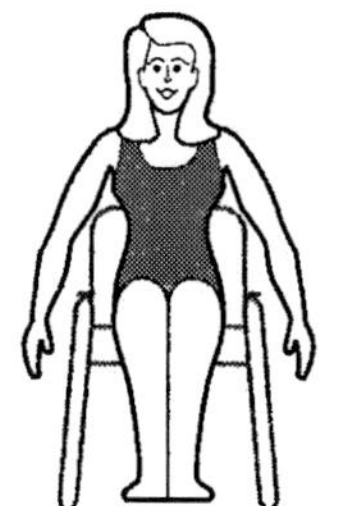
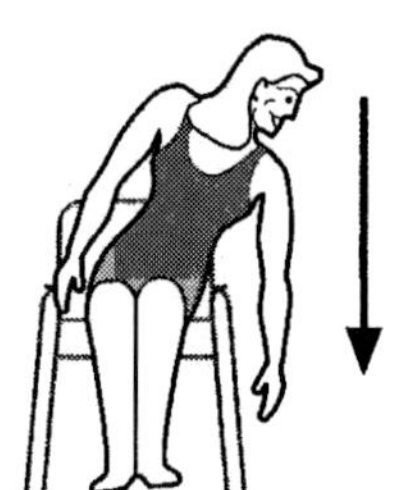
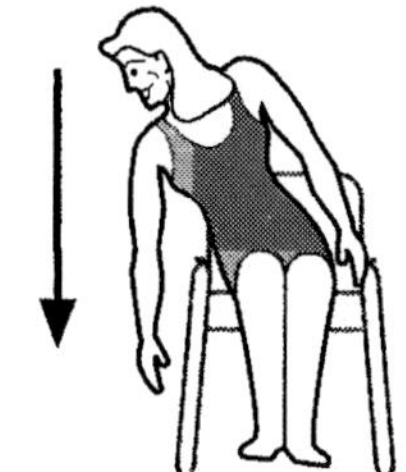

PURPOSE

To improve upper-body balance, stretch and strengthen the shoulder, back, and lateral (side) muscles.

STARTING POSITION

Sit straight or stand with your arms down at your sides. Inhale.

ACTION

1. Lean to the left and extend your left arm straight down. Point your head down, looking at your left hand. At the same time, raise your right shoulder up high. Let your right arm hang loose. Exhale simultaneously.
2. Return to the starting position while inhaling.
3. Repeat this action in the opposite direction.

COMMENTS

If you have limited upper-body strength, lean down only a short distance. Use the momentum of dropping your shoulder to help you sit up. Proceed slowly, stretching out the muscles. As you improve, lean down further.

Land Exercise 41

Lower-Arm Raises

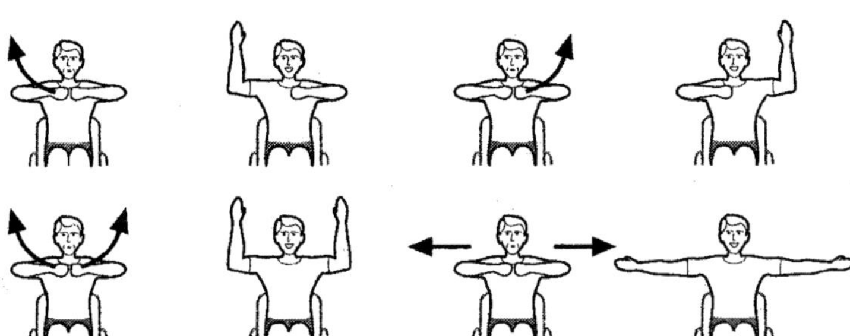

PURPOSE

To help restore motor skills. To strengthen arm muscles, improve upper-body balance and coordination, and increase range of motion in the shoulders, elbows, wrists, and hands.

STARTING POSITION

Sit straight or stand with your arms held up at shoulder level, elbows bent outward, and hands closed in front of your chest.

ACTION

1. Raise your right forearm, keeping your elbow in place at shoulder level, while opening your hand.
2. Return to starting position.
3. Raise your left forearm, keeping your elbow in place at shoulder level, while opening your hand.
4. Return to the starting position.
5. Raise both forearms, keeping elbows in place at shoulder level, while opening your hands.
6. Return to starting position.
7. Extend both arms straight out to the sides at shoulder level, while opening your hands.
8. Return to the starting position.

COMMENTS

Maintain body awareness while doing this exercise. Pay special attention to coordination. Be sure to fully extend your arms, wrists, and fingers.

Land Exercise 42

Diagonal Arm Circles

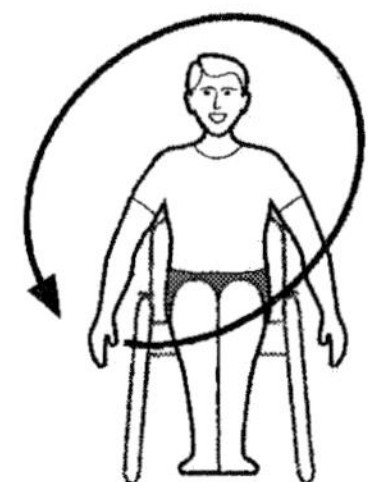

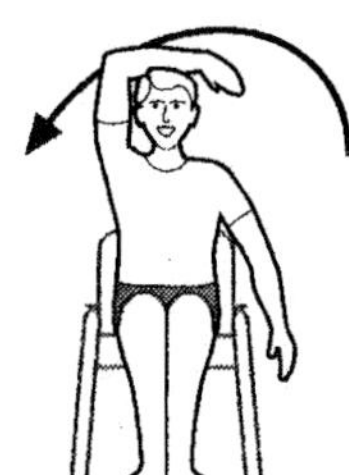

PURPOSE

To improve upper-body balance and increase range of motion in the shoulders.

STARTING POSITION

Sit straight or stand with arms down at your sides.

ACTION

Swing your right arm in a large diagonal circle:

1. Raise your right arm diagonally across your body in front of you.
2. Sweep your arm around in a large circle, raising it straight up, extending it out to the right, and returning your arm to starting position.
3. Perform several repetitions, then repeat with your left arm.

COMMENTS

Concentrate on balance. Keep your body straight as your arm moves. At first you may need to move very slowly in order to maintain stability.

VARIATIONS

1. Circle your arms in reverse.
2. While performing the movements, open and close your hand.

Land Exercise 43

Arm Cranks

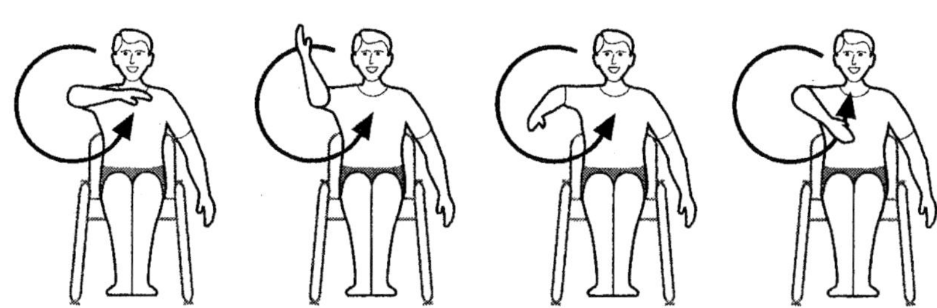

PURPOSE

To improve body balance and increase range of motion in the arms.

STARTING POSITION

Sit straight or stand with your left arm down at your side, and your right arm raised to shoulder level, with your elbow bent outward and forearm across your chest.

ACTION

1. Rotate your right forearm around in circles, pivoting at the elbow and keeping your upper arm out straight.
2. Perform several circular motions, then switch sides and repeat with the left arm.

COMMENTS

If you have difficulty maintaining balance at first, you can provide support with your unoccupied hand by hold on to your chair or a wall if you are standing. As your balance improves, let your other arm hang down at your side.

Land Exercise 44

Arm Circles in Front

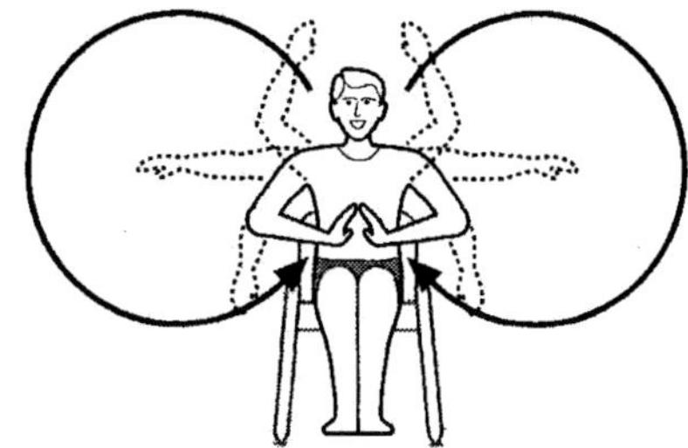

PURPOSE

To improve upper-body balance and speed, and increase range of motion in the neck, shoulders, and arms.

STARTING POSITION

Sit straight or stand with your arms at chest level, palms together in front, and fingers pointing upward.

ACTION

Swing your arms in large circles in opposite directions.

1. Bring your hands up to eye level, then raise your arms up over your head and then straight out to the sides.
2. As you lower your arms, point your hands down.
3. As you bring your arms back to the center, bend your elbows, and bring your hands back together.
4. Make circles in both directions. When reversing direction, place the backs of your hands together in front, with your fingers pointing down; then move your hands down, and circle out to the sides.

COMMENTS

As your hands go up, tilt your head back. As your hands go down, tilt your head down. Ensure you are breathing deeply.

Land Exercise 45

Arm Flutters

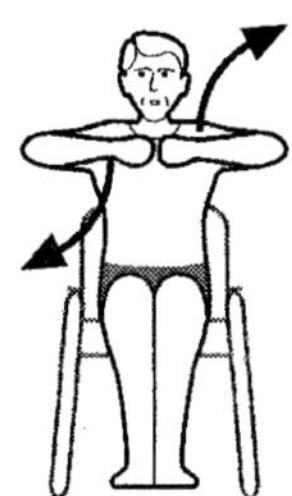 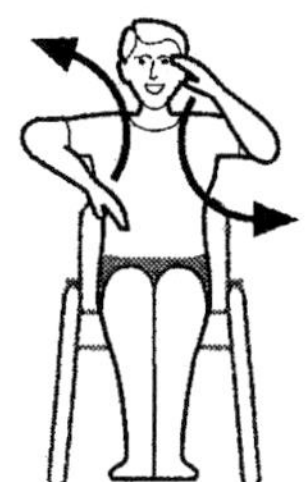 

PURPOSE

To improve balance and strengthen the shoulders, lower back, and abdominal muscles.

STARTING POSITION

Sit straight or stand with your arms held up at shoulder level and elbows bent outward, with hands closed in front of your chest.

ACTION

1. Pivoting at the elbows, rotate your arms 45 degrees up and down. Tilt one arm up as the other arm tilts down.
2. Continue fluttering your arms and slowly extend them out straight in front of you as you move them. Open and close your hands.
3. Continue fluttering your arms, and slowly return to the starting position.

COMMENTS

If you are not able to maintain balance, keep your arms in close to your chest. As you improve, extend your arms out farther.

Land Exercise 46

Twists

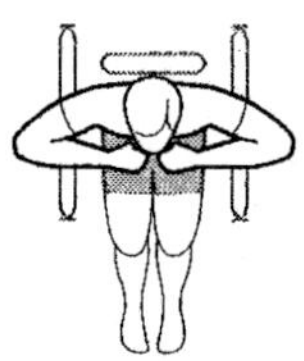

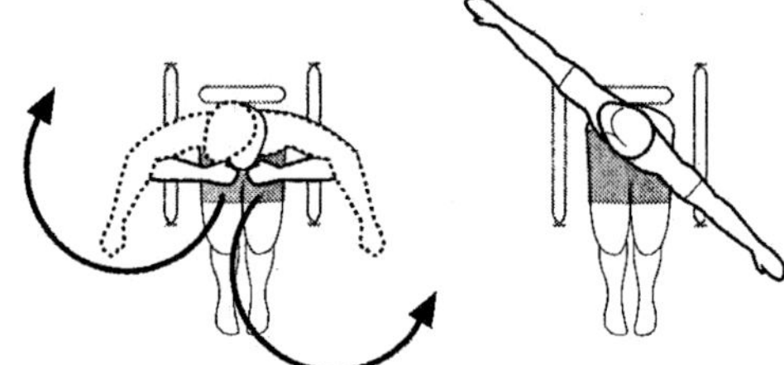

PURPOSE

To improve mobility and balance. To stretch the shoulder and lateral (side) muscles.

STARTING POSITION

Sit straight or stand with your arms at shoulder level, elbows bent out to the sides, and hands closed in front of your chest.

ACTION

1. Extend your arms straight out to the sides while opening your hands, and twist your body to the left while turning your head to the left. Hold this position for three to five seconds.
2. Return to starting position.
3. Repeat this action, turning and twisting to the right.

COMMENTS

Maintain body awareness while doing this exercise. Coordinate your arm movements with your twists. Pay attention to deep breathing. Keep your elbows at shoulder level, while lifting your diaphragm.

Land Exercise 47

Push and Pull

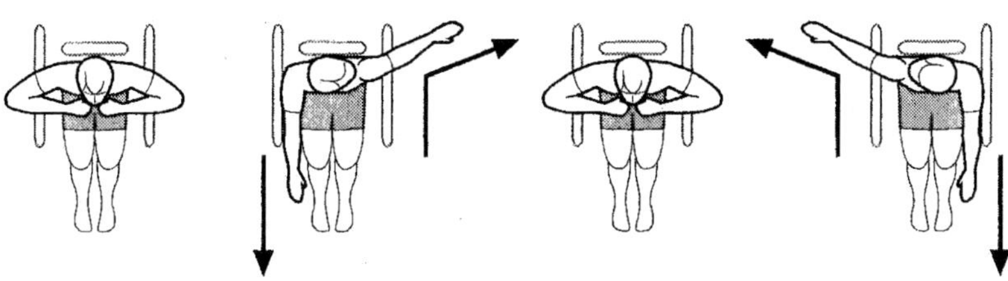

PURPOSE

To improve balance and increase range of motion in shoulder and arm muscles, and build strength in neck muscles.

STARTING POSITION

Sit straight or stand with your arms at shoulder level, elbows bent out to the sides, and hands closed in front of your chest.

ACTION

1. Slowly extend your right arm straight out in front of you with your hand forward and open, as if pushing against a wall. At the same time, turn your head to the left, pull back with your left arm and extend it out behind you.
2. Return to starting position.
3. Repeat this exercise with opposite arms.

COMMENTS

As you reach one arm behind you, twist your body. Perform this exercise slowly. Focus on moving the body, arm and neck simultaneously.

Land Exercise 48

Cross-Country Skiing

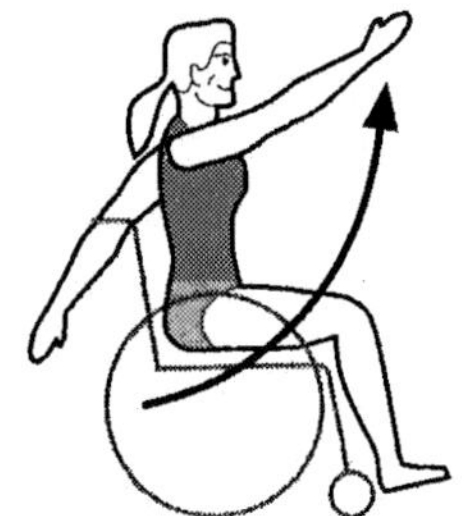

PURPOSE

To improve balance, coordination, and cardiovascular conditioning, and stretch the shoulder and arm muscles.

STARTING POSITION

Sit straight or stand with your left arm extended straight out in front of you, just above your head. Extend your right arm behind you, pointing down. Pretend you are gripping a ski pole in each hand and keep both hands clenched in fists.

ACTION

1. Keeping your arms straight, swing your left arm down and behind you, while swinging your right arm up in front.
2. Push your right arm down and back and your left arm forward and up.

COMMENTS

Keep your eyes on an object or an imaginary point straight ahead of you to maintain balance. Get into a rhythm of swinging, together with deep breathing.

Land Exercise 49

Lean Forward

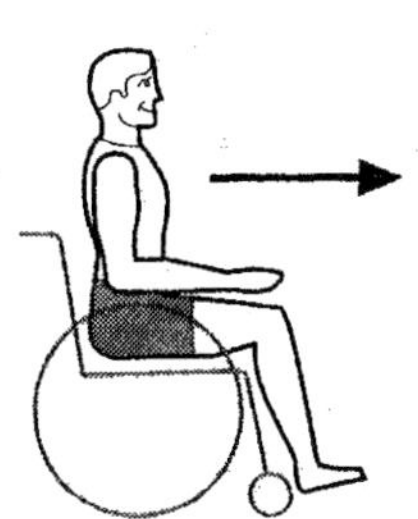
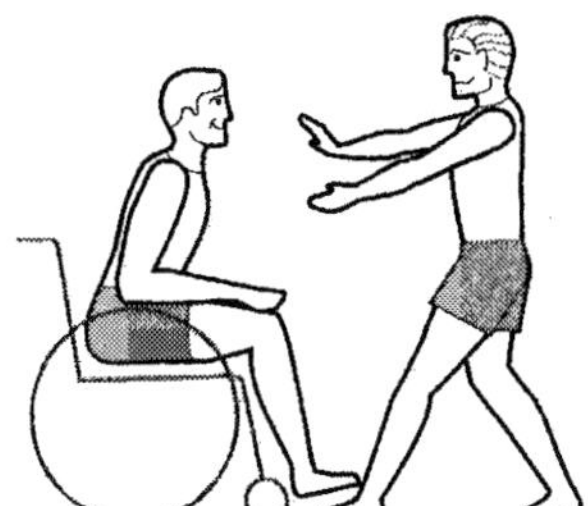
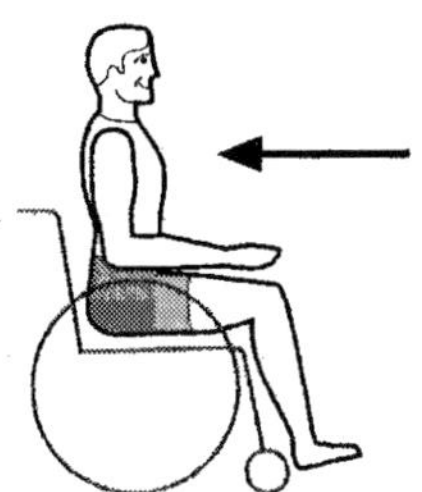

PURPOSE

To improve balance and strengthen the lower-back and abdominal muscles.

STARTING POSITION

Sit straight with your arms resting on your legs. Have an assistant stand in front of you.

ACTION

1. Keeping your chin up, slowly lean as far forward as you can without falling. Do not use your arms for support.
2. Return to the upright position.

IF LOWER EXTREMITY FUNCTION IS LIMITED

Recall which muscles you used to lean forward and back. Strain to make the movements, and visualize that you are doing the exercises with full range of motion, even if your movements are slight.

COMMENTS

Initially, your assistant should place his or her hands on your shoulders as you lean forward to prevent you from falling. As you practice, judge how far you can lean on your own. As your strength improves, have the assistant stand farther away.

Land Exercise 50

Downhill Skiing

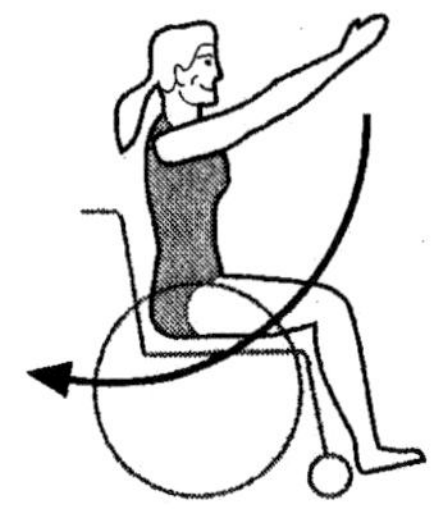

PURPOSE

To improve balance, coordination, and endurance. To stretch shoulder and arm muscles and build strength in back muscles.

STARTING POSITION

Sit straight with your arms stretched out in front of you and your hands clenched in fists.

ACTION

1. Swing both arms down and behind you, and lean forward. Keep your chin up, looking straight ahead.
2. Return to the starting position without using your arms.

COMMENTS

In the beginning, have an assistant stand in front of you to support your body if you fall forward. Do this exercise slowly, and limit the distance you lean forward and swing your arms. As you become more advanced, lean forward farther and fully extend your arms.

VARIATIONS

1. Perform the exercise while standing.
2. Pretend you are chopping wood. Do this exercise with your hands together, and bring your arms down between your knees.

Land Exercise 51

Clap Behind

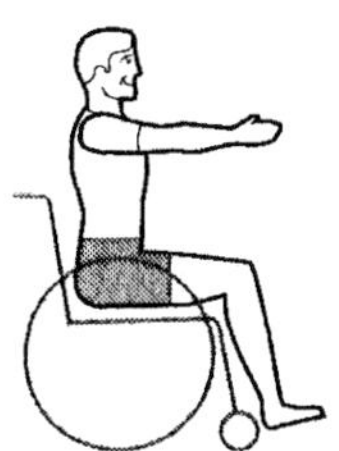
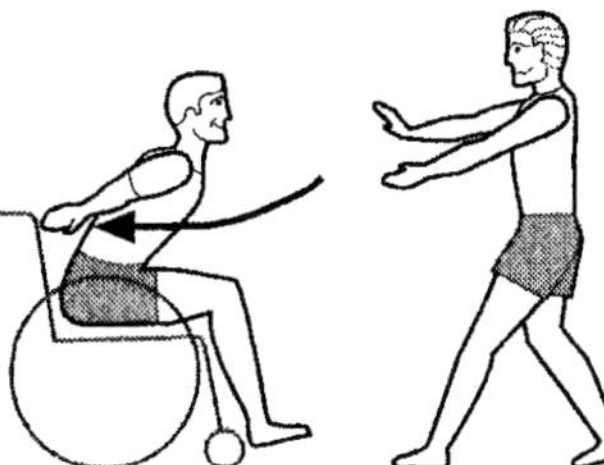
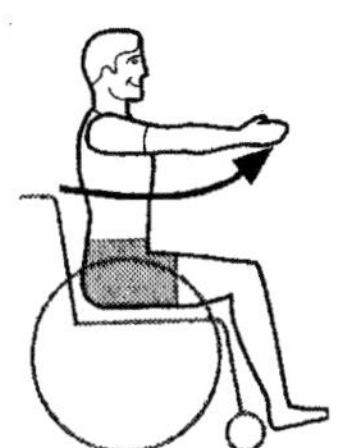

PURPOSE

To improve motor skills, speed, balance, and stretch your back, shoulder, and arm muscles.

STARTING POSITION

Sit straight or stand with your arms held straight out in front of you at shoulder level.

ACTION

1. Lean forward and clap your hands together behind your back. Keep your chin up, looking straight ahead.
2. Return to the starting position.

COMMENTS

Have an assistant stand in front of you to support your body if you fall forward. Get into a rhythm with your breathing and clapping. As your muscle control improves, increase difficulty by leaning farther forward, and raising your arms up higher behind you.

Land Exercise 52

Knee Pick-ups

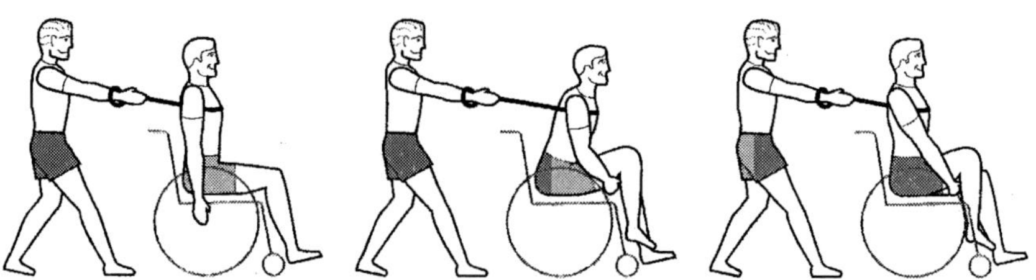

PURPOSE

To stimulate nerves in the legs and strengthen arm and leg muscles.

EQUIPMENT

A strap (a belt or exercise tubing). Have an assistant to help you with this exercise.

STARTING POSITION

Sit straight with your arms down at your sides and the strap around your chest. Have your assistant stand behind you holding the strap.

ACTION

1. Place your hands under your right leg. Maintain a straight position and lift your knee. Your assistant will prevent you from falling forward.
2. Lower your leg and relax.
3. Repeat the action with your left leg.

IF LOWER EXTREMITY FUNCTION IS LIMITED

Recall the muscles used to lift your knee. Stimulate those nerves! As you raise your knee, imagine that you lifted it without using your arms. In your mind, coordinate the leg movement you see with the effort to make it move.

VARIATIONS

1. Start by lifting your leg with help from both arms. As you improve, use one arm, then no arms.
2. Perform the exercise while standing.

Land Exercise 53

Leg Kicks

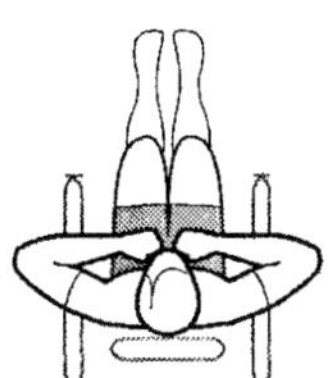

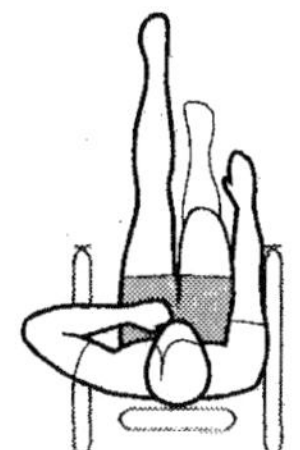

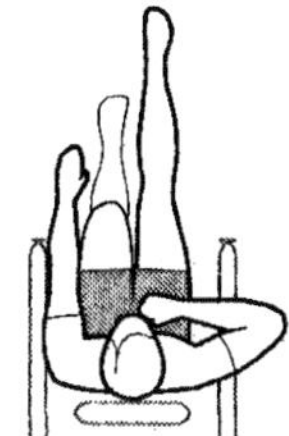

PURPOSE

To stimulate nerves, strengthen leg muscles, and develop coordination and motor skills.

STARTING POSITION

Sit straight with your hands in your lap.

ACTION

1. Kick your left leg out, and hold this position for three to five seconds. At the same time, extend your right arm in front of you.
2. Return to the starting position and relax.
3. Repeat this action with your right leg and left arm.

IF LOWER EXTREMITY FUNCTION IS LIMITED

Recall the muscles used to kick with your legs. Stimulate your nerves, and strain to make the kick. In your mind, visualize your leg out straight. Initially, you may not notice any movement, which is common. Keep trying! After a few months, have an assistant stand in front of you and watch closely for any micro-movements. The weight of gravity will make movement more difficult than when performed in water, but try, try, try!

Land Exercise 54

Knee Lifts

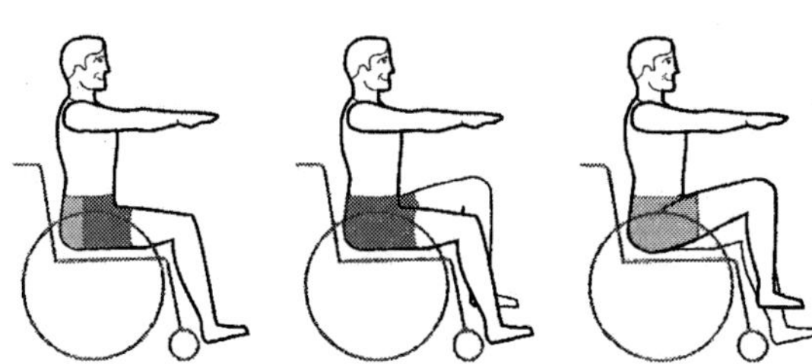

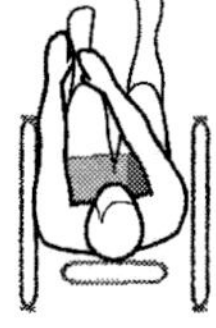

PURPOSE

To stimulate nerve and muscle function in the legs and build strength and muscle mass.

STARTING POSITION

Sit straight with your arms out in front of you.

ACTION

1. Lift your right knee up. Hold this position for three to five seconds.
2. Bring your knee and arms down.
3. Return to starting position and repeat this action with your left knee.

IF LOWER EXTREMITY FUNCTION IS LIMITED

Recall the muscles used to lift your knee. Strain to lift, and visualize the knee rising up to touch your hands. Initially, you may not notice any leg movement, which is common. Continue exercising, concentrating on making it happen.

VARIATION

As you raise one knee, extend both arms out, bringing your hands together above the raised knee.

Land Exercise 55

Arm Circles with Barbells

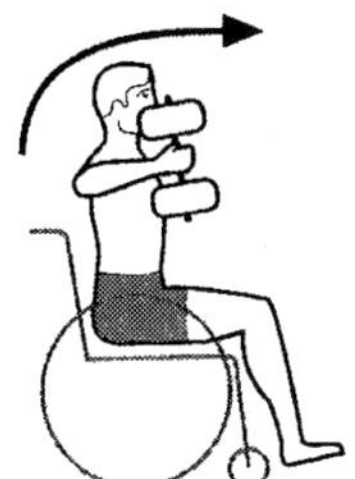
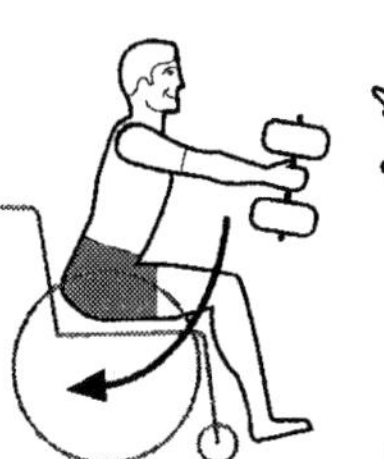

PURPOSE

To improve balance, strength, and increase range of motion in the arms.

EQUIPMENT

Two short water barbells or light weights. You may need an assistant to help you with this exercise.

STARTING POSITION

Sit straight or stand with arms down at your sides, holding a short water barbell or light weight in each hand.

ACTION

1. Circle your arms forward slowly, using a motion similar to the one used when moving wheels on a wheelchair.
2. Reverse direction.

COMMENTS

Your body may lean forward, throwing you off balance. In the beginning, have an assistant stand in front of you to support you. As your strength improves, make larger circles.

Land Exercise 56

Barbell Lift

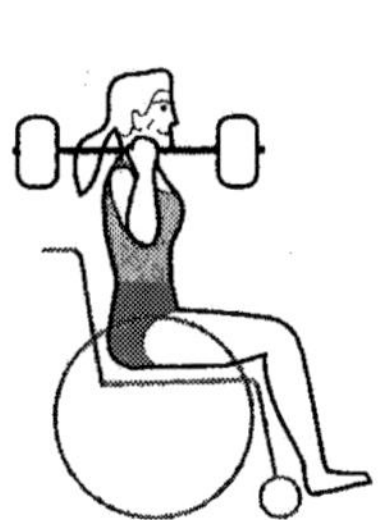
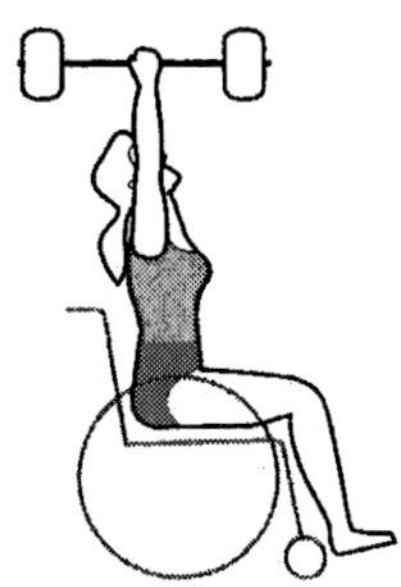

PURPOSE

To improve balance and strength, increase range of motion in arms, neck and shoulders.

EQUIPMENT

Two long water barbells

STARTING POSITION

Sit straight or stand with barbells held horizontally in each hand above your shoulders.

ACTION

1. Push the barbells straight up, fully extending your arms. At the same time, tilt your head back and look up, following the movement of your arms, and simultaneously inhale.
2. Return to starting position while exhaling.

COMMENTS

Maintain body awareness and pelvis stability throughout the exercise. Concentrate on deep breathing.

Land Exercise 57

Barbell Twists

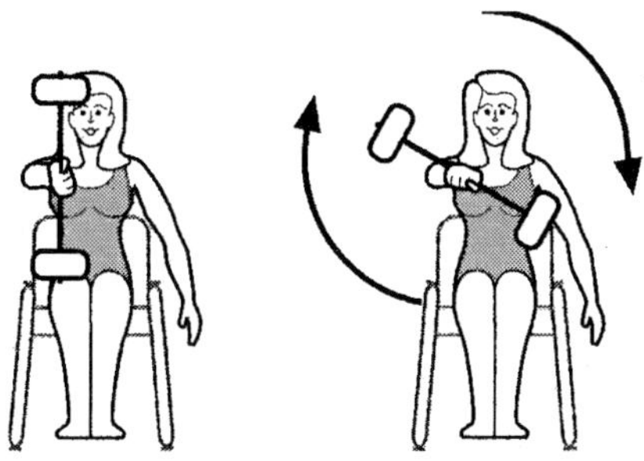

PURPOSE

To improve balance, increase range of motion in arms and wrists, and strengthen arm muscles.

EQUIPMENT

One long water barbell

STARTING POSITION

Sit straight or stand with your right arm extended in front of you, holding a barbell vertically in your right hand.

ACTION

1. Twist your right wrist and arm inward (counter-clockwise) as far as they will go.
2. Twist outward (clockwise) as far as your arm will go.
3. Repeat with your left arm

COMMENTS

Maintain body awareness. Pay attention to deep breathing. Keep your arm at the same height as you twist. Do not lock your elbows as you twist.

VARIATION

Twist the barbell using both arms. Place your hands close together in the center of bar.

Land Exercise 58

Barbell Grab

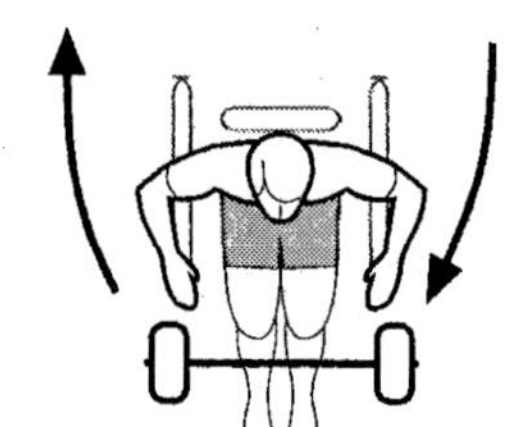

PURPOSE

To improve upper-body balance, increase range of motion in arms and shoulders, and improve speed and concentration.

EQUIPMENT

One long water barbell

STARTING POSITION

Sit straight or stand with your right arm stretched out behind you and your left arm holding the barbell straight in front of you.

ACTION

1. Let go of the barbell and switch arm positions, catching the barbell with your right hand before it falls.
2. Repeat the exercise switching arms.

COMMENTS

Maintain body awareness. Focus on hand-eye coordination.

Land Exercise 59

Curls

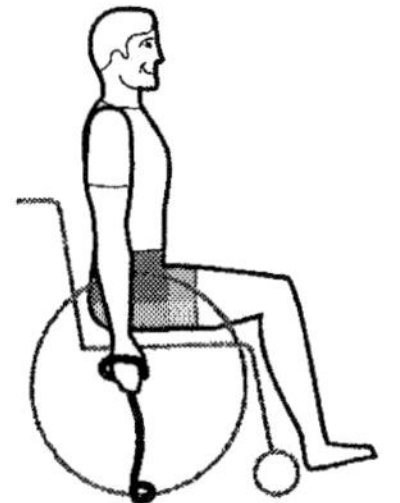

PURPOSE

To restore motor skills and strengthen the upper body.

EQUIPMENT

One or two pieces of short exercise tubing, chair

STARTING POSITION

Secure tubing to the right leg of your chair or wheel of your wheelchair. Sit straight with your arms down at your sides. Hold the tubing in your right hand.

ACTION

1. Bend your elbow, raising your right hand to your shoulder.
2. Return to starting position.
3. Repeat with your left arm.

COMMENTS

Keep your upper arm stationary, moving only your forearm. If you have difficulty maintaining balance, hold onto your armrest with your other hand.

Land Exercise 60

Triceps Extension

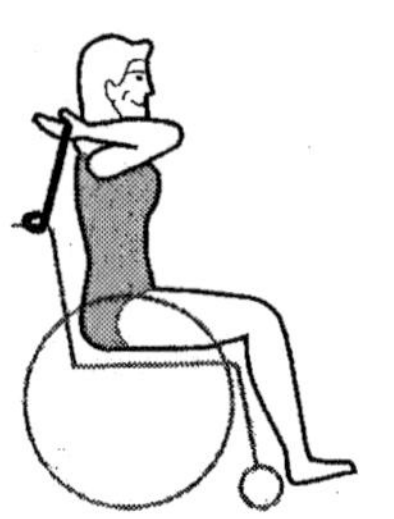

PURPOSE

To strengthen the lower back, triceps, and wrists.

EQUIPMENT

Two pieces of short exercise tubing, chair

STARTING POSITION

Secure tubing to the back of your chair. Sit straight. Reach your right arm up and back over your shoulder, holding the tubing in your hand.

ACTION

1. Bend your right elbow, extending your right arm up and forward.
2. Return to starting position.
3. Repeat with your left arm.

COMMENTS

Keep your upper arms stationary, moving only your forearms.

Land Exercise 61

Arm Raise

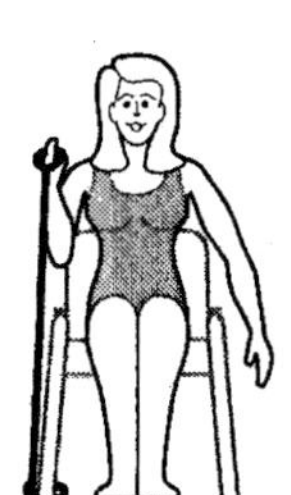
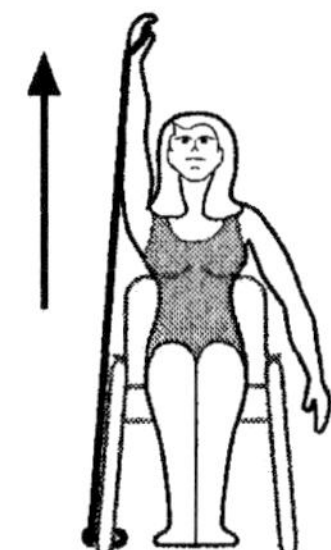

PURPOSE

To strengthen arm, shoulder, and neck muscles, and increase range of motion in elbows and shoulders.

EQUIPMENT

One or two pieces of short exercise tubing, chair

STARTING POSITION

Secure tubing to the right leg of your chair or wheel of your wheelchair. Sit straight. Hold the tubing in your right hand, with your elbow bent upward, and your left arm resting at your side.

ACTION

1. Raise your right arm straight up. Hold for two to three seconds. At the same time, turn your head upward, following the motion of your hand. Simultaneously inhale.
2. Return to starting position, lowering your arm while exhaling.
3. Repeat with your left arm.

COMMENTS

Keep your arms close to the side of your head while extending your arms.

VARIATIONS

1. Raise both arms at same time.
2. Turn your head alternately up, down, left, right, and straight while raising your arms.

Land Exercise 62

Arm Circles to the Sides

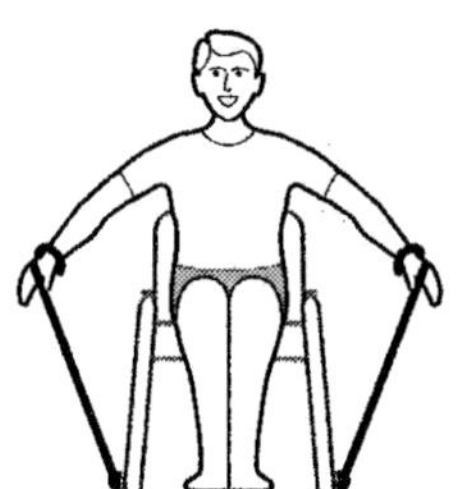

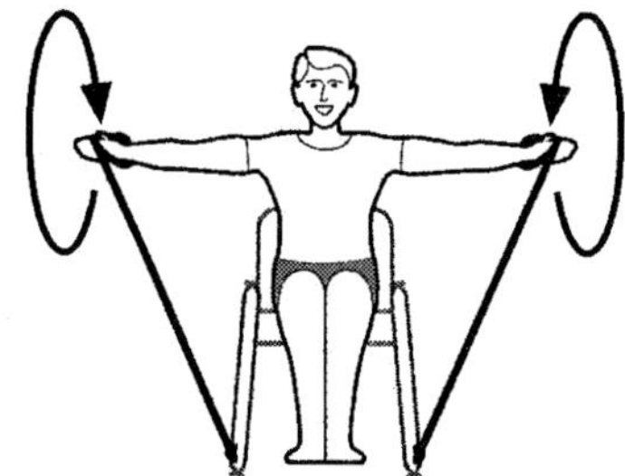

PURPOSE

To strengthen the shoulders, chest, and rib-cage muscles.

EQUIPMENT

Two pieces of short exercise tubing, chair

STARTING POSITION

Secure tubing to the right and left legs of your chair or wheel of your wheelchair. Sit straight with your arms fully extended at 45-degree angles, holding tubing in each hand.

ACTION

1. Raise your arms up to shoulder level
2. Rotate your arms in a forward circular motion.
3. Rotate your arms in the opposite direction.

COMMENTS

Maintain body stability while doing this exercise. Inhale as your arms go up, exhale as they go down.

VARIATION

Perform both small and large circles.

Land Exercise 63

Flying

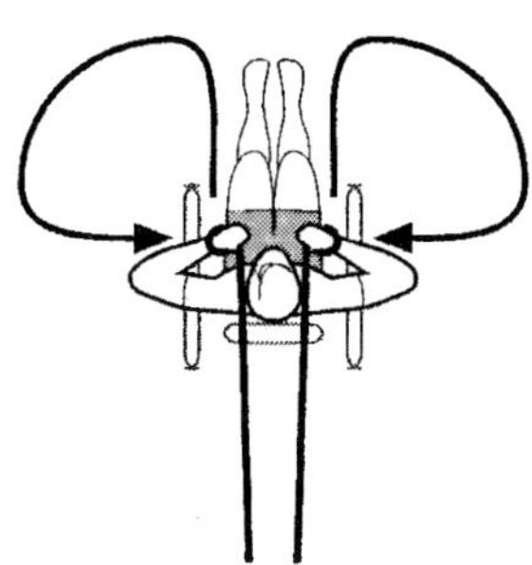

PURPOSE

To strengthen the upper-back, arm, and chest muscles, and improve posture.

EQUIPMENT

Two pieces of long exercise tubing

STARTING POSITION

Secure tubing just above shoulder level to a post behind you. Sit straight or stand with your arms at shoulder level and elbows bent to the sides. With your hands at the center and top of your chest, hold the tubing in each hand. The tubing should rest on the top of your shoulders.

ACTION

1. Reach your arms straight out in front and then out to the sides.
2. Return to starting position.
3. Perform this exercise in reverse.

COMMENTS

Maintain body awareness. Keep your elbows at shoulder level.

Land Exercise 64

Arm Circles with Tubing

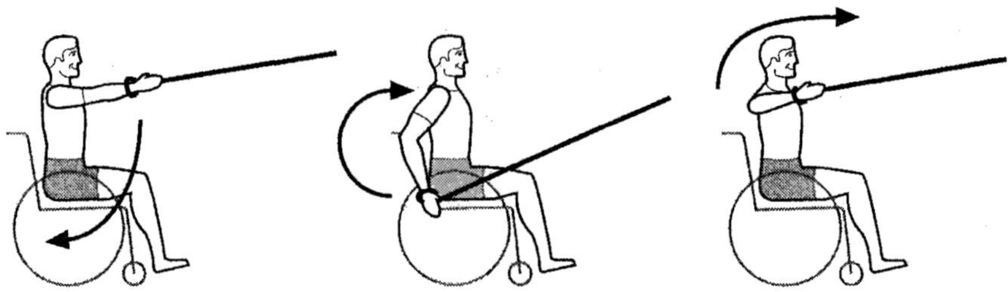

PURPOSE

To strengthen the shoulder, back, abdominal and arm muscles, and improve balance and range of motion in the upper body.

EQUIPMENT

One piece of long exercise tubing

STARTING POSITION

Secure tubing to a post three to four feet above shoulder level in front of you. Sit straight or stand. Put your hands through loops at the ends of the tubing and extend your arms straight out in front of you.

ACTION

1. Make circles with your arms, pulling the tubing down and back
2. Move your arms up and around to the front in large circular motions.

VARIATIONS

1. Circle in the reverse direction.
2. Perform this exercise facing the opposite direction.
3. Secure the tubing at different heights.

Land Exercise 65

Cross-Country Skiing with Tubing

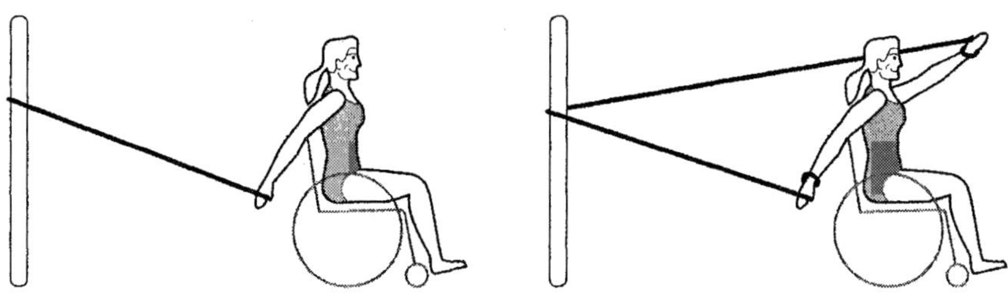

PURPOSE

To develop coordination, strengthen arm muscles, improve cardiovascular endurance, and stimulate deep breathing.

EQUIPMENT

One piece of long exercise tubing

STARTING POSITION

Secure the tubing to a post behind you just above shoulder level. Sit straight or stand with your arms extended behind you. Hold the tubing in both hands.

ACTION

1. Swing your left arm forward and your right arm back as if cross-country skiing.
2. Reverse arm positions.

COMMENTS

Keep your arms straight while doing this exercise. Be aware not to lock your elbows.

Land Exercise 66

Arm Stretch with Tubing

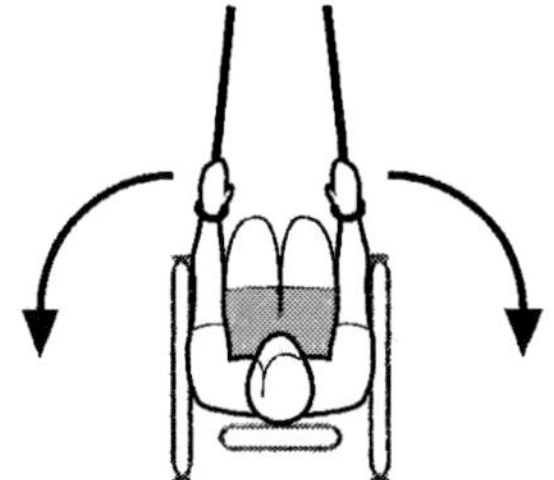

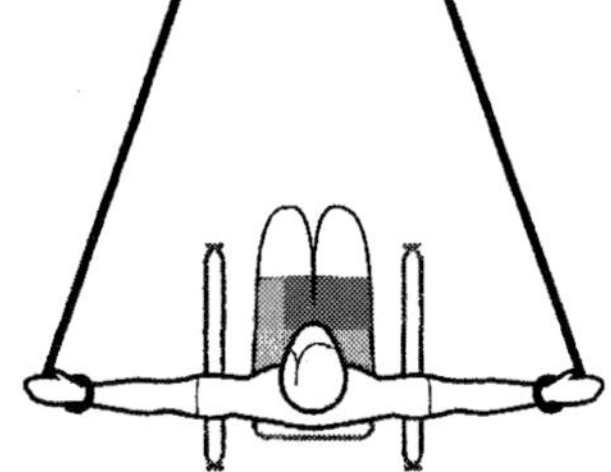

PURPOSE

To strengthen the chest, lower back, abdominal, and arm muscles. To improve balance and range of motion in the upper body, and stimulate deep breathing.

EQUIPMENT

Once piece of long exercise tubing

STARTING POSITION

Secure tubing to a post in front of you just above shoulder level. Sit straight or stand with your arms extended in front of you, holding the tubing.

ACTION

1. Spread your arms out to sides while inhaling. Hold this position for three to five seconds.
2. Return to starting position while exhaling.

COMMENTS

Work with your arms and elbows fully extended, but do not lock your elbows. Concentrate on deep breathing.

Land Exercise 67

Pull Downs

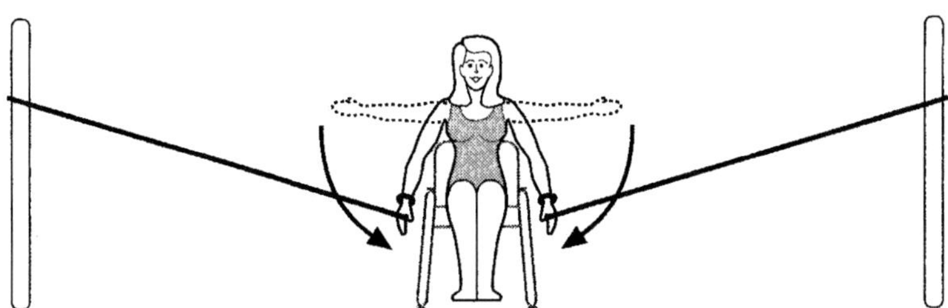

PURPOSE

To strengthen the chest, shoulder and arm muscles, and improve stability and body alignment.

EQUIPMENT

Two pieces of long exercise tubing

STARTING POSITION

Secure tubing to posts on each side of you, just above shoulder level. Sit straight or stand holding the tubing with your arms out to the sides. Inhale.

ACTION

1. Slowly pull your arms down simultaneously while exhaling.
2. Raise your arms up at your side as high as possible while inhaling.
3. Return to starting position.

Land Exercise 68

Cross Your Chest

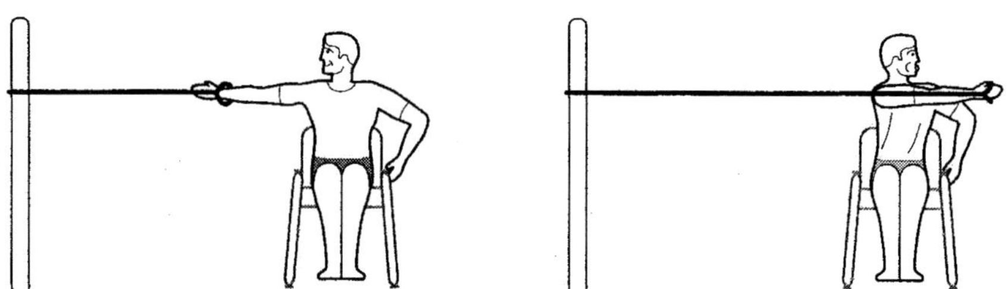

PURPOSE

To strengthen the chest and arm muscles, and improve stability.

EQUIPMENT

One piece of long exercise tubing

STARTING POSITION

Secure tubing to a post at your right side, just above shoulder level. Sit straight or stand. Hold the tubing in your right hand, extending your right arm to the side.

ACTION

1. Pull your right arm horizontally across your chest to the left as far as possible. Turn your head, following the movement of your hand.
2. Return to the starting position.
3. Repeat with your left arm.

COMMENTS

Move slowly. Keep your elbows at shoulder level.

Land Exercise 69

Hug Yourself

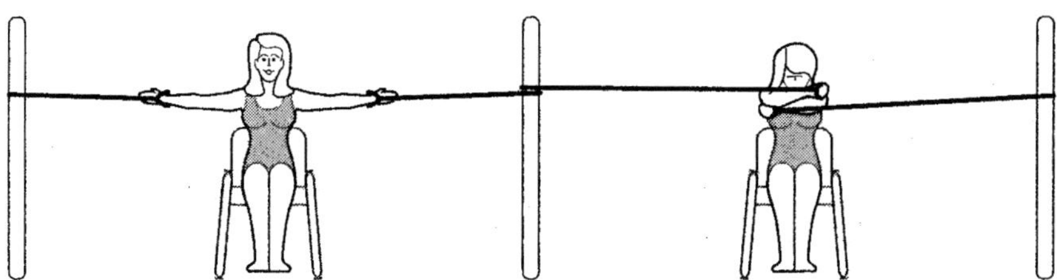

PURPOSE

To strengthen the shoulder and arm muscles, improve posture, coordination, and stimulate deep breathing.

EQUIPMENT

Two pieces of long exercise tubing

STARTING POSITION

Sit straight or stand. Secure tubing to posts on each side of you, just above shoulder level. Extend your arms straight out to the sides while holding on to the tubing. Inhale.

ACTION

1. Simultaneously bend both arms, crossing your chest, and hug yourself, bringing your wrists to your shoulders. Tilt your head down. Exhale.
2. Return to the starting position. Inhale.

COMMENTS

With each repetition, switch the position of your top and bottom arms. Maintain body awareness.

Land Exercise 70

Breaststroke

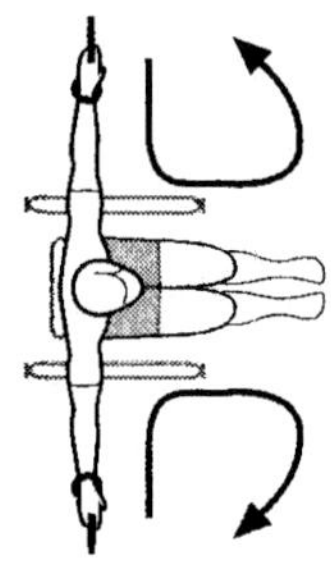
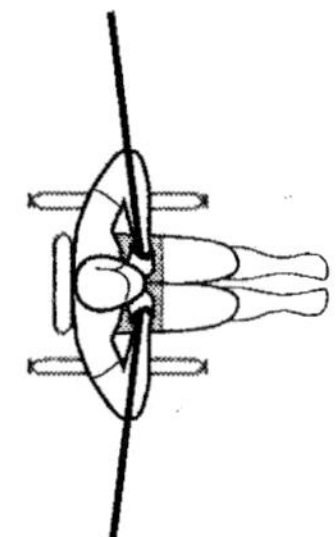
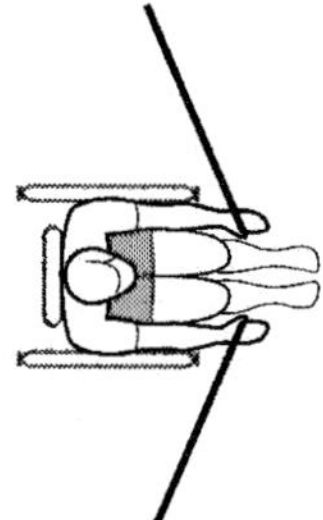
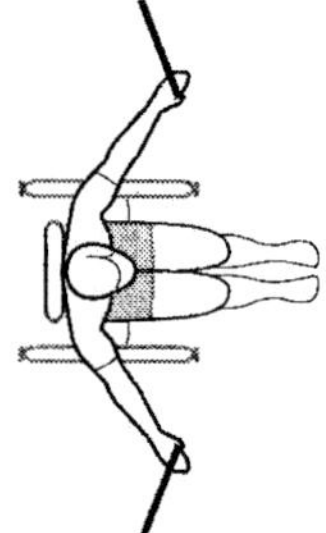

PURPOSE

To strengthen the chest, shoulder, and arm muscles, improve coordination, and stimulate deep breathing.

EQUIPMENT

Two pieces of long exercise tubing

STARTING POSITION

Secure the tubing at posts on each side of you, just above shoulder level. Sit straight or stand, holding the tubing with your arms out to the sides.

ACTION

1. Bend your elbows and bring them down to your sides.
2. Extend your arms forward to shoulder level.
3. Bring your arms back out to the sides (a forward breaststroke).
4. Reverse the action (a backward breaststroke).

COMMENTS

Pay attention to deep breathing. Maintain a straight body position.

About the Author

Dr. Igor Burdenko received his doctorate in Sports Medicine in his native Russia, where he was an athlete, trainer, coach, and sports medicine professional. He is a member of the American College of Sports Medicine and the National Athletic Trainer Association. Today, he runs the Burdenko Water and Sports Therapy Institute in Boston, Massachusetts. Dr. Burdenko has received numerous awards for his work and has a long list of prestigious clients, including Olympic gold-medalist Oksana Baiul, Olympic silver-medalists Nancy Kerrigan, Paul Wylie and Alex Despatie, Boston Celtic's Kevin McHale, NY Nicks Allan Houston and many others.

HYDRO-FIT
Exercise that feels good!
Your professional source for water exercise and aquatic therapy products and training
FREE catalog call 800-346-7295
SHOP anytime at hydrofit.com
HYDRO-FIT®

Aquatic Rehab at Home
Rent - Lease - Purchase
"Get Horizontal"
"Get Vertical"
"Move seated"
"Lift Compatible"
"Optional treadmill"
Build Anywhere - Modular - Assist Within - Assist from Without
928-300-9800
www.TheVerticalPool.com

CHANGING
THE WAY
WE TREAT
PAIN
Topricin
NEW Introducing
MyPainAway®
Powered by Topricin
MyPainAway™
AFTER BURN CREAM
MyPainAway™
FIBRO CREAM
TO RELIEVE PAINS ASSOCIATED WITH FIBROMYALGIA AND NEUROPATHY
Topricin for Children
Topricin Foot Therapy Cream
RAPID FOOT PAIN RELIEF
Topricin Pain Relief Cream
Moisturizing Relief for Arthritis and Joint Pain
Certified B Corporation
World Reowned Chairman of
Water and Sports Therapy Institute
Igor Burdenko Recommends
Topricin to Patients for Over 18yrs
30% OFF Topricin & MyPainAway Products
USE PROMOCODE: IGORB
(offer excludes 3/4oz tubes)
WWW.TOPRICIN.COM

For more information and to order
additional copies of "The Burdenko Method,"
please contact

The Burdenko Water and Sport Therapy Institute

617.467.4530
igor@burdenko.com
www.burdenko.com
www.tbmethod.com